FAT GIRL SINGS

DISCOVERING, EMBRACING, AND LEVERAGING RACIAL IDENTITY ON THE FOOTBALL FIELD, IN BUSINESS, AND IN LIFE

RAY SCHOENKE

Copyright © 2023 by Ray Schoenke LLC

All rights reserved. This book or any portion thereof may not be reproduced or used in any manner whatsoever without the express written permission of the publisher except for the use of brief quotations in a book review.

The name of my book is not intended to body shame anyone. This was my actual name as a child to many, and I own it as the adult who still carries this wounded child inside of him. Certain real individuals portrayed in this book may have memories of events depicted herein that differ from mine. I have made every effort to honestly, yet compassionately, portray the individuals and events discussed in this book. My objective was to grasp and consider why people behaved the way they did, what their actions or words meant, and how they affected me throughout my life. I have also considered why I am including specific people and events and the impact this inclusion will have on both the narrative and those included in it. Every effort has been made to trace or contact all copyright holders.

Publishing Services provided by Paper Raven Books LLC

Printed in the United States of America

First Printing, 2023

Cover Concept: Ray Schoenke
Cover Design: Iram Shahzadi (irfa6ster@gmail.com)

Paperback ISBN: 979-8-9879919-2-3
Hardback ISBN: 979-8-9879919-1-6
Ebook ISBN: 979-8-9879919-0-9

Hawaiʻi Edition Paperback ISBN: 979-8-9879919-3-0
Hawaiʻi Edition Hardback ISBN: 979-8-9879919-4-7

Praise for *Fat Girl Sings*

"Ray Schoenke has lived a fascinating life—from his upbringing in Hawaii, to his groundbreaking career as one of the first Polynesian players in the NFL, to his successful business career. Along the way, he has never failed to stand up or speak out for what he believes. I'll always be grateful for his support, and I'm glad he's finally telling his story."
—President Bill Clinton

"Ray Schoenke's story is an inspiration. His life and example provides us an important reachable lesson about honor and principle. I've written about hundreds of athletes but never one who carried himself with more dignity than Ray."
—Gare Joyce has written for publications including *The New York Times, The Athletic,* and ESPN for more than 30 years

"My dear friend, Ray Schoenke, far more than a standout NFL lineman, has left indelible marks on our country – champion of all underprivileged; powerful advocate for responsible gun safety; candidate for Governor. *Fat Girl Sings* is a funny, moving, fast and wonderful read about the life of a fierce American patriot."
—Joe R. Reeder, 14th Army Undersecretary & Chairman of the Panama Canal Commission (1993-97)

"*Fat Girl Sings* provides an evocative glimpse into the Hawaiian experience, touching on sports, culture, race, and a man's effort to discover, embrace, and accept all of himself. Even those who don't understand football will get excited by the detailed descriptions of plays on the field. This book is about a warrior engaged in a war without the killing, both on the football field and in life."

—Polynesian Football Hall of Fame

"As an 11 year veteran of the NFL, I had the opportunity to play against Ray Schoenke. The reality is that football requires physical skills that most people do not have and mental skills that are much higher than one would imagine. It is more than mass and muscle colliding. Ray and I were like two professors trapped in large bodies. What Ray and I did on the field was clearly a wonderful expression of two men plying their trade in different spheres, but our intellectual and mental approach to the game was what allowed us to truly appreciate each other. When you read *Fat Girl Sings*, I think you will enjoy and understand how profound a Sunday afternoon encounter was for Ray and I."

—Willie Lanier, Kansas City Chiefs. NFL Man of the Year (1972), Pro Football Hall of Fame (1986)

"Ray Schoenke, he's a champion. He was our best lineman the day we played Dallas in the play-offs in 1972. He got us to the Super Bowl."

—Billy Kilmer, Quarterback in the NFL for the San Francisco 49ers, New Orleans Saints, and Washington Redskins

"Ray Schoenke's life is a story of courage and strength, from the ferocity of the gridiron and the boardroom to his compassion and advocacy for the disadvantaged."

—Admiral William J. "Bud" Flanagan, Commander in Chief, U.S. Navy Atlantic Fleet (1994-96)

"*Fat Girl Sings* is a compelling book full of inspirational accounts of Ray's life experiences. Ray brings you along his journey as a young Hawaiian kid dealing with bullying and racial struggles as he triumphs over his challenging past and becomes an outstanding NFL football player and successful business owner. Ray was one of my most valued and dearest teammates. He is truly one of my treasured friends."

—Roy Jefferson, All-American All-Pro NFL wide receiver for 12 seasons with the Pittsburgh Steelers, Baltimore Colts, and Washington Redskins

Fat Girl Sings reveals battles for growth and inspiration
in pursuing and defining demanding realities of life
by a term that native Hawaiians refer to as *"MOʻOLELO"*
(history, tradition, recording, journal, story)

In the voice of Raymond Schoenke, native Hawaiian author,
his *"MOʻOLELO"* speaks:
his truth, his wonderment, his discernment,
his pain, his enlightenment, and his peace
in search of harmony with self, his environment, and his ancestors.

—Trustee S. Haunani Apoliona, MSW, Native Hawaiian Advocate for more than 45 years, and composer of mele ʻōiwi Hawaiʻi

"*Fat Girl Sings* is the story of a football player who gave it his all in the trenches - not just on the field, but in the battle to build a more just society. And his commitment to social activism wasn't just a flash in the pan during his years in celebrity - it was an enduring part of how he's continued to live his life. He played the game as he lived his life - with heart, purposefulness, and intentionality."

—Marc Elrich, Montgomery County Executive, a former teacher, still dreaming of playing middle linebacker

"Ray Schoenke's life story is one of inspiration, reflection, emotion, understanding, affirmation, and encouragement. From the opening moment to the conclusion, I was captivated by a story that basically described in great detail my own life experiences and those of many other Polynesian athletes, all of which had occurred well over two decades earlier… growing up in an environment of hostility and disconnect, but nonetheless finding a place of certainty, opportunity, and the inspiration to persevere. The "quiet voice" within us provided the attributes of ALOHA- Akahai- Kindness; Lokahi- Family (Unity); Olu'olu-to be agreeable; Ha'aha'a- Humility; Ahonu'i-Perseverance, which served as guideposts and brought clarity to the pathways of success that laid ahead for all of us to discover. Ray Schoenke, the man, myth, the legend, so special in many ways to so many."

—Corbett A. K. Kalama, former Kamehameha Schools Trustee, President of the Friends of Hawaii Charities - Sony Open in Hawaii, globally acclaimed Hawaiian Canoe Racing Outrigger Champion, one of 11 children born into a Hawaiian family with history dating back 64 generations, President and CEO of Resco, Inc. (Locations LLC)

"Ray Schoenke describes the NFL player experience realistically—the rush an athlete feels, the stress, the injuries….I clearly remember the incident with my thumb he writes about in *Fat Girl Sings*. I was just a young piglet at the time. Ray and I should compare pictures of our hands now. Every deformed joint is a story, and he is quite a story teller—a natural."

—George Starke, 13-year veteran with the Washington Redskins and three Super Bowl teams—affectionately known as the "Head Hog"

"I called Ray Schoenke a dumb Hawaiian, but he is really a tough Hawaiian. He paddled the Moloka'i Race with a dislocated shoulder."

—Nappy Napoleon, founder and head coach of the Anuenue Canoe Club and World Champion paddler and steersman.

"As I read this book, it reminded me of how the lessons that we all learned in the locker room and on the football field carry over to real life and winning off the field. In the end, it's what we give of ourselves to the team that truly matters. Ray gave his all, and it took him to a place of leadership in his business and in his community. And along the way, to a place of love for his family that was second to none. This book will touch everyone who reads it."

—June Jones, former head football coach, University of Hawaii (1999-2007); head football coach at Southern Methodist University (2008-14); XLFL offensive coordinator, Seattle Sea Dragons (2022)

"This is a book about an exceptional NFL lineman and an even better person. It's rare for a player to have the courage to stand up for his beliefs, but Ray Schoenke certainly did. Ray fought for racial justice with the same tenacity that he demonstrated on the field, and he was also an advocate for underserved children. *Fat Girl Sings* is a good read, and I particularly enjoyed hearing about Ray's firsthand experiences with coaches like George Allen, Tom Landry, and Vince Lombardi."

—Jerry Sherk, Defensive End, Cleveland Browns (1970-81)

"Ray Schoenke has been a friend of mine for 66 years. I've always admired his athletic ability. After reading *Fat Girl Sings,* I am also convinced that he is also a remarkable human being."

—Larry Johnson, Chairman & CEO Bank of Hawaii (Retired)

"Ray Schoenke is a true Keiki o Kaaina (Son of Hawaii). *Fat Girl Sings* is an incredible story of a young Polynesian man struggling through football and life. Told honestly and beautifully, it's an inspiration for future generations of Pacific islanders trying to break out and achieve greatness. He has set the stage for many bright futures but also reveals the price one has to pay. I loved the story."

—Walter Dods Jr., retired Chairman and CEO of First Hawaiian Bank and past Chairman of the American Bankers Association

"As a life-long Redskins fan, I found Ray Schoenke's book *Fat Girl Sings* a special treat. He puts you 'in the huddle and in the trenches' of NFL battles that led to the Skins first trip to the Super Bowl. His Warrior Ethos is the difference maker as he wrestled with constant fear of failure. That Can-Do-Never-Give-Up spirit led to huge success in football, business, and life. His candor in capturing and sharing each step of the journey makes this an invaluable addition to one's library."

—Lieutenant General Charles E. Domini, 3-Star General, U.S. Army

Table of Contents

Foreword by Don Graham....................xiii

Prologue xv

CHAPTER ONE
Trade Winds and Tumbleweeds (1941–1959) 1

CHAPTER TWO
Southern Methodist University—Cramming, Coaching, and Coeds (1959–1963) 61

CHAPTER THREE
Cowboy Up (1963–1964) 93

CHAPTER FOUR
Wisconsin Cheese to Ohio Buckeye Trees—Packers and Browns (1966) 127

CHAPTER FIVE
Fear, Trust, Service—Lombardi, Allen, and Special Olympics (1966–1975)... 147

CHAPTER SIX
Lessons from the Game (1953–1975) 217

CHAPTER SEVEN
The Silence After the Cheers—Schoenke & Associates
(1974–1980). 237

CHAPTER EIGHT
My Family and Hawaiʻi—Returning to My Ancestors
(1965–2000). 261

CHAPTER NINE
From One Blood Sport to Another (1992–2006). 291

CHAPTER TEN
To Have and to Hold (1986–2020). 319

CHAPTER ELEVEN
Still Stomping in the Puddles. 335

Photography Credits 339

About the Author 341

Acknowledgments

I would like to acknowledge the special relationships that are too numerous to mention individually that have tied together the threads of my life and run through it, without which this book would not exist. Within all of you are the experiences and connections that created the energy that led to this story—my life.

Foreword

Don Graham is the former publisher (and former sports editor) of The Washington Post. *He is now chairman of Graham Holdings Co.*

I got to know Ray Schoenke's name in the best possible context: he helped turn one of the all-time losing football teams into a winner.

I grew up in Washington, DC and it is difficult to describe just how bad our pro sports teams were. There were two, the baseball Senators, who regularly finished last in the American League, and the Redskins, who were, amazingly, just as bad. As a young fan, I lived through two years in a row when the team won just one game and other years that were almost as terrible. We were miles from the powerhouse teams in the league, like the Green Bay Packers and Cleveland Browns.

Ray wasn't the guy who singlehandedly turned those teams around, but he was part of the wonderful story. A dedicated owner, Edward Bennett Williams, wouldn't take no for an answer: he hired first the great Vince Lombardi and then (after Lombardi's death) George Allen to coach the team. So Ray can compare those two Hall of Fame coaches, and another—Tom Landry of Dallas—for whom he played earlier in his career.

Ray was not just a football player—he was a very, very successful one. He and a talented cast of teammates took the Redskins to a Super

Bowl, something I had never expected to see as a Washington football fan. I've read a lot of books about football players, few by offensive linemen. The only other one I can think of is Jerry Kramer's *Instant Replay*. Ray's enough of an intellectual to describe what was different about blocking Bob Lilly and Too Tall Jones.

I loved the college-football and NFL football parts of Ray's story. But the rest of this book is just as good. It is the story of a very, very unusual life. Ray grew up in Hawaiʻi, and the story of his childhood is impressively different from almost all those of his NFL teammates. He was a football player, but he always took his schoolwork seriously.

But the most surprising part of Ray's story takes place after his NFL career. So many famous NFL players, including more than one of Ray's teammates, have gone through financial collapse and bankruptcy. Ray did the opposite. Having started selling insurance during his off-seasons, Ray founded his own company, turned it into a huge success, managed it well, and ultimately sold it for a healthy price. Others made important contributions, but it's obvious that Ray was the driving force in the success of Ray Schoenke & Associates. Ray wasn't the only entrepreneur to come out of the NFL in his day, but he may have been the most successful.

Other parts of Ray's life took in famous Washingtonians from Ethel Kennedy to Bill Clinton. Ray enjoys telling the stories of his political ventures, and you'll enjoy reading them.

As a Washingtonian who always loved football, I'm glad I got to watch Ray Schoenke and his teammates play the game. Now, I'm glad I got to read this fine book, the story of a most unusual life.

Prologue

If you ask me how I felt about being called "Fat Girl" as a chubby, ten-year-old brown-skinned boy in a sea of White kids in a Texas schoolyard with my round belly expanding unforgivingly in a roll over the top of my belt, my answer would be a short one. I hated it. The warrior genes I inherited along with the unique gene variant on the Hawaiian half of my genetic pool that caused me to store fat[1] had not yet risen to the surface and stretched me into the six-foot-four, 250-pound NFL offensive lineman that I would become, so schools were battlefields—hallways were gauntlets formed of rows of boys I had to pass through, and playgrounds were anything but. In spite of my Hawaiian genes, I hadn't inherited the ancient warrior skills of Koa, or perhaps I didn't know it yet, but I clearly had the propensity to get fat.

Some studies have found that Pacific Islanders, especially Polynesians, and so Native Hawaiians, are more likely to have a unique kind

---

1 Sun, Hanxiau, et al. "The impact of global and local Polynesian genetic ancestry on complex traits in Native Hawaiians." *PLOS GENETICS*, 11 Feb 2021. https://journals.plos.org/plosgenetics/article?id=10.1371/journal.pgen.1009273.

Swain, Erik. "Genetics contributes to diabetes, HF, obesity risk in Native Hawaiian individuals." *Cardiology Today*, 11 Feb 2021. https://www.healio.com/news/cardiology/20210211/genetics-contributes-to-diabetes-hf-obesity-risk-in-native-hawaiian-individuals.

Maurice Wilkins Centre Diabetes for Molecular Biodiscovery. "New insights into diabetes, obesity risk among Polynesian people." 22 June 2018. https://www.mauricewilkinscentre.org/news/new-insights-into-diabetes,-obesity-risk-among-polynesian-people/.

Dvorsky, George. "How a Powerful Obesity Gene Helped Samoans Conquer the South Pacific." *GIZMODO*, 25 Jul 2016. https://gizmodo.com/how-a-powerful-obesity-gene-helped-samoans-conquer-the-1784266550.

Sonny, Julian. "Why Polynesians Are Genetically Engineered To Be The Best Football Players In The World." *Elite Daily Lifestyle*, 30 Sep 2013. https://www.elitedaily.com/sports/polynesians-genetically-engineered-best-football-players/778724.

of genetic predisposition to store fat, which has been theoretically attributed to the fact that they had to face food insecurity when sailing long voyages to and settling in the South Pacific islands. However, the only insecurity I was facing had nothing to do with food shortages. It had to do with surviving being chased by bullies, getting my face punched in, and being restrained and having my pants pulled down in front of my peers. I was like a fledgling bird. I had the equipment to fly, but I hadn't grown into my huge athletic body enough to keep me from being the target of predators. I was completely blindsided by the fact that I was singled out and had to learn that it had to do with my temperament, weight, and skin color. I was an easy target. Learning how to deal with bullies became a skill set I developed over a lifetime on the playground, on the football field, in business, and in politics.

Bullies are everywhere, in every facet of life. No one goes through the battle of life without getting bloodied, as I literally did on the playground as a child and on the field as an NFL lineman, but some of us come out victors. This is the story of Fat Girl, the sweet-natured little Polynesian boy who still lives inside the man who exploited the confidence he developed on those playgrounds as a dark-skinned boy in Texas to win at football, in business, and in life.

People have asked me lots of questions over the years about my success in sports and business and about what motivated my social commitment (in addition to wanting to know what happens in the huddle). I realized that my childhood experiences were critical in shaping the man I would become. I want this story to inspire those who are bullied, disenfranchised, or victims of racism and show them it is possible to overcome these difficult experiences. I especially want to be an inspiration to young athletes and young people to believe in themselves and have the courage and ability to take on bullies, which, as has been the case in my life, can be a lifetime challenge. I want to give real, meaningful insights into NFL football that fans would have no way of experiencing. I want to inspire great athletes to prepare a life for themselves outside of their sport that will give them options when they retire from the game, which the majority of them fail to do. I want to help readers understand the challenges in a marriage when one is faced with a critically ill partner.

I also want to reveal how negative experiences as a young boy have followed me into adulthood. Much of my life has been like being chased by a wild dog. Stability became an indication of impending doom. My frequent moves as a military brat exacerbated my sense that stability is a harbinger of instability. I have had difficulty fully relaxing and enjoying my successes. I have felt I had to stay ahead of what unknown enemies could be just around the corner—a coach who questioned my commitment, a defensive lineman who is prepared to play dirty, members of a board of directors of a large corporation who question the mental capacity of a football player, or competitors encroaching on my territory.

I have had to face the world in an atmosphere of what I call "controlled violence" both on the field and off. While this worked for me in sports and business, it has taken a toll on my personal life and my psyche. I am only now coming to terms with my inability to relax and enjoy the fruits of my labor. Fat Girl is my constant companion, and the two of us are finally learning that fear is not the best of motivators, that we can rise to the top without a dark, faceless enemy chasing us, and we can learn to live with one another—the big man and the scared little boy who are one and the same. This is the story of Fat Girl and the man who can now embrace that little boy as a valuable partner. I will leave it to the reader to decide if I have been successful.

CHAPTER ONE

Trade Winds and Tumbleweeds
(1941-1959)

I can only imagine the trepidation my mother must have been feeling when she was about to reveal to me and my two sisters a family and a culture that had been cloaked in secrecy for my entire life of 14 years. My mother, Olivia Haleaka Alapa Schoenke, was a petite, attractive officer's wife whose family was 100 percent Hawaiian. That made me, her son, half Hawaiian. But I had no idea what that meant. I had lived almost my entire life on the US mainland and in Europe. I had left Hawai'i as a baby after the bombing of Pearl Harbor.

The only hint that we had ever had that my Hawaiian mother missed Hawai'i had been the mournful sound of her voice drifting through the house as she played Hawaiian songs on her 'ukulele and an occasional visit from a family member whom she greeted in tears.

In late November 1955, we had just arrived in Hawai'i after my father's military transfer from Wolters Air Force Base in Mineral Wells, Texas and had gotten settled in our temporary residence in Waipahu on the island of O'ahu. Mom must have come to terms with the fact that her past was going to be exposed, and she wanted to control the situation as much as she could. On a perennially warm Hawaiian Sunday morning, she banged on my bedroom door and abruptly ordered me along with my sisters to put on our Sunday best. She oversaw us to make sure we did. She was dressed to impress—one of her nicest dinner party dresses, full makeup, her nicest jewelry, high heels.

Her face was contorted into a paradoxical mixture of anxiety and excitement, an odd combination I had never seen before. Her movements were abrupt and rushed. She had to have come to terms with the fact that certain members of our Hawaiian family could expose the secrets she had hidden from us for years. She was obviously trying to remain calm, but we could all feel the tension. She ushered us into our blue 1953 Oldsmobile with my father, Raymond Frederick Schoenke Sr., a six-foot-five major in the Air Force whose parents had emigrated from Germany, at the wheel.

We headed to the north shore to my Hawaiian family's home town of Lā'ie at the northernmost tip of O'ahu. We bypassed the town of Wahiawā and passed Schofield Barracks, the Army base where my father was stationed when Pearl Harbor was bombed. As we dipped down toward the northern coast, we drove through the tall, grassy sugarcane fields and neat rows of pineapple that lay in front of the backdrop of the Ko'olau mountain range, which, like all mountains in Hawai'i, was created by volcanic eruptions.[2] The mountains in the distance were covered with dense green tropical vegetation cut by crevices formed from dark red lava flows or waterfalls. The landscape gradually changed as we approached the coast and could see the dark blue ocean glistening in the sun as the huge waves hit the shore. I was seeing a natural beauty that I had no idea even existed.

My siblings' and my cultural understanding of Hawai'i was pretty much dictated by the same things everyone else saw on TV or in the movies. The only difference was that my mother's version was more authentic than the TV versions and intended to ensure that, with her dark skin, she *and* her children were viewed as Hawaiian. Living

---

2 *National Park Service.* "Geology & Volcanoes." https://www.nps.gov/locations/hawaii/geology.htm.

in Texas had taught all of us that race was an issue and that being Hawaiian was acceptable, at least most of the time.

We rounded the tip of the island and came to Kahuku. Most of the houses were wooden boxes on stilts or corrugated steel Quonset huts. Most had lanais—open-sided, roofed porches or verandas. The housing was extremely simple, but somehow radiated the warmth and beauty of the local culture.

We finally arrived at Aunty Alice Alapa's house. It was set in a group of typical small, weather-beaten, frame houses with tin roofs raised above the ground on stilts and surrounded by banana, coconut, and papaya trees. My sisters and I had acquired some sophistication after having lived in several states and England, so the idea of encountering a new culture was not foreign to us, but on top of our excitement, we were also nervous. We climbed out of the Oldsmobile. Animated, brown-skinned people, men and barefoot boys dressed in aloha shirts and shorts and girls and women wearing colorful, flowery *muʻumuʻu*, ran toward us and swarmed around us, crying, hugging and kissing us, giving us leis. There were more relatives than I ever imagined I had. They were speaking Hawaiian to my mother. More importantly, my mother, whom I'd never heard speaking anything but English, was speaking Hawaiian back to them.

Mom stood there crying, surrounded by her family, with white and yellow plumeria leis stacked to her ears. I couldn't believe that we were surrounded by all these people in this paradise, all of whom, previously unbeknownst to me, were my relatives. Why had my mother kept this all from us? It was a beautiful moment, but I couldn't understand why I knew nothing about this place. Why had these people, my relatives, been hidden from me? I already knew that my mother had been using being Hawaiian as a way to neutralize her race during a time when the color of your skin could work against you. What I didn't understand is why she would hide all this natural beauty and a loving family from us, a family that clearly adored her and welcomed us.

ALAPA FAMILY HISTORY

The Alapa family has deep roots in Lāʻie and Kahuku, where The Church of Jesus Christ of Latter-day Saints had its Pacific outreach headquarters and did a great deal of missionary work.[3] My Hawaiian family is mostly Mormon. My great-grandfather, Oliva Alapa, was born in the mid-1800s. Land owned by the family in Kahana, a remote coastal area on the island of Oʻahu, was sold when Oliva moved to a settlement of Hawaiian Mormons in Iosepa, Utah, which is pronounced "Yosepa," in the late 1800s. The settlement was named for the Mormon prophet Joseph F. Smith, who went to the Hawaiian Islands as a missionary in 1854.[4] In the settlement, Hawaiians spoke their language and read Mormon texts in Hawaiian. Oliva Alapa was considered a leader there. His wife, my great-grandmother, had died in Hawaiʻi. Their son, Harvey Alapa, was my grandfather.

Olivia Haleaka Alapa, my mother, was born in 1910 to Harvey and Mary Kahoohihi Luela. A smallpox epidemic decimated Iosepa in 1913,[5] taking her father and mother and orphaning her at the age of two. The settlement was disbanded by the Mormon Church shortly thereafter, and many of its inhabitants, who, like my great-grandfather, had homesteaded large tracts of land there, were forced to sell their land against their will. Others chose to sell and voluntarily return to Hawaiʻi.

My mother returned to Oʻahu along with her three sisters and her grandfather, Oliva Alapa, in 1917. Two of my mother's sisters, Ivy and Julia, stayed with their great aunts in Kahana with her mother's side of the family, which was the lighter-skinned side. The third sister, Nahinu, and my mother stayed in Kahuku with her father's side of the family, who comprised the darker-skinned side.

---

3 Note: My family history has been pieced together from family anecdotes. It is as accurate as is possible under the circumstances. Other members of the family may have different opinions as to the accuracy of this history.

4 Mays, Kenneth. "Picturing history: President Joseph F. Smith sites — missions to Hawaii." *Deseret News*, 18 Jul 2018. https://www.deseret.com/2018/7/18/20649297/picturing-history-president-joseph-f-smith-sites-missions-to-hawaii.

5 Panek, Tracey E. "Life at Iosepa, Utah's Polynesian Colony." *Utah Historical Quarterly* 60, no. 1. 1992. https://issuu.com/utah10/docs/uhq_volume60_1992_number1/s/162486.

My Hawiian grandparents, Harvey Alapa and Mary Kahoohihi Luela

My aunts tell me my great-grandfather left the Church and eventually went to the Big Island, where he raised my mother until she was a teenager. He received a Hawaiian homestead, close to Hilo. Hawaiian homelands were areas held in trust under the Hawaiian Homes Commission Act of 1921.[6] About 200,000 acres were set aside for Native

---

[6] *Department of Hawaiian Home Lands*. "Hawaiian Homes Commission Act." 09 Jul 1921. https://dhhl.hawaii.gov/hhc/laws-and-rules/.

Hawaiians, whose monarchy had been overthrown in 1893 and whose "crown lands" had been ceded to the US government.

Oliva died in 1924 when Olivia was 14. She was then sent to live with her Aunty Annie. It is rumored in the family that she was being abused sexually by Aunty Annie's husband, who was thought to be a drunk. She ran away to her sister Julia's home in Kona. Julia had been ostracized from the family because she had married a Filipino.

From 1924 to 1931, from the age of 14 to 21, Olivia was on her own, and it is uncertain what she did. We know she went to San Francisco. After she returned to Kahuku from San Francisco, she had a child fathered by a Jewish surveyor she had met in San Francisco. At that time, she was informed that her sister Julia had died of leprosy, which triggered a lifelong fear of the disease in Olivia. When she became pregnant with her youngest daughter, Lani, her skin became dry and flakey, and she was convinced she had leprosy, so much so that my father considered leaving the Army and taking her back to Hawai'i.

Members of the family believe, despite what Olivia was told, that Julia died at the Kalaupapa Leper Colony on the island of Moloka'i.[7] In 1865, the Hawaiian government began sentencing lepers to involuntary lifetime isolation on Kalaupapa Peninsula to reduce the spread of the disease, which is now often referred to as *Hansen's disease*, after the Norwegian bacteriologist who first identified the germ that causes it.

> *The patients were judged to be civilly dead, their spouses granted summary divorces, and their wills executed as if they were already in the grave. Soon thousands were in exile, and life within this lawless penitentiary came to resemble that aboard a crowded raft in the aftermath of a shipwreck, with epic battles erupting over food, water, blankets, and women.*[8]

---

7 Law, Anwei Skinsnes. *Kalaupapa: A Collective Memory*. (UH Press, 2012).

8 Taymen, John. *The Colony*, (Scribner, 2007), 2.

Gross, Terry. *Fear and Loathing in Hawaii: 'Colony'*, 06 Feb 2006; https://www.npr.org/2006/02/02/5183996/fear-and-loathing-in-hawaii-colony.

Because Olivia's sister, Julia, was exiled there when she was, the horrors of this situation were likely to have been much less than was the case originally, where those inflicted with Hansen's disease were dumped in the surf and had to swim to the peninsula and fend for themselves. Food was dropped in the ocean from time to time, and the residents had to swim out to retrieve it. It was a lawless, cruel existence.

Belgian missionary, Father Damien de Veuster, devoted his life to serving this unfortunate population, treating them, and helping provide them quality of life. So, Julia likely was treated, received care, had a social life, and died with dignity. The uncertainty as to how the disease was contracted and spread at the time of Julia's death most certainly led to my mother's overwhelming fear that she might contract the disease.

When I asked my mother about our family name, she said it was the name of a regiment of King Kamehameha's army on the Big Island. I learned that isn't exactly true. The Hawaiian word ʻālapa means "athlete" or "slender", and Kamehameha was often described with this adjective. However, it was actually the name of a company of warriors who fought with Kalaniʻopuʻu, Kamehemeha's uncle and predecessor as chief of the island.[9] [10]

My mother didn't talk a lot about our Hawaiian heritage, but she did give me the idea that we were descended from warriors. During many years of combat on the football field and in the business world, I could sometimes sense the spirit of my warrior ancestors' genes coursing through my blood, inspiring and empowering me. The football field and the boardroom were synonymous. They were both battlefields.

---

9 Translation by Queen Liliuokalani. *Sacred Texts.* "The Alapa Regiment, Chapter XIII." 1897 https://sacred-texts.com/pac/hhl/hhl17.htm.

10 Kulanui. *Wehewehe Wikiwiki.* https://hilo.hawaii.edu/wehe/?q=ʻālapa&l.

SPORTS IN HAWAI'I, SNOWSHOES SCHOENKE, AND THE ALLURE OF MILITARY MEN

Sports, at that time, were popular throughout the islands. High schools and all the services—Army, Navy, Air Force, Marines—took part in contests. Sports were a big deal, and games were attended by a lot of local people. Local Hawaiian women went in hopes of meeting and dating servicemen. They felt that marrying a serviceman (who typically at that time was White) would improve their station in life. They were looking for an upgrade.

One of those servicemen was my father, Raymond Frederick Schoenke. He was a big-time athlete who had joined the military at 17 after growing up in Chaska, a farming community about 30 miles west of Minneapolis. My grandparents had come to America from Germany when they were young. My grandfather and his brother landed in New York, but when they heard there was land available in Minnesota, they left to homestead a large tract outside of Minneapolis. They cleared the land, cut down trees, burned out roots, and extracted everything so that they had land to till.

My grandfather disliked farming, so he decided to go into the small town of Chaska, about 30 miles from the Twin Cities, to work at a brick factory. He was happy to have a job as a laborer. My grandmother's job was to take care of the kids and feed everybody. They had chickens and ducks and geese and 9 living kids. Several others had died at birth. My grandfather was a little bitty guy who didn't say much. My grandmother was the typical German country wife—on the stocky side at this stage of her life, sweet, loving, and caring.

My father was born on December 10, 1910, in Chaska, Minnesota. After he dropped out of high school, he enlisted in the Army Engineer Corps thinking that meant he would drive a train. They shipped him to Hawai'i in the late 1920s. When he showed up at the Schofield Barracks, the supply sergeant asked him if he played any sports. "The general," he said, "likes the sports teams."

My German grandparents, Anna and August Schoenke

My father said, "Well, I played in high school." Consequently, he became an Army jock known as "Snowshoes Schoenke."[11] He had large feet, but this nickname was mostly due to the style in which he shot the basketball. He set both of his feet apart like he had on snowshoes and fired at the basket.

---

11 Joyce, Gare. "The Game Beyond the Game." SPORTSNET. https://www.sportsnet.ca/nfl/longform/ray-schoenkes-journey-nfl-lineman-white-house-insider/.

He was recognized as one of the top basketball players on the island. In 1933, as a private first class, he was on the division championship team.[12] (In fact, he was on the division championship team for four years and on the department championship team for three.) He was an All-Star basketball player and held the Army record for 50 points in a single basketball game. This was back in the 30s, before jump shots and three-pointers; his specialty was the two-hand push. He was an All-Star in baseball, too. I have pictures of him in his All-Star sweater and a watch he was awarded.

All the maids at Schofield got together and went to the games. It was easier to meet a serviceman at a basketball game than at a club in Honolulu. My mother had dated more than one serviceman and had married one of my father's basketball teammates. She later divorced him.

No sooner had she and my dad gotten engaged than my mother started working on Dad to go to OCS (Officers Candidate School). She wanted to be an officer's wife, but he did not want to be an officer. All he wanted to do was play basketball and hang out. He had a great life. He had few responsibilities as a sergeant, and he was dating my mother, a beautiful Hawaiian lady, who by then was pregnant with his first child. He had it made. Unlike many of the enlisted men on base who impregnated the local women and abandoned them, he had accepted the responsibility of a family and married her.

My sister was born the May after my parents married in September of 1939, and I was born in September 1941. My mother finally succeeded in getting my father to go to OCS after the bombing of Pearl Harbor in December of 1941. He was commissioned as a Second Lieutenant in September 1942 for the "duration of the present emergency."[13] Afraid the Japanese were going to invade Hawai'i, he sent us to stay with his family in Chaska, Minnesota.

---

12 University of Illinois Library. "US Army Recruiting News." 1933, 13. See General Wells present the Department Medal and Bar to the team, including PFC Schoenke.

13 Note: From a document sent by R.O. Crawford, Brigadier General, US Army, Commandant.

*My father and mother, Raymond Frederick Schoenke Sr.
and Olivia Haleaka Alapa*

He was then shipped off to Europe to build bridges and roads with the 3rd Engineer Battalion.

When he married my mother, my father sent a letter to his parents saying, "I'm marrying this beautiful Hawaiian lady, but I don't think we will be coming back to visit. We're going to live in Hawai'i." What he really feared was that his family would not accept my mother because she was dark-skinned. My aunts later told me that in Minnesota at that time, it was considered a no-no for a White to marry any person of color, so they would have viewed my mother as non-White. Then, two years later, he shipped us all there because he thought the Japanese were going to attack Hawai'i.

MY LIFE AS A MILITARY BRAT : MOTHER'S WILD DOG

Like my father, my aunts—his sisters—were concerned about their mother's reaction and how my mother would be treated in Chaska. We went there in May 1942—my mother, me, my sister Marilyn, and my older brother Walter.[14] We went by boat to San Francisco and then took a train to Minneapolis, Minnesota. Walter later told us that when we arrived, the assembled aunts and uncles viewed my mother as an officer's wife, not as a maid. And she came off strutting. She had taken on the persona of the generals' wives she had worked for. My aunts, simple housewives and first-generation children of immigrants, were blown away by her because she was so proud and conducted herself in such a sophisticated manner. She walked and talked like she was a queen. Walter said they practically bowed to her.

My mother worked throughout the 1930s as a maid in the homes of generals. At that time, officers usually came from well-to-do families and were West Point graduates. She was taught to serve, talk, and conduct herself with proper etiquette. She was expected to understand the protocol in an officer's home.

We settled in what was a little German community, where at the time, several of the Germans in the community were not looking kindly upon Jews and were supportive of Germany and Hitler. However, my mother quickly befriended the Coopersteins, the Jewish grocers, with whom the family remained friends for years, so she could get sugar

---

14 Moffitt, Kelly. "75 Years Later: St. Louis Memories of the Pearl Harbor Attacks." *All Things Considered*, St. Louis Public Radio, 07 Dec 2016.

St. Louis Post-Dispatch. "Walter Schoenke Obituary." Jan 2016. https://www.legacy.com/us/obituaries/stltoday/name/walter-schoenke-obituary?pid=177249954.

and butter and other special items that were being rationed at the time. She needed these items to entertain, which she promptly started doing. She had learned how to throw elaborate parties in Hawai'i as a maid to the general. She threw tea parties and wined and dined the residents of Chaska. Everybody was impressed with the wife of Second Lt. Raymond F. Schoenke. They just assumed that she was well-educated and came from the upper middle class.

I never saw my mom treated with racism. She befriended people in the community, and they adored her. She worked hard to please people, though, and she put on airs by trying to seem very sophisticated and more educated than she really was. When I left for school, she was in a bathrobe and slippers. When I returned from school, she was transformed. She had on a nice dress, makeup, high heels. She knew how to be a classy hostess, and she entertained people who were economically a few stations above us, the people who owned the hardware store, the banker, the minister. You wouldn't believe how expert my mother was at convincing everyone that she was much more than a country girl and an orphan from Hawai'i.

However, things were different at home. She could be a terror. At one point when I was maybe four, my brother Walter, a young teenager, was going around the community saying, "It's all bullshit. My mother's a maid." She got so mad that she took my father's belt and tried to beat the hell out of him, and when my dad came back from the war, they shipped Walter out of town to some private school. She didn't want him around blowing her cover. At that time, I was too young to really understand that she even had a cover. I didn't understand this until we went back to Hawai'i, and her past was exposed to me as a teenager.

As a military family, we went from Minnesota to Missouri, Washington, New Mexico, New York, England, and then Texas. My dad stayed in the US Army Corps of Engineers, but at some point, sometime after 1947 when the Air Force was separated from the Army, he had to make a choice. He decided to join the Air Force because he would have a higher rank.

One of his first assignments after the war was in Tacoma, Washington, where I went to kindergarten. One of my first memories is from kindergarten in Tacoma. I sang a little ditty I'd learned, "Little Duckie Duddle," on the way home from school:

Little Duckie Duddle
Went swimmin' in a puddle,
A puddle, a puddle
Quite small
He said it doesn't matter
How much I splash and splatter
I'm only
A little duckie after all
Quack, quack

Every puddle that I came across, I jumped in. When we were adults, my brother Walter sentimentally recalled watching me splashing my way home singing that song. It's because of his retelling that I remember it.

I was a sweet little boy then, not the warrior I later became.

My sister Olivia Pualani, whom we call Lani, was born in Tacoma. Walter, Marilyn, and I were close to each other, but Lani was the baby, and she ended up being very close to my mother, who lived with her in her old age. Lani, perhaps due to her long relationship with my mother as an adult, has a distinct perspective of her and even identifies with her. Like my mother, Lani is artistically inclined. She built a major wholesale manufacturing business in luxury decorative pillows that reflected her impeccable taste. She, like my mother, is concerned about appearances and is consequently very protective of her mother's memory. To this day, she is deeply concerned about how Mother will be perceived by others who knew her, even after her death.

Family photo in Rome, New York in the late 1940s

My older sister, Marilyn, has assumed the calm, centered personality of my father, and has raised her children without raising her voice, as she recalls Mom doing frequently. She says that when she was angry as a young mother, she softened her voice. The softer her voice, the more concerned her children got about the consequences of their behavior. She, like myself, played a role in calming my mother when she was out of control, and her son, Neil, also became a calming influence. She also inherited my mother's artistic gifts, and, although by her account, she is less talented, she did pass this talent on to her own daughter.

I had both very negative and very positive experiences with my mother, and even though those experiences are depicted here in the harsh light of my memories, I had enormous love and affection for this very complex, strong, resilient, intelligent, and gifted woman, a sentiment that is shared by all of us except Walter, now deceased, who had a strained relationship with her, bore the brunt of Mother's volatility, and was also very much like her. He shared many of her worst and best characteristics. He was a problem for my mother, and they had a very negative relationship. But he was like a father to me, and I worshipped him as a child. As an adult, he assumed many of the negative qualities of my mother. But I did appreciate his professional capabilities and later hired him as a lead marketer representing my company in the Midwest.

We moved to Hobbs, New Mexico when I was in first grade. We lived in a Quonset hut at Hobbs Army Airfield, which was used during World War II by the United States Army Air Forces Air Training Command as part of the Western Flight Training Center. The military base was in the middle of nowhere in the desert. There were jackrabbits running everywhere, which my father enjoyed hunting. My first experiences with guns and hunting included carrying an unloaded shotgun while he hunted rabbits and in the officer's "club," which was nothing more than a glorified Quonset hut on the base. The base commander was a colonel who was a sharpshooter. He often demonstrated his ability after dinner or an event by shooting live ammo at circles of glass normally used as outdoor targets inside the hut near the fireplace. When he hit them, they shattered, and pieces of broken glass littered the floor around the fireplace. From my perspective as a small child, the only thing I can liken this experience to is the Wild West.

We next moved to Rome, New York, while I was still in first grade. I remember we had two- or three-foot snows. There was an ice rink—tennis courts they'd hose down with water and freeze, and everybody would skate. One time, I decided to skate back to my house on the roads. Part of the way home, I got so tired that I crawled the rest of the way in the snow on the road on my hands and knees. My older and far wiser sister, who was all of eight years old at the time, asked me why I didn't just take off the skates, put my shoes back on, and walk home. I had somehow failed to recognize that I had that option.

In New York, when I was in the second grade, an older kid, maybe 10 years old, showed me how to start a fire. I was fascinated by this new ability, and some friends of mine and I got the wise idea when we were hiking that we could start a campfire underneath a row of pine trees in the back of a farm behind our subdivision. We got so excited by the fire that one kid got more brush to stoke it. Before we knew it, there was a full blaze going. I peeked out from under the branches of the trees and saw fire trucks and neighbors heading for the blaze. I'm seven years old, and the only thought I have is that I need to get out of there and go home.

I race back to my house, where someone is on the phone telling my mother that I had started a fire. She was so embarrassed, she started wailing on me, and then she lit matches, grabbing me forcefully by the arm, holding my fingers up to the flames, saying, "That'll teach you to start another fire." I was fighting her hard, and, while it was difficult, she still was able to burn my fingers. I ran to my room crying and went to bed. My sister Marilyn heard me crying and came in and asked me what was wrong. I said, "Mommy burnt my fingers." She slowly backed away with her head down like I had a disease she didn't want to catch. Mom certainly got her point across. "Don't start fires." The next day, Mom brought me breakfast in bed and told me she was going to take us to the fair. She put bandages on my fingers, and we went to the fairgrounds. I sat in the backseat with Marilyn, still in shock. It was raining, so we never got out of the car. The contrast between what had happened the day before and what was happening then made no sense to me. I wasn't sure what to expect. As an adult, whenever I lit a fire in my fireplace, I felt my mother looking over my shoulder.

Another time, I was sitting at the table pouring water into a glass and not paying attention, and next thing I knew, the water streamed out of the glass all over the table and the floor. She walked up behind me and lashed me across the back with her hand. I was eight or nine at the time. She would just snap. It was not predictable. Any innocently stupid thing I did could result in an explosion. She had quick hands. It wasn't unusual at all for her to slap me. She had created an image of herself that she did not want betrayed by her history in Hawai'i, where she had no social standing, and any kind of embarrassment triggered her fear of being outed. Any behavior on my part that threatened her carefully constructed image could be met with severe and potentially violent outbursts. My father was often away on assignments at other locations in the US as well as in Europe, so she had to contend with my sister and me and Walter, who was in high school and really only slept at the house and otherwise was absent.

Soon after Walter was taken out of private school and sent to a public school in Rome, New York, he decided to leave home, telling me he was going to Minnesota to live with my father's mother, who adored him. He said, "I can't take Mom anymore." He just walked out. I ran after him and jumped in his arms.

"You gotta take me with you," I said, crying.

"You gotta stay here," he stated emphatically.

"I'm *not* gonna stay here," I screamed. He took me back home and then left. This became common behavior on his part. He left and returned after my mother tracked him down. When my mother was alone during my father's frequent absences, she carefully hid her past, constructed stories, and tried to be 'somebody.' She was always afraid someone would find out she was hiding her humble background. When Walter or I embarrassed her by doing things that drew negative attention to the family or suggested she wasn't a good mother, she'd snap and tear the house apart by throwing anything within reach, breaking dishes against the walls and turning over furniture. These outbursts were incredibly frightening to witness, and I often felt guilty afterwards if I believed I had triggered them. Often, after these explosions, she would go into a funk, put on her pajamas and robe, go into her bedroom, and wouldn't come out for several days except to prepare food, remaining mostly silent and then returning to her room. She left the door open and appeared to be sleeping. We walked on eggshells until her depression lifted. We worried about her but were afraid to bother her. She also became remorseful and depressed after outbursts when she punished us physically. It was obvious that she loved us and felt badly about her behavior, but it was very confusing. This pattern lasted throughout our childhoods.

Her background in Hawai'i was a wild dog chasing her that at any moment could catch up with her, rip her apart, and destroy her. The pressure on her must have been tremendous, and in turn, the pressure not to reveal her past or uncover her falsehoods was transferred to us, especially Walter and me, the two loose cannons—he because he openly broadcasted her background, and me because I, in my youthful innocence, could unwittingly embarrass her. The frequent moves also contributed to upending our stability. It was difficult to ever view the world as stable or predictable. My mother's wild dog followed us wherever we went.

We moved to England in the late '40s. My father was assigned to the 3rd Air Force in Ruislip, England, working for the Berlin Airlift. We lived in a small town called Beaconsfield, about 30 minutes by car outside of London. The remnants of the war were still very much in evidence. When we took the train to London, we could still see bombed-out parts of the city in ruins. The Germans had also directed rockets without targets into the English countryside, and people talked about how the rockets had flown indiscriminately and crashed all over the place.

With my sisters, Marilyn and Lani, when we lived in Beaconsfield, England

There were a variety of schools, where those with higher status required uniforms and were segregated by sex. We lived in a middle-class neighborhood on the fringes of London. The school I attended backed up to the apartment complexes where maids and other common laborers lived. Their kids lined up on the fence and yelled at me to come over to the fence, which I did. I was friendly with them because some of their parents worked for us. That was a no-no to my mother. They were the children of the people who worked in our home. I wasn't to play with them (but I did).

My mother was very eager for us to take on the habits of the English—the styles, the language, and the mannerisms. Coming from the US, we didn't know the protocols. I remember going to the homes of middle-class kids for tea. My manners were extremely unrefined in terms of British culture, while they had been completely acceptable in the States. For example, the bread was baked in fresh loaves and was delicious. I started sopping the buttered bread in my tea, and when I looked up, everyone was staring at me, and Marilyn was side-eyeing me. I have no idea how she knew what to do and what not to do. They served dainty little cucumber finger sandwiches with tea, with which I was unfamiliar. I opened my sandwich to see what was in it and still required an explanation. They used a knife to scoot food onto the back of their forks, which seemed very strange to me. Breakfast was simply bread and tea, unlike the eggs and bacon or cereal that I was used to. At first, I didn't realize I was being ill-mannered, but after watching other children, I realized that there were certain ways to conduct yourself in Great Britain, and I was not adhering to the protocols.

Walter attended and graduated from the High Wycombe Oxford Prep School. He graduated in 1950 and then tried to get into Oxford, passing four of the five tests, but failing one, so he went back to the States and enrolled at the University of Minnesota. My guess is that he partied and didn't go to class. It was the first time he had been totally independent. He flunked out, so he enlisted in the Air Force to avoid facing my parents.

My parents sent me to a private school, Davenies. It was in a beautiful, pastoral setting, with historic formal gardens in a small valley surrounded by trees. The classrooms were situated in a cluster of beautiful buildings.[15] I had to wear a uniform consisting of a blue

---

15 *ARCI TONIC.* "Davenies Day Preparatory School." https://www.architonic.com/en/project/dsdha-davenies-school/5104570.

blazer and brown shorts, green stockings, and an orange-and-brown cap with a bumblebee on it or khaki slacks, dress shoes, blue blazer, white dress shirt, and tie. I took French, Latin, Geometry, and World Geography. It had been part of the curriculum for these kids since they were four years old. I was eight years old, and needless to say, I did very poorly. I spent a lot of time in the "dunce" chair. We played cricket, rugby, soccer, and boxed and swam. My dad had taught me the crawl, whereas everyone else only did the breaststroke. At swim meets, I won all my races. We had to take horseback riding lessons, and when they asked if I rode, I assumed it was cowboys and Indians, and I said, "Yes." But you had to wear the little black cap, and you couldn't ride Western style deep in the saddle and respond naturally to the horse's movement. You had to bounce up and down when you trotted, which seemed unnatural to me, and I had to learn to do it. I really got a taste of the Old World.

Music was required at Davenies, and when they asked me what instrument I played, I had to admit that I didn't play an instrument. I agreed to do piano because that appealed to me, but they said I had to have one at home to practice. I told my parents, and they arranged at a nearby church to "rent" a piano for me to practice on. I had to walk almost every day at the age of eight and nine at dusk along a fencerow backing up a row of houses to the back of an empty church and use the key given to me to gain access and practice the piano by myself. As I walked, beyond the fence, I could see into the windows of the nearby houses as the lights in the homes went on. I knew a child in one family, comprising what appeared to be a large group of Irish blue-collar workers—robust, young, lean, strong men with their sleeves rolled up, passing large plates of what looked like meat and potatoes around the table every time I walked by. I remember thinking they looked very happy, as if they were all really digging in and enjoying the meal. I always wondered why there were so many people eating there. I practiced for an hour, but occasionally, I walked to the sanctuary and peeked in to see if anyone was in there. There never was anyone. I was scared a lot while I was in that building.

At the time, the English were still on food rations, but we could buy whatever and as much as we wanted at the military commissary. We had a big American car, which was impressive in the little town of Beaconsfield. We even had an English maid and gardener, Mr. and Mrs. Weston. My mother made a point to go to estate sales and buy silver with our American dollars. She put on parties for officers and their wives at our house with all these silver settings. A former employer had sent her to Honolulu to cooking school, and now she had the serving utensils that made it possible for her to entertain in style. When she entertained, which was often, she exhausted herself and the maid with polishing all that silver and preparing the food.

In England, my father was often away, but when he came home, we ran and met him as soon as he had parked the car. We hugged and kissed, and inside, he let us climb up his belly while he flipped us over like beached whales. Then, at some point, and quite suddenly, he said, "Raymond, we can't do that anymore. Now we have to shake hands." I was a little happy-go-lucky kid—eight or nine years old—shaking hands with this giant. I wanted him to be my daddy. I wanted to play! But he came from a different world. He never had a close relationship with his own father, and from that point forward, there was a formality between us.

Meantime, my mother got it in her head that she had to go to the European Continent, insisting she couldn't go by herself, so she took my sister and me along. We were eight and nine years old, going through France and Switzerland, alone among adult travelers. This was shortly after the war, and the water wasn't good to drink. Servers at restaurants brought glasses of wine for us, and my mother said, "They can't drink wine."

"Well, you don't drink the water here. You'll get sick," they replied. So, we drank the wine. It was sort of a crazy trip for two young kids. My mother wasn't hungry for experience or knowledge; she just wanted to be able to impress people later by telling them that she'd traveled through Europe. I remember being in Lucerne, Switzerland, in a little paddle boat in the middle of a lake. My mother was screaming trying to get me back to shore. I was having the time of my life out there all by myself.

TOO FAT, TOO BROWN, AND TOO TALL

In 1951, we moved to Weatherford, Texas, just west of Fort Worth, where I started in the middle of fifth grade and continued for sixth, seventh, eighth, and part of ninth grade. I got a good taste of Texas. While England was the Old World, Texas was a new world, where you could ride a horse the right way. It was filled with cowboys, country music, square dancing, and, unfortunately, segregation. For the first time, I started to become aware of how my skin color would play a huge role in my life. At first, I was oblivious. I was a nice kid and fairly popular. But during my first year in Texas, my belly hung over my belt, and guys who were bigger or more mature got other kids to start calling me "Fat Girl" to try to humiliate me. I was an easy target, and they got a lot of their friends to go along with them to surround me and tease me.

In fifth grade, I was under constant assault by sixth-grade boys, and the kids in my class were in no position to defend me. I was on my own. I had never felt so totally helpless and alone. A few times, I was abruptly surrounded outside near the building while several guys held my arms, and someone undid my belt while two or three other guys pulled my pants down. They left me with my pants around my ankles, laughing as they ran away. Other students were always happy to serve as the jeering gallery, some from inside the classroom looking out the windows, while I rushed to get my pants back up—in shock and humiliated beyond belief. I felt violated and traumatized. I still feel an emotional charge remembering it. I don't remember exactly what they said to me, but I do recall that there was a racial overtone to their taunts. For the most part, I tried to dismiss it, but I was confused about why I was being singled out and physically attacked.

When I got to junior high, I had a paper route. I had bought a new bike, thrilled about the first day of school, and was looking forward to junior high. My elementary school experience had been colored by some incidents, but I had blown them off, and as a whole, I had a good elementary school experience and was fairly popular. However, I soon learned from other kids that the big thing at junior high was yet again to pull someone's pants down in front of everybody to embarrass them, and I was marked. As before, kids tougher and older felt they could pick on me. The first week of school, the word went out that a gang of older kids was going to take my pants off in front of everyone.

All around me, I heard, "They're going to get you."

I still felt confused. "Why *me*?" But internally, I knew I was different and that they perceived me as weak. I never told my parents this was going on. I spent a whole week dodging my oppressors—parking my bike in the back of the school so I could leave from there while they waited for me in front. They didn't catch me, but I knew I would eventually have to stand up to them. A teacher ultimately asked me why I was parking my bike in back of the school and told me I had to park it in front where everyone else did. I no longer could hide and run away.

"*To hell with it. I'll just meet 'em,*" I bravely said to myself. I parked my bike in front of the school and, after school, walked out to my bike. They all surrounded me and started calling me names and teasing me. Some kids pushed me off of my bike, and one kid came over and punched me in the face and bloodied my nose. I think I went into shock. I had no idea why this was happening to me. Then, the principal came, broke it up, and tried to figure out what started it all. He took us into his office. He let the other guys go but kept me back and said, "Raymond, you're going to have to learn to stand up to them." My confusion deepened. I still couldn't quite grasp why they were picking on me and no one else. I just wanted to be the nice kid that I knew I was but also knew that there was something different about me that was provoking some of the more aggressive kids and causing them to single me out. The only thing that was noticeably different about me was the color of my skin.

Parker County, where Weatherford is located, has an extensive history of the relations between the American Indians[16] and the ranchers and settlers there. Indigenous Americans have been labeled a number of ways throughout history, but the Bureau of Indian Affairs has suggested the term "American Indian." I identified with the American Indians because of my dark skin because they were the only people I knew of who looked like me. I studied Indian tribes; I knew about the Comanche and Navajo. That was my world. My identification with them said something about my growing consciousness of my own race.

Because I identified with American Indians, I took up hunting in the fifth and sixth grades. I joined the Youth Center, where the National Rifle Association held contests, providing BB guns and targets, and won several of the competitions. As a ten-year-old, I asked for a gun for Christmas, and though I thought I got it across to my parents how badly I wanted it, the present I thought was a gun turned out to be a baseball bat. I was a good athlete and might have appreciated the bat, but I started crying. Walter, who had come back from the service for Christmas leave, went out and bought me my first gun, a used, single-shot .22 rifle, for $10.

My dad started to indulge my passion. Hunting doves was a big thing in Texas. My father got me a hunting license, and together, we bought a bolt-action 20-gauge shotgun. I befriended classmates whose families lived on the outskirts of town, and Dad took me out to their farms to hunt doves, rabbits, and quail. From that point on, I was immersed in developing hunting skills—not just sharpshooting, but also the patience to track animals and sit in blinds.

---

16 Oliver, Pamela. "Race Names." *Race, Politics, Justice*. 16 Sep 2017. https://www.ssc.wisc.edu/soc/racepoliticsjustice/2017/09/16/race-names/.

Native Sun News Today Editorial Board. "Indian, Native, or Indigenous. Which One Would You Choose?" 16 Aug 2018. https://www.indianz.com/News/2018/08/16/indian-native-or-indigenous-which-one-wo.asp.

My little league baseball team (it's not hard to find me)

I was also beginning to like sports. It wasn't as easy for me as it had been for my father, who had excelled at baseball and basketball. I joined Little League when I was 11, for which the age requirement was 10 through 12, but soon there was a new problem. There's a picture of the Little League team at that time with this monster in the background, which is me. I mean, all the other boys are below my shoulders! When I was 12, coaches accused me of being older, requiring me to bring my birth certificate. When I got up to bat, opposing coaches came over and grabbed the bat and chewed me out or told my coaches to kick me off the team. As assistant coach, my dad always stood up for me. When I'd hit a home run, opposing coaches would start screaming again, doubting my age and accusing my father and me of cheating. I wasn't doing anything wrong. I was just big, and I could hit the ball out of the park. By the end of the eighth grade, I was over six feet tall.

By 13, I was six foot three. It was just a matter of time until the day of reckoning. I was becoming a warrior because I had to. It started in football. At first, I didn't know how to tackle or block people hard with a great deal of intensity; I turned my head away and often completely missed. During recess, my friends and I played catch with a football on the cement tennis courts, and older boys—my nemeses—came over and stole the football away and laughed. I ran after them and tackled them so hard I scraped my cheek on the surface of the court. While I only scraped my face, when they hit the ground, their faces, arms, and legs slid unforgivingly across the cement. They had bloodied abrasions on their arms and faces, bits of gravel stuck to their skin, and pain in their chest, backs, or stomach from being tackled. I had small pieces of gravel lodged in my face, but the guys I hit were far more bruised and bloodied. I felt powerful and vindicated. Any pain I felt was worth it, and the gouges in my skin were badges of honor. I looked as tough as I felt, and everyone knew it. They stopped stealing our football.

Then, on the football team, I realized I could really hurt these guys. If I led with my head, the helmet protected me, and it functioned like a battering ram. I became a wild man. The harder I hit 'em, the more the coaches exclaimed how great I was, and I just kicked it up a notch. From that point on, nobody messed with me. I became more confident in who I was, particularly against the bullies.

In the seventh grade, it was the eighth and ninth graders who were my enemies. I hit them. I got moved to the eighth-grade team, up to the ninth-grade team, and then as a ninth grader, to the junior varsity team. I hit them. Then, I had to face seniors on the high school team. Once, when I walked into the locker room, a senior walked up to me and punched me right in the stomach. It took my breath away. As I was bending over, gasping for air, he laughed. I sprang up and tried to punch him in the face. He didn't expect a counter.

"Don't ever do that again," I said. I then went after him and anyone else who challenged me on the football field. I was realizing that bullies are everywhere. It just never stops. Bullies are inherently cowards. You have to take them down immediately, or they become emboldened and feel they are invincible. Later on in the NFL, as violent as that world was, I couldn't believe that I encountered teammates who hadn't learned how to take down a bully and thus could be bullied on the field. I had learned how to do it, and it has served me well. I also know that you can still be a nice guy while not tolerating any form of bullying.

Weatherford was a very White community. There was a small population of Blacks who lived in Black neighborhoods. Nothing was integrated. They went to segregated schools in Fort Worth. I could go to the White school because I wasn't Black, but the irony was that I could be singled out and bullied because I wasn't *White*. My mother was very dark-complected, but she had figured out how to survive, how to fool others about her identity. She made sure everybody knew she was an officer's wife and Hawaiian. She told everybody that she had attended the University of Hawai'i and had formal training in art, and these false credentials appeared in the local papers. She used her "Hawaiianness" in subtle ways and capitalized on the mystique of being Hawaiian to prevent people from viewing our ethnicity as negative. She was trying to project a romantic image of Hawai'i and Hawaiians based on people's ideas from movies and television. She taught my older sister a hula, and she had me sing a simple Hawaiian song at a women's club event. I had no idea I was being manipulated to support her efforts to neutralize our ethnicity. Later, at an event in junior high school, Marilyn danced the hula in a bathing suit and cellophane skirt. My sister was really pretty, and everybody thought that her dance was cool. My mother's efforts were working.

But with us, my mother didn't really talk about being Hawaiian. I only knew that Hawai'i existed. There was an officer, a dentist, who was Japanese, from Hawai'i, and he and his family came over and brought us Asian food they had cooked. It was festive, and they reminisced about Hawai'i. But Hawai'i seemed to me like it could have been on Mars; the conversations never really centered around *us* or our relationship to Hawai'i.

Being Hawaiian did function in a certain way for me. When a new kid would come into school, and say, "Hey, what's the name of that spic over there?" my schoolmates would say, "Nah, he's not a spic. He's a Hawaiian." But I knew I was dark, and I knew that that was a problem. I knew that I was a "spic," or a "half-ass nigger" when I went out of the city limits, where nobody knew me.

But within the confines of this town, I developed a positive reputation. I wasn't a troublemaker. I was a good student, a good athlete, quite popular, president of my eighth grade class and vice president of my ninth grade class. My size helped me, and athletics. I felt secure, but I knew the minute I stepped outside the city limits—boom—I was no longer this favored child. I knew I would be pigeonholed. I knew that racism existed, but I still didn't really know about truly being Hawaiian.

I applied myself academically, starting in grade school at T.W. Stanley in Weatherford. My teachers, Mrs. Lidell in fifth grade and Miss Ragell in sixth, were supportive, encouraging me and praising me for my work. However, this was a time when corporal punishment was allowed in public schools, and Miss Ragell enjoyed this dubious 'privilege' of her station at every opportunity when it came to me. If I was drifting away and looking out of a window, my reverie was abruptly interrupted by Miss Ragell slapping me across the face or back. I felt clearly singled out when I got slapped for looking out of a window during class when other students did not. Other teachers, the male teachers and the principal, would decide to punish me for some minor infraction and would make me go into an office and bend over a chair or table and hit me sharply on the butt with a large paddle a few times. I always felt singled out. In spite of this, when I got to junior high, I was a straight-A student.

By the ninth grade, I was in the top classes. I won't say it wasn't hard, but I loved reading history. When Walter flunked out of college and joined the service, he left all his college books at our house. I read his history book; it was for a survey course, from the caveman to the

Renaissance. I read it when I was in the fifth grade. I was intrigued by these stories, and when I had the chance to learn, it really thrilled me. I studied the history of Weatherford, where the Comanche and the White settlers had battled. Because I was fascinated by this, I started drawing Indians. When they'd ask me to draw something for the class, I drew all these Indians. They were good portraits.

HAWAI'I: NOT JUST ANOTHER MILITARY TOUR

In 1955, my father requested an assignment to Hawai'i and was transferred to Hickam Air Force Base. I was in the middle of the ninth-grade year; I was popular; I was one of the best athletes in the school, and I had a girlfriend. I cried when we left Weatherford. We returned to Hawai'i toward the end of football season. I had played most of the games in Weatherford, but I left before the season was over. The idea of traveling to Hawai'i to most people would be enchanting, but to me, it was just another military tour. My whole life was being disrupted. We went up to Minneapolis to see my dad's mother and father because he was fearful that his mother was going to die before he got back from Hawai'i. I went to a couple of football games with my cousins. Then, we drove to California.

Our passage to Hawai'i was paid for by the military on the US naval ship *Shanks*. My father was the ranking officer, and our quarters were on the main deck.

I could not have anticipated how beautiful Hawai'i would be. The most astonishing thing about my relatives was their generosity every time we visited Lā'ie. There was always a big pot of corned beef on the stove and poi in the refrigerator at Aunty Alice's house. There was always fresh fish. Anyone who showed up at dinnertime was welcomed.

"Oh, Raymond, come in, get something to eat," were the first words I heard. I'd bring friends, and they would go straight to the refrigerator and start pulling food out. I was chagrined because I knew it was food the family needed. These were not wealthy people, but it was that way. Everything my family had, they wanted to share. I'm like that, too, and I attribute it to my Hawaiian roots, of which I am enormously proud. I have shared and continue to share my resources, however big or small, with my family, those I have become close to, and with those who have helped me on my journey.

We arrived in Hawaiʻi in the middle of the school year, before Christmas. We couldn't get housing at first, so we lived in Waipahu. I went to Pearl Harbor Junior High.

On one of the first days there, I found out who really ran the school: the Samoans. Lanu Tutufuli was the big dog. His brother Lesi was his sidekick, and they strung along a few other Samoans and a couple of White kids, the court jesters who propped them up.

I'm walking down the hall the first day, and here comes the Samoans and their crew walking shoulder to shoulder down the hallway, wall to wall. There's no room to pass. They aren't moving. I say to myself, "*Oh shit, here we go again.*" I choose the one in the middle and barrel right into him, knocking him over. I go straight through and keep on walking.

The next time I meet them walking down the hallway, we get to the same spot, and they just part and let me through. Then, they say, "Hey, come walk with us. Don't be a loner." We became buddies. One of the jesters, a hāʻole[17] (White) guy, says, "Yeah, these guys, they control everything, man. Nobody messes with me now. I go to lunch, and they make guys give me money!"

I see it happen—they go up to this hāʻole kid who's sitting down, eating his lunch. Lanu whispers in his ear; the guy takes out his wallet and hands this White kid some money. The hāʻole says, "Ain't it cool?"

---

17 *Surfer Today*, ""The origin of the word "haole."" https://www.surfertoday.com/surfing/the-origin-of-the-word-haole. It literally means "foreigner" in Hawaiian and over two centuries has come to mean "White." It can be used disparagingly as a racial slur and can carry the connotations of words like *honky* or *cracker*, or simply used to differentiate someone as a White foreigner. There is also a word, kamaʻāina, used to describe a Caucasian local who has lived on the islands for several years or generations. It literally means "child or person of the land." A person of native ancestry is called a kānaka.

I got to run with them. Somebody in their family was in the military, which was why they were in the school, so they could get on the bases. They showed me how everything worked there—how I could use the swimming pool and the gyms. The noncommissioned guys used the weight room at Hickam to become muscle men. They were real bodybuilders. They started showing me how to lift weights. Not only was I getting taller, but I was becoming lean and muscular. I had lost the baby fat that had made me a target for bullying and was developing a good physique. I put two buckets full of rocks in my bedroom. Every night I did curls with the buckets of rocks and did a few hundred push-ups. Mom wanted me to get rid of the buckets of rocks, but I refused.

SPORTS IN HAWAI'I: "ROOTS" TO SUCCESS

Because I was big, the coach of the Pearl Harbor basketball team asked if I'd play basketball, and I agreed to join the team. We played public school teams in Honolulu, as well as private schools: St. Louis, 'Iolani, Kamehameha, and Punahou, the most prestigious of them all. My dad helped the coach out when he had time since he had more experience with basketball, and we both became aware that private schools were dominating the athletic programs in Hawai'i at the time and were actively recruiting talented players, who could qualify for athletic scholarships if they were unable to pay the tuition and qualified scholastically.

My older cousin, Al Lolotai, on the side of the family who had married Samoans, was a professional wrestler and one of the first Polynesians to play in the NFL. When we went to Kahuku, he asked my father if he could take me to one of the family outings where they played football with all the kids from Kahuku. On the football field, and when we wanted something to drink, they called a time out, ran up a coconut tree, and chopped off some coconuts with machetes that were lying on the side of the field. I say to myself, "*This is unbelievable!*

You play football barefoot on these grass fields; the kids are really great athletes, and we get to drink coconut juice. We never did that in Texas."

Al was a graduate of 'Iolani. He started talking to my father. "He needs to go to 'Iolani." My dad at the time was a major at Hickam, responsible for all the installations on the base (buildings, remodels, air hangars).

His second lieutenant, Lt. Grey, was a graduate of Punahou. "Would you consider having Ray go to Punahou?" he asked.

"Sure, I don't care, as long as we don't have to pay his tuition," my father replied.

"Well, when Pearl Harbor basketball plays Punahou, why don't you check it out and see if you like it?" Lt. Grey suggested.

We played Punahou, where when I first saw the gym, I saw it as just another gym. However, it was in actuality a stark contrast to Pearl Harbor Junior High School's outdoor asphalt basketball courts surrounded by open playgrounds and Quonset huts that served as classrooms. This campus was pristine, with beautiful buildings that housed the classrooms and library, lush landscaping with coconut and palm trees, hibiscus with bright red flowers, huge monkeypod trees that afforded shade, and fully equipped gyms with a swimming pool, dormitories, and baseball, soccer, and football fields. I was just into sports at the time and oblivious to the power and influence that private schools had on sports programs in Hawai'i. The Texas public schools I had attended didn't have any of these resources either.

My sister was going to Roosevelt—a public high school that was about a mile from Punahou, in the Makiki neighborhood of Honolulu. She was a sophomore, and she said, "We don't like kids from Punahou; they're real rich and snotty, and we don't want to be with them." All I knew by then was that the campus was gorgeous—76 acres, three athletic fields, beautiful old buildings that were built by Hawai'i's first missionaries.

My dad and I met with Jim Iams, the athletic director at Punahou. He sat us down and talked about the school, its legacy, what I could do there. I had taken a scholastic exam, and Iams looked at my scores.

"He's proficient," he said. "We'd like Raymond to go here, but we can't give him a full scholarship." My dad had an officer's income, so I didn't qualify for financial aid.

"He can go to Roosevelt for nothing," my father responded.

Iams said optimistically, "Well, let's see if we can come up with a way to do this." He found me a sponsor, a wealthy alum. Harrison Cooke was a descendant of one of the original missionary families and owned Honolulu Sporting Goods.[18] He was also on the board of the Bank of Hawai'i. Iams said Cooke would pay for half of my tuition.

"You need to meet him and let him know how you're doing in school and in sports," Iams told me. "Don't just take the money and run." It was about more than finding me a sponsor. Iams wanted me to understand what the school was all about, how the scholarships for athletes worked, how you were expected to perform. Harrison Cooke paid only half my tuition. Iams suggested I get a summer job to make up the other half.

My dad's lieutenant back when he was an enlisted man at Schofield Barracks now ran a construction company, AC Chock. My dad called him, and he said, "Yeah, Ray can work for us in the summertime." The company had contracts with the Defense Department to build installations and reinforce the docks and radar facilities and expand the airfields on the islands. I went to work for AC Chock doing manual labor.

The first day I showed up at a Marine military base as a hulky 15-year-old, the crew was trying to figure out whether I would work hard or was some prima donna friend of the owner, and they wouldn't even talk to me, explain anything to me, or explain directions I was given that I obviously didn't understand. The foreman got mad at me because he thought I wasn't following his instructions. The crew was

---

18 *Honolulu Star Bulletin*. "Harrison R. Cooke Purchases Honolulu Sporting Goods Co., Ltd." 03 July 1946. https://www.newspapers.com/clip/31162684/honolulu-star-bulletin/.

extending the airfield, and the foreman gestured to an area that had been graded and told me to dig a ditch four feet wide and four feet deep. I really had no idea how to do what he was asking me to do, and he called me stupid when he saw how I was doing it.

"What's the hole for?" I asked.

"It's not your job to know what it's for. Your job is to dig the ditch," he snarled. I basically got assigned to every nasty job on the project. I dug ditches, spread gravel, hauled and spread cement, and spread hot tar. I never complained, and, over time, the crew started to appreciate what a hard worker I was, especially once I knew what I was doing. The next summer when I came back, after I got some local press for being an All Star, I was viewed as being really cool. They let me drive a dump truck that I legally wasn't allowed to drive. The money I made went to Punahou, so my dad didn't pay anything. My football buddy and good friend Joe Muller joined me at AC Chock. He needed a summer job to make extra money, and we both needed the friendship.

Jim Iams also explained to my dad how they selected athletes for scholarships. It seems like stereotyping today, but coaches looked at ethnicity to see the strengths in each group. He explained how the coaches felt that Asians tended to mature early. They played the skilled positions, the guard in basketball, the shortstop and third baseman in baseball, running backs and sometimes quarterbacks, maybe ends in football. But they never got big. Then, he talked about the Whites. They matured late. It wasn't until their senior year that they shone in sports in various positions. The coaches loved the Polynesians because they matured early, and they stayed good for all three years. I fit the mold. I was naturally born big-boned with a frame that is perfect for any NFL position.

After I began playing for Punahou, I ran into coaches who had known my dad when he was "Snowshoes Schoenke," and they asked me if I was related to him. One of the coaches from the University of Hawai'i, Tommy Kaulukukui, knew my dad from those days. I was pleased to hear stories about my father, and it was good for me to establish connections with the University of Hawai'i. I was starting to be recognized because of my dad, but also in my own right as an athlete. I was meeting some of the former graduates from Punahou, hearing their life stories and how they had become successful athletes and learning about what it meant to go to this prestigious school that was founded in 1841 specifically to educate the children of missionaries and the children of Hawaiian chiefs. It was known as a rich White school, but Hawaiians had always had a place there.

Punahou had many rules that athletes had to comply with. First, it was very demanding scholastically. I was a good student, so I knew how to study, whereas a lot of the scholarship boys did not have good study skills. They were just there to play sports. In Weatherford, my teachers complimented me and asked me to answer questions in class. Academics were harder at Punahou, so I had to play catch-up. Second, at lunchtime, I had to work as part of the serving crew to earn my free lunches. A lot of Punahou students—not just athletes—were on scholarship, so there was a normality about working in the cafeteria or in the school offices.

In my sophomore year, I went out for football. There was one guy, Danny Ane, who was this great running back. He was the younger brother of Charles "Charlie" Teetai Ane, Jr., who had played for USC and ultimately the Detroit Lions. The Ane family was—and still is—legendary at Punahou. Charlie's other brothers, Gilbert and David, were also outstanding athletes. I looked up to all of them. The coaches showed films of Charlie Ane—he became my inspiration.

I decided not to go for running back because Danny was the running back, and I wanted to make the varsity team. So I went out for lineman. Then, Bill Monahan, my coach, saw Paul Hornung in the Hula Bowl. He was a big strong running back and winner of the Heisman Trophy. I reminded him of Hornung, and because I was in his English class and a good student, he knew I was smart, so Monahan decided to make me into a quarterback. I was tall, and I went from being a lineman to

My Punahou football team—I'm #76

trying to figure out how to be a quarterback, how to throw a ball. I was either second or third team behind the starter, Alex Jamile.[19]

Monahan was experimenting with me. When we had drills, I sometimes played safety on defense, which is the last man left to make a tackle if a runner breaks out in the open. We had open field tackling, and Danny Ane came through, 230 pounds, like a galloping bull. I jumped on him, clubbed him, and pulled him down. I thought nothing of doing that. I think the coaches were impressed. That ended my career as a quarterback. I'm sure they were saying, "Why do we have this guy throwing passes? Let's get him in the line where he can tear people up."

My junior year became a huge year for me in football. Bill Monahan had been a Punahou grad, and he went to Dartmouth and served as a Marine in Korea, earning a Purple Heart and a Bronze Star for valor. He had a quiet demeanor both as a teacher and a coach, but when he spoke, he was demanding, and you listened. I once asked to get a paper extended until after a championship game with Roosevelt.

"Raymond, if football interferes with your schoolwork, I suggest you quit football," he said as he walked away.

---

19 *Star Advertiser Obituaries.* "WILLIAM 'BILL' WELSH MONAHAN, JR. Obituary: Honolulu Star." https://obits.staradvertiser.com/2020/07/05/william-bill-welsh-monahan-jr/.

In my junior year, I reached my full height, six foot four, and Monahan decided for sure to make me a lineman. Like other Polynesians, I'm naturally suited for that position, with my height and weight, and I was well ahead of other Punahou students since I'd started lifting weights at Hickam Air Force Base. The surfing and paddling helped, too. I was one of the most muscular athletes on campus and a fierce defensive player. I started dominating the line. I played wherever they put me, and I took on everybody. I was still trying to prove myself now as a Hawaiian football player. By that year, my junior year, football was my sport, and the Buff 'n' Blues my team. I simply tried to annihilate the player in front of me, and because I was strong and quick, I became good at it. We had a great team, and the only game we lost was to Roosevelt. That was a bit of a sore point because my sister was still at Roosevelt, and she was dating their second team quarterback, Raymond Correa. Roosevelt was a powerhouse. The competition between the two schools, particularly in football, was fierce. It was either Punahou or Roosevelt. They dominated.

There were fights, not so much with Roosevelt guys but with other public-school guys. There was a lot of resentment toward Punahou, which was viewed as a rich kids' school.

During a football game against McKinley, this Japanese American football player, Matsuda, starts punching me in the face.

"I want to take this guy on," I say to Coach Monahan.

"No, you can't do that. I don't want you to get kicked out of the game. Just ignore it."

As soon as the game's over, I take off after this guy, and he runs to the school bus. He gets in, and they close the door, and I'm screaming at him, telling him, "Get your ass out here!" I go up to where he is sitting. I smash the bus window, and all hell breaks loose. They drag me off, and I'm giving them the finger and cussing.

When I came back to Hawai'i to play in the Hula Bowl my senior year in college, Matsuda was on our team, representing the University of Hawai'i. We laughed about that incident.

There was this other guy, Lindsey Kinney, a teammate and a bully. He liked to go after people who were smaller. Great athlete, a natural on the basketball court, but with a mean streak. He could hurt people. I made it a point to go one-on-one with him in blocking drills on the football field, where I dominated. We had to come to terms with who was the kingpin and where. I became the higher-up on the football field and acknowledged him as the kingpin on the basketball court. We became friends. When the local boys drove through the Punahou campus at the end of most days, whistling at the girls and taunting us, Lindsey Kinney decided he'd had enough of it, so he went after one of the cars and punched a guy in the face. He hit the guy in the mouth, and the guy's teeth cut his hand wide open.

"Why'd you do that? There's gonna be a hundred guys over here!" I said.

Benny and I told Lindsey that he needed to see a doctor. Then, Benny and I sat there waiting for the local boys to show up. Sure enough, they came in their souped-up cars. Several cars showed up, and three or four guys got out. They were looking for Lindsey.

"I got a hundred guys up on the hill, up on Dillingham Field, and all I gotta do is whistle, and they'll be down here, and we'll have a brawl," I said.

They were cussing me out.

"Why don't you guys just leave?" I lied and said, "Lindsey apologizes." So they left.

I also started to learn what it meant to date cute girls—who you can date and who you can't date as a Hawaiian. There were dances, and many times, the hā'ole girls would ask *you* to dance, would ask *you* if you'd go out with them. Many hā'ole girls were forbidden by their parents to date Hawaiians, so we were like brown sugar cookies. This was new to me. It wasn't just about me, or about Hawaiians; I was surprised by the various racial taboos. One of my teammates, who said he was Puerto Rican and obviously had African-American ancestry, was sought after by a lot of girls. One classmate was the daughter of a Pacific World War II veteran who had been a POW, and he forbade her to date Japanese boys. Some Chinese parents didn't accept interracial dating, so the kids hid it from their parents. The racial attitudes came out in other contexts, as well. When I went over to a hā'ole friend's house in Kahala to lift weights, I was never invited inside. Such was Punahou.

I was just beginning to understand Hawai'i and what it means to be Hawaiian, and once I got used to these byzantine rules, I started to realize one thing about myself—being Hawaiian gave you a mystique. It made you something special; it was something to be *proud* of. The Hawaiians at Punahou had status: They were great athletes; they sang in the school choirs; they played guitar and 'ukulele; they danced the hula. They were put on a pedestal.

When I had lived in Texas, I had been looking for an identity, and I identified with American Indians. But in Hawai'i, Hawaiians are the natives. That whole thing changed. I said, "Whoa, I like this idea better, being Hawaiian." When I was walking around on Kalākaua Avenue, the main thoroughfare through Waikīkī, with my surfboard, at my height, I looked more mature than a 15-year-old—and all these wahines (pronounced wa-hee-neighs), college coeds coming in from the mainland, whistled at me. I thought I was really cool. I imagined being a Hawaiian beach boy and a great surfer even though I was neither. I wanted to become more Hawaiian than the Hawaiians.

I did surf, but I was never in the category of real surfers. I just got on the wave, and I went one way: either right or left, and that was it. And I stayed on the wave. Anyone in my way got crushed. I'd just yell at 'em, "Get out of my way!" And if there were canoes, I'd say, "Jump out of the canoe 'cause I'm coming at ya." I was behind as a Hawaiian in the dress, song, dance, and the sports that defined Hawaiians—surfing, paddling, and sailing.

Close to Pearl Harbor, in ʻEwa Beach, my mom had a cousin, Evangeline. Aunty Evanne worked at the telephone company, and so did her husband, Uncle Mel, who was Portuguese. She was a proud Hawaiian. Both were professionals—executives—who lived in a beach home in ʻEwa. Aunty Evanne had a lot in common with my mother. She felt we needed to stand up, conduct ourselves in a respectable way, take on the refinements of the hāʻole, and speak proper English. She had a beautiful home, very clean, two or three bedrooms, right near the beach. It was a small lot, but it was immaculate, with coconut trees, a yard, and a pond. She was extremely proud of her yard, and she was also quite proud of my mother for what she had accomplished. Next door to her were some Filipino families who had fighting roosters, which she abhorred because they had cages for the roosters along her property line, and they made a lot of noise. She had a son named Leonard, given to her in hānai by her sister. Leonard was gay. Sweet, sassy, tall, skinny, and very effeminate, he was known as a *māhū*.

When I went to the beach on that side of the island, or if my friends and I were going to surf at Makaha, we always stopped there. I showed up with these big guys, football players. Leonard met us with his apron on and his hair all coiffed, "Oh Raymond, come over here; give me a big hug and kiss!" And then, "Raymond! Who are these good-looking guys?" As he hugged them, he said things like, "Oh, your muscles are so big. Aren't you so manly, so big, so strong?" And every one of them hugged him back.

Nobody ever said, "Oh my god, I'm not gonna touch him!" In most cases, they had a *māhū* in the family, too, so it wasn't a big deal. It was common in Hawaiian families at that time to accept openly gay members in the family. Unlike on the mainland, it was not an embarrassment.[20]

Once I went down to Waikīkī with my sister Marilyn and Leonard and one of his boyfriends, who was in the Navy. Marilyn was extremely

---

20 Diamond, Milton. "Sexual Behavior in Pre-contact Hawaiʻi: A Sexological Ethnography." (2004), 16:37-58; https://www.hawaii.edu/PCSS/biblio/articles/2000to2004/2004-sexual-behavior-in-pre-contact-hawaii.html.

attractive, and she was getting a lot of attention from soldiers and sailors on leave—and from locals, too. I was also getting looks. Leonard and his boyfriend were sort of protecting us as they walked behind us. Leonard was enjoying the attention that Marilyn and I were drawing to us all.

A whole new world was starting to open up, going down to Waikīkī with all the hotels and tourists and finding out that I have this cousin who's a *māhū*, and he's a sweet, nice guy. I was learning about a level of tolerance that I had never observed in Texas.

There were lots of pecking orders to figure out—in the classroom, at dances, in sports, and off campus. I was learning a lot, including identifying potential adversaries, and observing how all the guys at public schools hated us and how we hated them. The local guys drove through the campus, and sometimes fights broke out. You always had to be ready. I was trying to figure out how I could fit in playing all of the different sports that I liked, just how I would fit in, and which ones I would perform well in. Some sports overlapped, and I had to make a choice. In football, I had to determine what position I would play. When I started at Punahou, my freshman year, I was on the basketball team. Then, it was track season, and I decided to do track instead of baseball, even though I loved baseball. I threw shotput and ran the 220. I was on the JV basketball team the next year. Instead of doing track my sophomore year, I decided to do baseball. But the track people still wanted me to throw the shot, so I came up and threw the shot.

When I arrived in Hawai'i, I already knew that I was becoming bigger and stronger and faster. In Hawai'i at the time, the fighting was boys being boys, trying to be men. I was learning that you never back down, and you gotta be ready to mix it up anytime. You learned to exist in that atmosphere. There was always going to be a struggle over who was gonna be the big dog.

The big dog in our class was a guy by the name of Benny Sampson, a Black Puerto Rican boxer. He was smaller than I was. Benny was, I wanna say, five foot, 10 inches tops, maybe 175 pounds. But he was a boxer. He was a tough guy, arrogant, and he came from the projects. He was the kingpin. I wasn't trying to be the kingpin—I was just trying to be a good student, a good football player. But I was a big guy, a new guy, and I wasn't going to genuflect to Benny. The guys thought it was cool that I wasn't kissing Benny's ass, but they were thinking it was just a matter of time before something would break. Benny and I always played around like we were fighting, but we weren't fighting. We played a slapping game, but then it escalated during my sophomore year. We finally had to square off. We got into a fight. The JV basketball coach, who was also the baseball coach, Jim Doole,[21] sat us down and said, "It might be better for you guys to work together than to be at each other's throats all the time." Out of that, for some reason, Benny and I suddenly became buddies, and we could take on the world.

One day, we're playing basketball against Maryknoll School. A forward named Mel Tom pushes or gets into a fight with one of our players, and I sprint off the bench and dive at him and knock him to the ground and start punching him. In the meantime, his whole team jumps on me, and I'm screaming for Benny. "Benny! Where are you?"

Benny was on the outside looking at some girl up in the stands. He's trying to get in, but he can't. I'm getting killed. So finally, the referees break us up, and Benny says, "Ray, I'm sorry." He and I made a good team, and we became very close. We are friends to this day. You lived in that world. In Hawai'i, when somebody just looked at you cross-eyed, you said, in Pidgin English, "Eh, brah, what you lookin' at?" or "You like beef?" It's standard. It was a macho world, and you had to learn how to stand up and take on tough situations.

It carried over to everything I did. I remember being on Hotel Street, which was in the red-light district; that's where I transferred to the bus for Pearl Harbor to get home. A lot of military men hung out there. Some servicemen walked by. One of them had an expression

---

21 *Chelmsford High School Alumni Association*, "James E. Doole, Jr.". 1941. https://chsalumni.org/hall-of-fame-members/32-hall-of-fame/hall-of-fame-members/1995/108-james-e-doole-jr-1941-d.

on his face that seemed threatening to me. At 16, I was ready to take on an adult serviceman.

"What are ya lookin' at?" I yelled. I went after him.

"Hey, man, I wasn't looking at anything. Sorry if I offended you," he said, and then he walked off. I felt a little embarrassed. Hawai'i builds that fighting instinct. It's Hawai'i, but it's also life. It's part of this code that we have among men, particularly young men. That carried over when I went back to Texas. That attitude stuck with me.

FUN, FIGHTS, AND FEUDS

While I was attending Punahou, as a freshman, I had a Texas driver's license, but I had to ride the bus because I didn't have a car. My sophomore year, my father helped me buy an old '46 Plymouth sedan. On weekends, I got up early, put a surfboard on top of that old car, and headed to the beach. Or I loaded up the car with friends to go bodysurfing at Makapu'u. We took off our shirts and pranced around and tried to look like the older guys who worked for the hotels and catered to the tourists. They were often great surfers, but they were basically glorified servants to the guests of the hotels they worked for. It was well known that in addition to teaching tourists to surf, they also were available to their female clients as escorts. To us as young guys, this somewhat demeaning career choice seemed really cool and exciting.

In addition to dealing with the social complexities of football, my burgeoning interest in girls, and my surrounding environment, I also had to deal with my volatile mother, who feared that I would succumb to the beach, quit school, and become a beach bum, which really appealed to me at the time.

Just before daybreak one morning, as I left to pick up my friends to go bodysurfing, my mother ran out of our duplex in the officer's quarters in the military compound and chased down the street after my car past the two-level brick duplexes housing other officers and their families in her light blue, sheer nylon nightgown screaming at me at the top of her lungs, "YOU'RE GONNA BE A BUM...YOU'RE GONNA BE A BUM!"

I yelled, "NO, I'M NAHHHhhhhhht..." back out of my window as I drove away. Her panic-stricken screams slowly faded into the distance as I tried to wipe out the memory of her running behind me with the early light revealing her body through her nightgown to both me and any neighbors awakened by the commotion.

In the summertime between my sophomore and junior year, I worked construction, and then I went down to Waikīkī and paddled for Healani Canoe Club, which was on the Ala Wai Canal. Ancient Hawaiians paddled the channel waters for food, fun, trade, and war. Mythical demigods did it, surfers did it, modern heroes did it—proved their athletic prowess on the oceans. Paddling in modern Hawai'i is a demanding, total-body sport. If you paddle, you are a real Hawaiian. I thought I was the coolest thing ever.

Afterwards, I'd go down to the beach, where there was always a bunch of my classmates. I hung out with the group and then went to parties. Once, a good-looking guy classmate, Sandy Kahanamoku, Duke Kahanamoku's nephew, invited me and a bunch of guys to drive up Punahou Street toward Mānoa. We pulled over next to a beautiful woman driving a sports car. She was older—probably married. I was in the backseat of my friend's car.

The guys tell me, "Schoenke, stay put and watch. Be cool. Sandy's trying to make his move here." Sandy gets out and says a few words, gets in the car with this woman, and takes off.

"*That's interesting,*" I think to myself. I'm learning a new way of being—daring, romantic.

At Waikīkī Beach, there were women who came over from college on the mainland, primarily from southern schools. One of the things they liked to do before graduating from college was to go to Hawai'i for six weeks and date a beach boy. It was a mob scene. I was 15 or 16 at the time. I was a kid who looked like a grown man. These women just wanted to be able to say that they knew someone who was Hawaiian and a beach boy, and I decided to play along. After all, I had already had some practice at this. I grabbed my surfboard, walked around without a shirt, and let the coeds whistle at me.

"I can't introduce myself as Ray Schoenke; that doesn't sound Hawaiian," I thought. I asked my buddy to give me a Hawaiian name.

"Call yourself Napua," he said. I think that's a flower, or maybe it means "the flowers." It seemed like kind of a *māhū* name, but what did I know?

So I met these women and told them my name was Napua. I always had a surfboard—part of it was walking around with a surfboard, being big and dark and attractive, thinking I was really cool. I even managed to talk to a couple of co-eds. I never really dated any of them, but I wanted to. I'd be walking down Kalākaua and I'd hear, "Napua! Napua!" I didn't answer because I had forgotten that my name was Napua!

That summer after my sophomore year, I'm walking near Punahou, and my classmate Kehau Kea comes by in her MG. We're talking, and she says, "You want to take a ride with me?"

I say, "Sure!" So I jump in her sports car, and we drive around. That sort of broke the ice. I started dating her. I became totally infatuated. I just went hook, line, and sinker. She was a tandem surfer. She surfed Makaha and eventually won the Makaha Championship. And she was more sophisticated than me about life and things in general. I was thinking, *This woman's for me*. We dated, but I think she felt that I was lacking in some ways, immature, not macho enough. I didn't press her to have sex, but she wanted to. I was all for it, but on a New Year's Eve after too much drinking and trying to figure out how to do all that, my first time, well, it was a little complicated. After that, she gave me back my paddling medal, which meant that it was over.

SKELETONS IN THE CLOSET

Aunty Alice, who had raised my half brother, was Samoan, married to my Uncle George Oliva Alapa. Her maiden name was Alice Aipata

Faliuga Savaiinaea. She was a kind, thoughtful woman who brought with her a certain distinction, a certain aura of respect—Samoan royalty, but she never thought she was better than anyone else. She was really the matriarch, and she gave us a connection to the Samoan community.

The Alapa family had some other really solid citizens who were well respected. I was proud of them. My cousin, Elwood, kept an impeccable house, dressed immaculately, and insisted that we take pride in ourselves. I met my Aunty Hopiana at her home in Kahana. I got to know my cousins. One of them, Gordon Broad, went to Kahuku High School. He and I were All Stars (which was equivalent to being All State on the Mainland) the same year, he in the country and me in the city.

On our first visit to Lāʻie, when I was 14, Marilyn and I noticed a picture of a handsome young man. "Who's that?" I asked.

Our cousins looked stunned. They didn't know what to say. Somebody finally said, "Well, that's Stanley. That's your brother."

"Really?" I said. They couldn't believe that I didn't recognize Stanley. Later, I asked my mother about the good-looking guy in the picture. She didn't say anything.

Shortly thereafter—we were still at our temporary place in Waipahu—my dad took Marilyn and me to the back of the house, to a back bedroom, and sat me down. "Stanley isn't your cousin," he said. He explained how I had acquired a brother I didn't know about.

Stanley was then in the service. My father told me that my mother had had a relationship with another serviceman, a naval officer, that she had gotten pregnant, and that her boyfriend had been shipped out when his commanding officer learned of the attachment. Stanley was hānaiʻd to my aunt. Hānai is an informal adoption in Hawaiʻi. It was common in those days. When a child was born to a mother who for one reason or another wasn't able to raise the child, the child was raised by another member of the extended family. Stanley was adopted by my Aunty Alice. But my dad didn't tell me at that time that my other brother, Walter, was also a half brother. He told me about that shortly after. It turns out that Mother had a child by the basketball player she had married prior to dating my father—another secret she kept from me for many years. My mother had separated from Walter's father before the war and then had developed a relationship with my father, who raised Walter as his child.

In those days, when you were hānai'd, you knew who your mother was. When we finally met Stanley, he interacted with us as though we were siblings, which we were. We were all part of a large family. I thought it was cool that he was my brother. He had played football at Kahuku High School, where he was an All-Star and also in the service. He was even offered a scholarship to UCLA. But he decided to come back to Hawai'i. Stanley was six foot four, an outstanding athlete, a good-looking guy. I had a big brother with connections and ties to the Samoan community. That was cool. But Stanley told me that one night in 1941, when I was three months old, after the Japanese had bombed Pearl Harbor, we left.

My mother never told my aunty or him that we were leaving. He couldn't believe we just left. My mother always took a lot of interest in him, and he must have established a maternal bond with her even though he was being raised by someone else. He said that the day he found out we had moved—he would have been ten—was the worst day of his life.

"I'll never forget how terrible I felt when they told me she had left," he said. I have since realized that she would have had to "explain" him to Dad's family if they had taken him with them. Dad had never told his family that Stanley was her child, and she would have had to tell them about her past history if he came to live with us. Abandoning her child was how she chose to insulate herself from her past.

TWO SIDES OF THE PARENTAL COIN

My mother was an oddity in the family. She could be incredibly sweet and kind, but her family knew that she could be very combative. In Kahuku and Lā'ie, they knew that you didn't mess with her by questioning her authenticity. When we lived in Hawai'i, she was known as an accomplished *lauhala* weaver, and she was quite proud of her artistic talents, sometimes inflating her level of expertise. In Hawai'i, she went to Moloka'i and harvested hala (screw pine) leaves, which are used to weave baskets, floor coverings, hats, and roofs. She was astute in Hawaiian crafts and weaving and wove in the traditional Hawaiian way. She bragged about studying porcelain techniques and oil painting in England.[22]

She was truly an artist—oils, all mediums, and sculpting. She was always painting with oils, painting china, working with porcelain, and firing her work in a kiln. While she was incredibly talented, it all felt to me as if everything she did to distinguish herself was a race to stay ahead of her past, and she simply could not just relax and enjoy her many and varied accomplishments. Her past, especially the fact that she had a child out of wedlock and only a public elementary school education, if even that, could at any time uncloak her and reveal who she really was: an uneducated, orphaned, former maid, who had created a façade of social elitism.

She was strong and ambitious and driven and demanding. She wanted to be wealthy; she wanted to have nice things. My dad could never make enough money. We were broke all the time. She always wanted more. It upset my father. She wanted nice clothes, bigger cars, a nicer home. However, she was also always looking for another source of income, and because she wanted more money, she was willing to sacrifice. When we were in Hawai'i in the 1950s, she wanted a mink stole, so she went to work as a nurse aide at the Nu'uanu Convalescent Home[23] so she could have a mink stole. In Hawai'i that didn't make any sense whatsoever, but she got that mink stole and went out to parties wearing it.

She was never satisfied because she was chasing a dream intended to erase her past. If she could become sophisticated and was viewed as

---

22 *Honolulu Star Bulletin*. "Mrs. Olivia Alapa Schoenke, 81, obituary." 04 Mar 1992, 37. https://www.newspapers.com/clip/25958228/mrs-olivia-haleaka-alapa-schoenke-81/.

23 Olivia Alapa Schoenke obituary, 1992.

well-off, no one would question her. She was always fearful of being embarrassed in front of anybody in town. We were a good, straight family, building a reputation.

But there was another side to all this. My mother could be like a bull, but she was actually very fragile, which was a big part of my later experiences with her. I think she got burned early. She had been orphaned, and she had to learn how to take care of herself. She also saw examples, both good and bad, I'm guessing, on the military bases, of how people improved their station. She also saw that some people weren't willing to work as hard as she was. She saw that through hard work and sacrifice, you could elevate your position and get somewhere.

My father was also very disciplined and very confident in his own quiet way. Unlike my mother, who wanted to be seen and heard, my father stayed behind the scenes and let his performance speak for him. As an accomplished athlete, my dad had the discipline to perform on the field and also to keep his cool. Pressure didn't bother him. Once I decided that I was interested in sports and took an interest in baseball, my dad was very supportive. He was an assistant coach when I was in Little League. Later, he went to all my games. I didn't look to him to coach me, and I didn't like the fact that he'd come and tell me how to do things, but he was always there for me.

My father was not a physically demonstrative man. He became less so as we got older, and when we did something that warranted punishment, unlike my mother, he found it difficult to punish us physically. When I was eight or nine, I accidentally left the doors to the rabbit cage open. They got out in the yard, and the dog killed one of them. Dad felt he should punish me for being irresponsible, so he told me to go get a belt. I went upstairs and hunted for the flimsiest nylon belt I could find. I certainly wasn't going to bring him a strong leather belt. He made me bend over, and every time he hit me (it didn't hurt at all), I yelled out. It was clear he couldn't bring himself to hurt me. He wasn't a man who got angry a lot. He balanced out my mother.

In addition to the complex nuances of my parents' personalities and family histories, my siblings and I were also having to learn to adjust to the frequent changes in our housing and school situations. We were constantly having to adjust quickly and to fit in—to learn the personalities and expectations of new teachers and trying to make new friends in sometimes hostile environments.

This period was when I also found out that after my half brother Stanley was born, my mother had the relationship that led to the birth of my other half brother, Walter. I don't know why she didn't hānai Walter. He stayed with her. He told me he remembered my mother taking him out to Lāi'e, and he remembered playing with Stanley. They knew each other, but Stanley was with Aunty Alice, and Walter was with my mother.

I speculate that maybe my mother gave up Stanley temporarily because she was still young and trying to find herself, and maybe she was looking for another relationship, or maybe because he was born out of wedlock, and Walter wasn't. Walter told stories of men coming to the maids' quarters and banging on the door and asking for my mom.

As he matured, Stanley came to view Aunty Alice as his mother and his family in Lāi'e as his nuclear family. By the time I was a junior at Punahou, Stanley had come back from the service, gotten a job, and was working at a nightclub. He rented a cottage between Kalākaua and the Ala Wai Canal, where I paddled with the Healani Canoe Club. Stanley let me stay at his house and drive his two-door, olive-colored T-Bird convertible. I would never give my 16-year-old brother, cousin, or relative the use of my brand-new Thunderbird convertible! But that was just part of the culture in Hawai'i. Some people say Hawaiians don't have anything because they give everything away. That's the way it is in Hawai'i. Everything mine is yours! So here I am, a 16-year-old working a construction job, drinking beer with the guys after work, a little tipsy, driving down Kalākaua Avenue, waving at all the wahines in a T-Bird convertible.

Stanley even let me bring my girlfriends over to his house when he and his wife weren't there. I made the mistake of leaving the front door of his apartment open because that was common in Hawai'i to get a breeze, while I was making out on the living room sofa with a girl (I had become a little more adept by now).

Stanley comes in later and says, "Raymond, do me a favor. Just close the door. Everybody sitting out on their patios at the apartments across from our cottage was watching you!"

MEANWHILE, BACK IN TEXAS

In my two years at Punahou (1957 and 1958), I won five letters: two in football, two in track, and one in baseball. On the varsity football first team, I played offensive and defensive guard, winning All-Star Mention honors in 1958. As the track team's championship shot-putter, I established a state record in 1957. I was known as a powerful batter in baseball and played as an outfielder on the varsity squad. I was inducted into the Punahou Hall of Fame in 1992.[24]

Then, halfway through my junior year, my parents abruptly decided to return to Texas, where my father retired. I spent my senior year at Weatherford High School. But Hawai'i had put its stamp on me. Before I had arrived in Hawai'i in 1955, I knew I was Hawaiian, but my mother hadn't talked much about it. When I left Hawai'i in 1958, I was Hawaiian all the way. I knew the drill. I knew the history, and I was proud of it. I was Hawaiian from that point on.

I hadn't known that being Hawaiian was special until I got to Punahou. It gave me credibility about who I am—this brown-skinned person who was not only respected, but something special. If you're attractive and a good athlete, that's a couple extra notches on your belt. I had Hawaiians and Samoans in my family, and they were from Kahuku, Lā'ie—which gave me street cred. I surfed at Waikīkī; I paddled for

---

[24] *Punahou Hall of Fame*. "Raymond E. 'Ray' Schoenke (1959)." Punahou School, 16 July 1959. www.punahou.edu/hall-of-fame-detail?pk=1115254.

Healani, and my brother let me drive his T-bird convertible. On top of all that, I was an All-Star on the Buff 'N' Blue team for Punahou.

At Weatherford High in Texas, you had Whites, and you had some Mexicans, but you had no Blacks. There certainly weren't biracial kids like there were in Hawai'i. (The saying was, "If you're brown, stick around. If you're Black, stand back. If you're White, you're all right.") And, typically, you didn't cross these boundaries. You didn't hang out with Mexicans, and you didn't hang out with Blacks. That was the culture. In Hawai'i, the culture was open. But there was a sort of code. You were ready to fight at the drop of a hat, and everyone knew that. How do you exist in that? The way I dealt with it was to give the impression, "I'm a big guy; I want to be strong, fair, and nice. But don't mess with me."

In Weatherford, Texas, during my senior year of high school, when we played basketball against Brownwood, a powerhouse rival in football, several kids who knew my reputation in football sat in the bleachers and began chanting "Hula Hoop, Hula Hoop, Hula Hoop," whenever I touched the ball. They pounded their feet on the bleachers and made all kinds of noises. I was just boiling.

"They are only making fun of *me* and no one else," I'm thinking.

"Schoenke, calm down," my team members keep saying.

As soon as that game is over, I sprint right up into the stands, yelling, "C'mon, let's get at it. Who wants a piece of me?"

Everybody just freezes. I realize they are kids, ninth and tenth graders, who are having fun at my expense, who now are scared out of their minds.

Finally, the coaches run up and grab me, and say, "C'mon, let's get out of here." As I got bigger and stronger and faster, everything changed. I knew that if I had to, I could deal with anything. I went after anyone who was bullying me or attempting to bully me, and if they didn't back off, I made sure they paid a price.

Luckily, my experiences motivated me. I *wanted* to become big and strong. I was starting to play football, and I learned how to tackle hard and knock people down in football. Get two people running full speed into each other, and even with helmets on, it's scary—it's not natural. As a young player, I learned by accident that if I put my head in there, that if I didn't close my eyes, I wouldn't miss, and if I led with my head and my helmet, I could easily knock my opponent down. A player might be coming at me, but if I took him on head-on with my helmet, I became the aggressor. I started excelling at it.

On top of these issues, my hormones began to rage, and I was thinking about dating, which is intimidating and difficult. Any attempt to connect with someone you are interested in can lead to rejection, and you are incredibly fragile. You try to look for some kind of interest or indication, either directly from her or through her friends, before you even attempt to connect with a girl.

I didn't have any dates when I first got back to Weatherford, but I soon had a girlfriend, Janet. She was a natural blonde, very popular, a cheerleader and homecoming queen, but her circumstances were difficult. Her father had passed away, and her mother was raising her and her two brothers. She was very popular, but she was in a sort of desperate situation. She was going steady with a guy who worked in town—one of those guys with a long car with the fins and mufflers who wore his hair slicked back. A greaser. Even though she was taken, the head baton twirler basically coaxed me into calling her.

"I'm going steady," Janet said.

"Well, it's Thursday, and I don't have a date for the game on Friday. I don't know what I'm going to do," I replied.

I saw her the next morning, and she said, "I broke up with my boyfriend."

Back then, a boy sent a chrysanthemum with a few ribbons—and if you were a player, with your number—to a date, who wore the floral brooch to the game. I sent a big white mum with a blue #35 across it. Janet showed up at the football game as a cheerleader with my mum. It was a huge deal. She was effectively telling all the girls that I was dating her.

With my high school girlfriend, Janet, and friends in Weatherford, Texas

In Texas, you might have 3,000 people at a high school football game. When you went to Honolulu Stadium to play a game, there were 25,000 people there. And when you were an All-Star, you were like an All-American; you were king. So it was this incredible world. Hawai'i was small, but high school sports was the biggest game in town.

For a 16-year-old kid, it was heaven on earth. Everybody knows who you are. I'm out working construction, and I hear, "Eh, I seen your picture in the paper. You one All-Star, huh?" These are the laborers who were big, tough guys I was afraid of. The whole thing was beyond belief. On this small island, out in the middle of the ocean, that's not any bigger than the county that I live in today. That's the world. As a 16-year-old kid, it was more than heady. At 16, I was a celebrity.

As a football player, it is difficult to achieve a balance between being a warrior on the field and shedding that persona when you get home because on the field, you have to be in a warrior mindset, and at home, you have to be caring, thoughtful, warm, loving, and compassionate. The way that I dealt with this issue in my childhood in Texas was to embrace the warrior attitudes of Native Americans. What they brought to me was this fierce warrior mentality combined with a sense of tribal obligation.

Earlier in my childhood, I had been obsessed with the Comanche and the Cherokee. When I returned to Weatherford for my senior year, though, I was obsessed with being Hawaiian. I let people know I was Hawaiian, and in spite of the fact that I had left Texas, I was proud to return as a Hawaiian. I still wasn't versed in the long history and rich culture of the Hawaiian people—that would come later. But I already understood, at some level, my dual identity as a relentless fighter on the field and a softie off, which epitomized both the native American and Polynesian warrior. I was adept at tackling, and I was a good teammate. I was a tough guy, but I carried around a ʻukulele. The juxtaposition between these two aspects of me was often confusing to my teammates, but they came to respect and admire this paradox. Not all football players can let go of their warrior mentality when they leave the locker room. They take it to restaurants, bars, parties, and home. It's very hard to make that adjustment.

Meanwhile, I still couldn't believe my family had forced me to leave Hawaiʻi my senior year. It had devastated me. Why would *anyone* want to go back to Weatherford?

Well, there had been some problems to address. My sister was dating Raymond Correa, the quarterback at Roosevelt High School, and they didn't want her to marry him. My father had put in his 28 years, but he hadn't made Colonel, and he had to decide whether to stay and forever be a Lieutenant Colonel or get out and start a new career. He was looking at job options in Hawaiʻi, and also the cost of buying a home. My parents still owned a home in Weatherford, and the job opportunities in Texas offered a better income, so they decided to return. My mom was comfortable with the decision because she had built a reputation in Weatherford. Apparently, my opinion on the matter didn't count. I guess they felt it would be an easy transition because I had lived there and played football there before. It wasn't.

Now that we were back in Weatherford, my friends who knew me before couldn't understand why I was so sullen. Like, "What happened? You were really cool, and now you're this unhappy person."

Once I got into football and joined the Weatherford Kangaroos, I started gaining praise from my teammates. From a physical standpoint, I was strong, fast, and quick, and I was angry. I had a mean side that served me on the football field because I was so upset about having to leave Hawai'i.

In Texas, football was not limited to three yards and a cloud of dust. It was wide-open football. What was surprising to me, unlike in Hawai'i, the players were very gentlemanly. In Hawai'i, it was all blood and guts. You had to be ready to get into fisticuffs when you played Farrington and McKinley in Honolulu because a lot of the scholarship guys at Punahou came from their districts. We had a great rivalry with Roosevelt, too.[25]

I played fullback on offense and a down lineman and linebacker on defense. The harder and better I played, the better I felt. I was trying to get Hawai'i out of my mind. I had only been there three years, but I breathed it; I talked it; I acted it. I took my disappointments and feelings about leaving Hawai'i out onto the football field. I became—not a wild man, but driven to the max. From being the nicest person off the field to being a badass on the football field. When we played Garland High School, a larger high school in a suburb of Dallas and a highly ranked team in the state, I was labeled after our victory as "the Hawaiian Bomber."

Once in a preseason scrimmage game against another high school, I blocked a guy; he went down, and he jumped back up. I hit him again and knocked him back down, and he jumped back up. I just kept pounding him. His coaches finally ran out and grabbed me.

---

25 Kwon, Bill. "Schoenke Does Honor to His Heritage." *Honolulu Star-Bulletin*, 10 May 1990, D-1-D-3.

Me with some of my Weatherford High School teammates

They dragged me off while screaming at me, "Leave him alone!"

"Tell him to stay down!" I yelled back. As a blocking back, my job was to take the guy out of the play. That's how football is played.

Our team was becoming a powerhouse. We were at the top of Division 3-A, with schools of between 300 and 400 students, but we were also playing schools in 4-A, with more students, and we were beating everybody. The team was getting recognition, and I started getting some recognition myself, especially from visiting college scouts.

I never thought of myself as better than anybody else, but I was a very good player and team member. I became close to the guys on the team. We were ranked the #2 team in the state within our high school division, and we were highly ranked in the state for all schools, regardless of size. It so happened that the #1 team in the state, Breckinridge, was in our division. We both also played teams outside our division, from larger schools, but still, when we met Breckinridge in the ninth game of the year, we were both undefeated. Unfortunately, they won and went on to capture the state title for Division 3-A.

CHAPTER TWO

Southern Methodist University— Cramming, Coaching, and Coeds (1959–1963)

As a potential All-State high school football player with the Weatherford Kangaroos, I started noticing coaches showing up from colleges like the University of Texas, Southern Methodist University, Rice University, University of Oklahoma, Texas Christian University, and Texas A&M. They asked to take me out to lunch, wanting to introduce themselves to me because they were interested in my going to their school. That didn't happen at Punahou—it was so insular. Suddenly, I started getting a lot of attention. I wouldn't say I was overly excited, but I was flattered. One of the coaches mentioned Charlie Ane because I had a reputation in Texas as a Hawaiian. He had played with him with the Detroit Lions. The inspiration that allowed me to dream of a career in pro football was suddenly rekindled.

One of those coaches was an assistant coach from Southern Methodist University. At the time, Head Coach Bill Meek was compiling a good record at SMU. He looked like George Washington, with his gray hair and air of dignity. He had recruited quarterback Don Meredith, who earned All-American honors in 1958 and 1959, with his .610 career completion percentage, making him the best of any passer in SMU history.

My fifth grade teacher, Mrs. Lidell, often read stories to the class at lunch, and she once read a story about Doak Walker,[26] a football player who had gone to SMU and was an outstanding runner. He won the Heisman Trophy in 1948 and played for the Detroit Lions. Doak had gone to high school with Bobby Layne, she said, building up to her story. Bobby went to the University of Texas, and Doak went to SMU. They ended up playing against each other. Bobby Layne was a hellraiser; he drank and partied hard. He was an outstanding quarterback in spite of his social failings, but I didn't consider him to be a role model. Doak, on the other hand, was a straight arrow. He was clean and didn't drink. That story stayed with me and was one of the reasons why I later looked favorably upon SMU. On top of that, Charlie Ane, one of my heroes, also played with Doak in Detroit. The story felt like a Marvel comic story to me—all my heroes coming together.

When I visited SMU, I wanted to see if there was anything about Doak Walker on the campus. I don't remember if I found anything, but I liked the school. It reminded me of Punahou—small upper-middle-class student body, good academics, and good football. It appealed to me. I also noticed there was one Mexican on the football team, Rene Medellin,[27] who dated a White girl. That said to me, "If he can do it, maybe I can do it, too." It also told me that maybe the racial attitudes were different there from elsewhere in the South.

SMU was in the Southwest Conference. Back then, all of the teams in the Southwest conference were segregated, and they seldom played schools that were integrated. In the Bowl games, the Southwest conference team played teams that were integrated, but within the conference, none of the schools were, with the exception of some Mexican players. But SMU also played against schools outside the

---

26 *SMU*. "About Doak Walker." https://www.smu.edu/DoakWalkerAward/AboutUs/AboutDoakWalker. *Michigan Sports Hall of Fame*. "Robert Lawrence (Bobby) Layne." https://michigansportshof.org/inductee/bobby-layne/.

27 Payne, Darwin. "In Honor Of The Mustangs: The Centennial History Of SMU Athletics 1911-2010." *SMU DeGolyer Library*, 2010. https://www.amazon.com/Honor-Mustangs-Centennial-Athletics-1911-2010/dp/1878516906.

conference, so even if I was a rarity as a dark-skinned person at SMU, I wouldn't always be the only one on the field.

I was also being recruited heavily by the University of Texas. My high school coach at Weatherford was going to be a coach at the University of Texas, so it was assumed that I'd go with him. But when I went down there to visit, I roomed with a couple of football players who seemed to have some animosity toward Blacks. And they didn't speak highly of a Mexican player, Rene Ramirez, a running back on their team who was a star and sort of a lover boy and good-looking. They called him the "Galloping Gaucho."[28] I said to myself, "*What are you gonna call ME?*" Although the University of Texas was an outstanding university and eventually had the #1 team in the country, that interaction turned me off.

I was aware of racial issues at all the universities, and I noticed whether or not they played integrated schools—typically those from the North, the East, and the West. Not just because I was dark-skinned and didn't want to be at a disadvantage, but also because the teams that were integrated were the very best, and I wanted to play against the very best. The Southwest Conference included Texas, Arkansas, Baylor, SMU, Texas Christian University, Texas A&M, Texas Tech, and Rice. But SMU, unlike the others, also played schools that were ranked nationally in the Big 10—Ohio State, Missouri, USC, Navy. If I went to SMU, I knew I would play against the best.

I visited some of the other schools in the conference, and I started getting feelers from the West Coast, East Coast, and some of the military academies because some of my Punahou friends had gone to Stanford, and they put the word out. I also got calls from Notre Dame and Oklahoma, and I visited both. But Oklahoma pushed the hardest for me. Bud Wilkinson, the Head Coach of the University of Oklahoma was very impressive. At the time, Oklahoma had won

---

28 Mata, Mary. "Mexican-American college football legend honored at UT Hall of Honor." News Taco, 04 11 2013. https://newstaco.com/2013/11/04/mexican-american-college-football-legend-honored-at-ut-hall-of-honor/.

40 games in a row. His reputation was extremely good as both a coach and a mentor to young men.

My father had decided that we should also ask the schools that were trying to recruit me to help my sister, Marilyn, by offering her a scholarship to attend the school with me. For a while, Oklahoma was a contender—because Marilyn could go there. They offered to pay her tuition, and when I visited with my entire family, they set her up with a date with the captain of the football team.

The military academies reached out because I was such a good student. I think it was the football connection, but my dad's military background didn't hurt. My father discouraged me from going there.

"If you want to go to the military, there's nothing wrong with it," he said, "but Raymond, you gotta recognize that they're in charge of your life, not you." Which was interesting for a guy who put in 28 years and did well and appreciated what he'd gotten out of the service. I met with the recruiters from West Point and the Air Force Academy.

They urged me to go to a military academy and assured me it would be a good decision.

But I said "No."

There was another reason not to go to West Point: I wanted to go to a school that was close enough to home so that my parents could see me play, but far enough away so that they wouldn't be banging on my door all the time.

SMU had great appeal to me. The players were a bunch of tough guys, and I liked that. And I liked the fact that they played a great schedule: Big 10, West Coast schools, University of Maryland, the Naval and the Air Force Academies. Great school, and there were beautiful women. I thought, "That's the place for me." Marilyn did not feel comfortable at SMU, as she clearly wanted to go to Oklahoma. I felt bad for Marilyn, but I didn't want to go to Oklahoma. Marilyn eventually went to North Texas University. She dropped out after her freshman year and got married.

I'D DATE HIM, BUT I'D NEVER TAKE HIM HOME

As soon as my freshman year at SMU started, I became painfully aware of being different. I was the only dark-skinned kid in my classes, and in fact, there were only a couple of other non-White students on campus. It was an upper-middle class, White, privileged, school. I wasn't upper-middle class or White or privileged, but I was a good football player. Sometimes jocks were considered a catch, but not in my case because of my skin color. And football players had a reputation for not being very bright, so even though I worked hard at academics, and there were several players on the team who were outstanding students, my smarts didn't exactly work in my favor, either.

Then there were the fraternities. Eventually, it dawned on me that they were an important part of campus life. My team members were being rushed. Although I was one of the best football players, I was not being rushed. I assumed that it was because I was Hawaiian. I held that against them, even though I was friends with several fraternity guys. I became increasingly aware that I was being discriminated against by some of the best fraternities because of my race. There were even altercations where fraternity boys would try to ridicule me in the student union in front of other students. I didn't want to punch them in the face and make a spectacle of myself, so I just had to take the public humiliation. I figured out fast that everybody didn't love me, and I acquired a little edginess. I managed to find a way to turn the other cheek—after giving them a look that said I could cut them up if I wanted to.

I had felt like something special at Punahou. In Hawai'i, being Hawaiian had made me almost a romantic figure, and being a star athlete made it even easier. I had become comfortable with the looser, more playful, less Judeo-Christian sense of sexuality and love that I encountered while at Punahou. Then, I was back in Texas, where sexual mores were stricter. As if to try to reclaim some of the identity I'd gained at Punahou, I'd wear my black-and-white oxfords and carry my 'ukulele around. I even sat on a wall and played it, and the girls

I was accused of murder in a mock trial at SMU, and I won an ugly man contest in this outfit

would come around and listen. I was not your typical Texan football player. I was the *Hawaiian* football player.

But at SMU, I heard that girls would say about me, "I might date him, but I'd never take him home." I felt nothing short of inadequate. I was some dorky kid that, I felt, nobody liked. I turned inward, becoming somewhat reclusive.

To make matters worse, when I arrived at SMU, I had an embarrassing situation with my teeth—I had a tooth kicked out my freshman year in high school, and the military dentists that fixed it just jammed it back in there, not bothering to align it correctly. So I had this space in my teeth, sort of like the former New York Giant Michael Strahan—only he came by his naturally; his teeth were aligned, and it actually enhanced his looks. But not mine.

My parents assured me that no one cared about it. But *I* cared about it. I was constantly trying to figure out how I could make my teeth look better. It consumed me. I ended up going to Baylor Dental School in Dallas to be a guinea pig for students at the dental school. They experimented on me, and they botched it. There was a big space, *and* the tooth was crooked. I smiled, but I wouldn't show my teeth—I felt ashamed, even inferior. I just shut down. I wouldn't have anything to do with the coeds, and I started dating women off campus. I dated beautiful girls, but I felt less judged somehow about my social status because they were working-class girls, not privileged rich girls.

I got depressed about the whole scene—being excluded from fraternities, feeling on the outside, feeling socially rejected, and too embarrassed to even smile. I went to a psychologist during my freshman year. He asked me to draw what I thought life was all about. I drew a picture with the three crosses depicting the crucifixion of Christ, a noose hanging from a tree symbolizing death, and a baby symbolizing new life.

"What the hell is this?" the psychologist asked incredulously. He encouraged me to appreciate the situation I was in—I was in a good school; I was a star football player; I had a lot of things going for me. I didn't need to feel sorry for myself. He didn't think the majority of the students viewed me as different. I walked out of there feeling better.

I ended up pledging to Phi Gamma Delta my sophomore year, which was a good fraternity. I still didn't have enough money to join, but they said that I could finance the initiation fee; they took me up to the university bank to sign a promissory note for the fraternity dues.

SAVING GRACE

Football saved me. My freshman year, I was a running back. I made the second team All-Southwest Conference Freshmen Team. We practiced on a hill above the stadium. I built a bit of a reputation because every time the freshman team went down the hill to scrimmage the varsity, I'd end up in a fight. The upper-class football players could get brutal. Since I was a running back, as I ran through the hole, two guys, one on each side, would grab me, slam into me to tackle me, and then another guy would come in with a forearm and hit me right in the face. Needless to say, I didn't appreciate that, and I started fights.

After a few episodes like this, the head coach looked at me and said, "Leave him up on the top of the hill." So the freshman coach and I stood there together playing catch while the rest of the freshmen went down to scrimmage. I can't say I was "special," but there was something gratifying about being singled out this way because everybody knew if I went down the hill, there was going to be mayhem.

At first, during my sophomore year, I was a running back on the varsity team. I was on the second team for offense but the first team for defense. The first three games were against Missouri, Ohio State, and Navy, all rated among the top teams in the country at the time. I was starting to get noticed. I heard later that guys from Missouri and Ohio State had my press clippings up on the board in the locker room. However, I didn't break away from the defensive player in the Ohio State game, who got ahold of my ankle. I failed to pull it out and went down.

At Monday practice, the line coaches came over and told me they were putting me as center. I was so angry that I wasn't playing in the backfield I refused to work out. I was wearing low-cut shoes. The line coach, Royal Price, who was known as "Sharky" by all of us, a name that lay somewhere between respect and hostility, brought over high-top shoes and said, "You're a lineman now; you gotta wear these." I took them and threw them over the fence. He didn't know what to do.

When I used my head as a battering ram (my face took a beating)

That evening, he came to my room and told me I should be grateful because the kids in Europe after WWII didn't have any shoes. I failed to understand the parallel.

But I went from a second-string running back to a first-string center. As a way to mitigate my anger, they moved a senior out and moved me in. I became a starter on offense and defense. I played all the time. I played nose guard, tackle, defensive end, and linebacker. I led the team in tackles my sophomore and junior year. I think we played six

All American and All-Southwest Conference lineman for SMU, 1962

of the top 10 teams in the nation. I was named Sophomore Lineman of the Year in the Southwest Conference for the 1960 season because I had outstanding games—I blocked punts, I had a lot of tackles, and I really had a super year, even though we lost nine games and tied one. In 1961, I was All-Southwest Conference on a team that only won two games. My senior year, however, the new coaches decided to play me at defensive end or tackle.

All those losses made the 1960 season disheartening, and after the 1961 season, Coach Bill Meek was replaced by Hayden Fry. He had been at Baylor and Arkansas before SMU tapped him as head coach for the 1962 season. At Arkansas, where Fry was an assistant coach, there was a system where all the linemen assumed a four-point stance, both offensively and defensively. Fry brought this system to SMU.

Initially, it was hard to block in a four-point stance, but with time, we learned how to scramble block to tie up the defensive linemen for several seconds on either a run play or a pass play. On defense, the primary goal is to take out the player who is assigned to block you as well as other defensive linemen who are close to you. The play is accomplished by rapidly angling to your left or right based on the call made by the defensive captain and trying to grab a defensive player while you are being blocked by the tackle in front of you. My job was to slant down with great speed—moving down the line past the tackle who was trying to block me and through the guard to get to the center. As the tackle was trying to block me, I was moving to the left or right. He actually contributed to my momentum by hitting me at an angle. I tried to grab the guard and, if I could, the center. The guy who was blocking me, usually a tackle, went with me. If I was lucky, I could take three men out in the play, which allowed the small, quick linebackers to make the tackles. I made very few tackles my senior year. My job was to knock people down.

On offense, in a scramble block, you fire your head into the tackle and crawl forward by digging your hands into the turf and pushing off your feet under him like a crab, tying him up, with him on top of you trying to get free. I was the only guy over 200 pounds on the line. Fry believed in small, swift, strong guys, partly because you're playing in hot weather, and the idea is to wear people out.

In the Big 10 when it's cold in the winter, a big guy who weighs 250-260 can operate. But when it's 110 degrees, that big guy is worthless. And sometimes the heat is an enemy that is related to more than your size. On the first day of practice, during Fry's first day as head coach, in the morning there had been a shower; steam was rising off the field, and the temperature rose to between 80 and 95 degrees. The rule he had was that you run between all drills. You never stop moving. Everything is 100 percent.

We were only on the field for maybe an hour and a half, and if we got tired, we were permitted to raise our hand, take a knee, and take a 60-second break. Mike Kelsey, who had roomed with me in the summertime in the oil fields, was running with me in the same drills. Because we had roomed together in South Texas during the summer recess from college, I knew he wasn't in the best shape. As I ran past him in drills, I noticed that his face was becoming increasingly flushed.

"Take a knee!" I kept screaming at him as I went past him.

"No. They are going to have to carry me out of here," he yelled as I passed him. Which they did. I saw him drop on the field. I was completely panicked when I saw him go down. The trainer packed him in ice and sent him to the hospital. His temperature had risen to over 105. I was wakened at six the next morning, and Fry told me to wake up the team and tell them that Mike had passed away early that morning. Occasionally, after that, during these practice drills that year, I dropped to my knees and wept.

When I was playing in the Southwestern Conference for SMU, the schools in the conference included all the schools in Texas plus Arkansas, where the weather ranges from 80-100 degrees throughout the football season. You tend to have players who are no larger than 220-230 pounds. You have a lot of linemen who are around 205. They are fast, quick, and strong. When you block somebody, you only block them for a couple seconds; then the back is gone. Everything happens in split seconds. Big guys are at a disadvantage, but I could play well at 220. Trying to get up to 230-250 was a no-no. But that weight works in the pros because, in the pros, you only play offense or defense, so your time on the field is half as long.

Fry won the conference coach of the year award that 1962 season, and I won conference honors in my junior and senior years. But our team was terrible. Fry, however, assured us that our team was improving and building for the future. Two years later, his team was in the Cotton Bowl. I was despondent about our record, but as a player, I was determined to play well. And I was going to go after people in front of me. We played teams that were in the Top 10—Southern Cal, Arkansas, Texas, TCU in our conference, and then USC, Maryland, and the Air Force Academy. I built a reputation, and that was good, but I was still on a losing team.

DATING "ICE BOX"

My high school years in Hawai'i had given me some confidence in terms of my looks, but after I'd had a tooth kicked out, I thought that the space in my teeth just ruined me. I hated my smile. I'm sure my lack of confidence was related to other things at SMU, but the teeth didn't help. Finally, I went to a real dentist.

"I can fix that for you," he said. And he did!

From that point on, in my junior year, I suddenly felt, "Hell, I'm as good-looking as anybody here, and I'm physically better than most." I was of course still dark-complected, but I was playing the Hawaiian theme to work in my favor, like my mother. I was confident, a good student, a good football player. It seemed like as soon as I realized that my looks weren't bad, women actually started approaching *me*.

I met Nancy Box my first week at SMU. We were in English class together, and she was sitting in the first seat in the back row when I came in. Most of the seats were filled in front of her, so I walked all the way down to the end of the row she was in and sat down. I turned and looked at her. She was looking at me.

I was viewed as the "Hawaiian," the "I'd maybe date him, but I'd never take him home" type, but she took me home, although it did take a couple of years.

Throughout my freshman year, I was still dating Janet from Weatherford, and she was desperate for me to marry her. When I went off to SMU, she was afraid that I was never going to come back. I came back from my freshman year and worked the oil fields in Houma, Louisiana in the summer. I didn't see Janet. I worked night shifts because none of the older, married guys wanted those shifts. I came in at 10 at night and worked 'til six in the morning.

The rig was like a boat set up out in the swamps. On the boat, there was a big derrick, with pipes all lined up on the deck. They were leaned up against the derrick using a crane so they could be screwed into the pipe being drilled into the ground. There was a crew of five people—the driller and four assistants. I was in charge of securing huge clamps that were moved into place by a machine to hold the new pipe in place while it was screwed in. To screw the pipe in, someone had to lasso it with a chain and pull it tight. The machine would wind the chain around the new pipe, and as the chain turned the pipe, it screwed the pipe into place. Most of the guys who threw the chain or held the clamp were missing fingers because their fingers got caught under the chain as the pipe was being screwed in. I managed to avoid this injury.

The rest of the time, we did maintenance work on the equipment. I was once tasked with unscrewing a lid on a piece of equipment, and when I got it unscrewed, I had no idea how heavy it was, and it dropped onto my thumb and crushed it. I also got a crushed toe from a similar incident. It was easy to get injured because there were lots of opportunities to get hurt. When people didn't react fast enough in this very dangerous, volatile environment, fights would often break out. The job paid two to three times more than the hourly wage for a laborer, and jobs like this were hard to come by.

Janet eventually asked when we would get married.

"Well, I gotta graduate; I gotta go to grad school, law school. So, seven or eight years from now," I said. (These words much later came back to haunt me when I was on the *other* end of that conversation.)

"That's it." Janet was done with me. She was engaged to be married within a couple of months.

I came back for my sophomore year and was still viewed as off-limits, not someone to take home by the SMU coeds. I started dating Miss Dallas, Kay Sutton. One of my teammates and his wife had gone to high school with her. She was classically beautiful for the time, statuesque, with dark hair and fair skin. She later became a Playboy Playmate. I got some kudos for bringing her to the after-game parties.

Nancy and I were eyeing each other from afar—this went on for a year and a half! She was one of the great beauties on campus. But she had a date every other night. Back then, there were these guys who were upper-middle class and popular; they had the confidence, the money, the car. She was going out with guys like that. She was constantly being chosen as queen at dances and social events—she was named Engineer Queen and ROTC Queen. Nancy was a woman who was nice to everybody, even a dorky-looking engineer. *All* the guys had designs on her.

I was nice, but I was independent, uneasy, and still a little reclusive. And I wasn't into the Greek society thing—I couldn't afford it, for one thing, but also, I was turned off by elitism. Some of the sorority and fraternity members wouldn't have anything to do with me—I assumed because I was Hawaiian. There were racial overtones in the fraternities and sororities, but also throughout the school. The only school that was integrated was the divinity school. Otherwise, there were no Black students in the undergraduate school.

One time, there was an open house for my dormitory, and Nancy came. Other guys in the dorm had eyes on her, too, but I think she came to the open house to see me. I had an old girlfriend's picture up in my room, which I later discovered that Nancy had definitely noticed. She didn't ask me who it was, but that put a freeze on things for a while.

There was a sock hop every Friday afternoon, and I'd go occasionally and dance with Nancy. Once I walked her back to the dorm afterward, and I realized she was one of the sweetest, most thoughtful and caring people I had ever met. She was nice to me and incredibly open. She and I had a connection. I invited her out.

"I'm busy, but please ask me again," she said. I did. I think we may have gone out for a milkshake or something.

No one could believe that she'd even go out for a milkshake with a guy like me who played football, was angry most of the time, and ended up in a lot of fights. I was an odd duck—non-White, low-income, and lacking in decorum, whereas Nancy was a beautiful, friendly, sweet person who was my exact opposite in terms of social graces.

One weekend, in March 1961, our sophomore year, when football spring training was in full session, Nancy asked me to escort her to an ROTC ball. I said yes, of course. That night, some of the football players were gonna get together with their dates and go out to a lake and have a blanket party—that's where you lie down, eat, drink, and make out.

But that day, in a live scrimmage game, my shoulder was dislocated. The team doctor we had wasn't a medical doctor, and he couldn't put the shoulder back. He was standing on my chest, pulling on my arm. I was screaming bloody murder. Finally, he sent me to a real doctor who gave me a shot and popped it back in. He told me to wear a sling and rest.

"I'm supposed to go to a dance," I told him.

"I don't think you should do that," he said.

I went back to my dorm and called Nancy.

"I don't know if I'm gonna be able to come to your dance tonight."

She was disappointed. I decided to go and meet her afterward. I was outside in the parking lot, drinking beer with some of the guys on the team, who also had girlfriends involved in the ball. Nancy came out, and her parents were standing outside, too. She hadn't known they were coming, but they had wanted to see her be presented. I came over with a sling on in shorts and a T-shirt, all disheveled. Her father was a doctor, Chief of Staff of the VA Hospital, the biggest employer in her hometown, and her mother was this refined-looking Southern lady. Nancy presses me to go over and meet her parents. She greets them and says, "Oh, hi! This is Ray Schoenke."

I hung back and did not do the traditional, "Hi, so nice to meet you." Instead, I was dismissive and disrespectful. I showed a lack of interest. I didn't even really speak. I just sort of grunted. I was injured and in pain. The whole thing was a surprise. I felt no obligation to try to impress them. They didn't send their daughter to SMU to meet the likes of *me*. I was clearly not *dressed* to impress, and I didn't want to seem like someone who was going to kiss up to them and try to impress *them*. I didn't care *what* they thought. They looked taken aback. Unfortunately, that's how I met her parents.

Nancy and I still went out to the lake. Nancy's last name was Box. She was known as Nancy "Ice Box." You didn't do anything with Nancy. You're not gonna put your hands up her dress. Nancy didn't mind this label because men knew if they went out with her, they weren't going to get very far. But we're out there at the blanket party, having a marvelous time. We're with three or four other couples. They were surprised—here was Nancy, with this Hawaiian nobody, at a blanket party.

We started seeing each other, and Nancy started working on me. She urged me to conduct myself in a more gentlemanly manner. When I ate dinner, she said I should look at her, not just at the food. She didn't like that I drank alcohol. She was very demanding, and I had to come to terms with her standards, which weren't mine. All of this combined made me feel insecure. I wanted the world to know, "Hey, World, I'm somebody," but she didn't want me to enjoy my celebrity on campus by acknowledging people who wanted to talk to me because I was a football player. I wasn't acting like I was special, and in my innocence, I thought it was really cool that everyone on campus knew who I was. If someone stopped to talk to me, Nancy would keep on walking.

A lot of the guys who knew Nancy and knew me couldn't believe that we were making it. But we were dating, and then it moved into the summertime, and I went to the oil fields. Nancy was working as a secretary in Dallas, and I drove up every other weekend from South Texas to see her. It became a very intense relationship.

By my junior year, I'd asked her to go steady. At first, we kept it a secret. Then, we decided to announce it at a pinning party at the sorority where both sorority and fraternity members serenaded the pinning couple. I fixed my fraternity pin on Nancy's blouse; there was a ceremony—it was like being engaged. After that, Nancy and I became sort of The Couple. She was a straight arrow. I was trying to mesh my ideas about the Hawaiian way of doing things with her very Southern way of doing things.

I said, "Why don't we get married?"

She said, "Are you crazy? We're still in school!"

"C'mon, you're the one and only."

"Yeah, but we've got things to do, and school to go to." She wasn't about to bend.

In the summer between my junior and senior year, in 1962, I lived in a garage apartment at the palatial North Dallas home of a woman nicknamed Peppy, who said she was related to the founder of Dr. Pepper. She needed somebody at her home because she traveled out of town to Europe for the summer. She was very patronizing and treated me as if I were a servant.

If I was leaning over a shovel working in her garden, she typically remarked something like, "People who lean on shovels are lazy."

I took offense and defended myself, "I'm not lazy."

One weekend Nancy came over, and months and months of frustration boiled over. The first issue was that Nancy had some lofty expectations of me, in terms of how I conducted myself. She came from a Southern home where people were polite, didn't swear, didn't drink. Everything had to be calm because her father had had a heart attack, and an older brother had died when he was a teenager after a swimming pool accident. Everything was quiet in the house, tranquil. Her family wasn't especially wealthy, but they were classy and

Nancy and I on our way to a college dance

gentrified. I certainly wasn't. In terms of material things, compared to the other SMU students, I had nothing. I came from a family where turbulence was common, unlike Nancy's home, and also, my mother put on appearances to be accepted. Nancy's parents didn't have to. They were the real deal.

While I treasured Nancy for her kindness and her principles and her sexual self-control, I felt caught in a situation that was becoming untenable. I was totally devoted to her, but Nancy refused to have sex until we were married. This was the '60s, and for a Southern girl like Nancy, the fear of pregnancy overpowered everything. It would have ruined her life.

Finally, I blurt out, "So when are we gonna get married?"

"It'll be years yet!" she said. "You still have to graduate and go to law school—it'll be at least four years." Janet's response to almost those same words coming out of *my* mouth my freshman year were coming back to haunt me. Given the reverse of the situation, in retrospect, maybe I should have been more empathetic toward Janet when she asked me that same question. My reaction to Nancy's comment was similar to Janet's reaction to mine. I became infuriated.

My question led to a huge argument between Nancy and me. Her response felt like a rejection. It also sounded like a prison sentence without parole for our sexual relationship. I think her hesitation to marry me stemmed from a contradiction between her finding being with someone who was off-limits and unacceptable to her parents as exciting and her Southern mandate to shape me into someone who was *not* off-limits to her parents. She would be making a huge leap marrying a mixed-race man who didn't conform to the social standards expected of someone she would be predicted to choose to marry.

As a football player, she saw me as having a lack of direction that made her hesitate to marry me until I proved myself. She must have felt the burden of adding social value to me. And she must have been questioning what value I was going to add to her life in the future. It must have shown through in my posture, the habits she felt I needed to refine. Somehow, the entire situation was emasculating to me, turning my insecurities into the sex that was being withheld and holding them over me, controlling me, and keeping me from seeing my way forward for myself in any other way than being with Nancy.

I completely lost it, and the argument that erupted between us became so intense and hostile, it led to her saying she didn't want anything more to do with me. She turned around, went downstairs. I chased after her, begging her not to leave.

"Nancy, I'm sorry. Don't leave. Wait. Let's talk about it." I felt heartsick. She got into her car and drove off. I took off in my car, following her. I managed to get her to pull over.

She looked me hard in the eye. "I want nothing to do with you." She drove off.

For the first time in the rank darkness of this devastating loss of the woman I loved, I had to shine a light onto myself, to illuminate the man I could become and find what I lacked that had kept Nancy from agreeing to marry me. I felt I had lost everything. She was the most important thing in my life. She brought everything to me—principles, prestige, rank—because, at the time, I didn't feel I had any of those things without her. And she was so genteel, which was an attribute I had sought out in her and wanted for myself.

To have Nancy, I had to relieve her of the burden of carrying my insecurities, face them, and overcome them on my own, alone, as a result of a few moments of pent-up anger that led to her walking away.

I called her at her family's house in Bonham that night. Eventually, her father answered and wouldn't allow me to speak with her. He must have felt that he needed to protect her from me.

I called my parents and told them about the argument and that Nancy had broken up with me.

"Oh my god," was their response.

I quit my summer job and went home. Nancy wouldn't have anything to do with me. I was deeply sad and dejected.

To help get me out of my funk, my parents suggested I go to a pre-football event in August in Fort Worth. Because I was expected to be an All-Conference player, I was introduced along with players from other schools and the University of Texas. They also introduced Miss Texas, Penny Lee Rudd.[29]

---

29 *Miss Texas Scholarship Organization*. "Miss Texas Alumnae – 1960's. 03 March 2017. https://www.misstexas.org/alumnae-blog/miss-texas-alumnae-1960s

As I was walking out, a Texas football player says, "Would you mind waiting a second, Ray? Miss Texas wants to meet you." Penny came up to me.

"Hey, I really think you're cool," she said. I was taken aback. Nancy and I had split, and suddenly, I'm at a function, and Miss Texas walks up and decides she wants to go out with this big Hawaiian guy.

She started calling me, saying, "We've just got to get together."

A shift happened. I knew that I was appealing as a football player because I was muscled up, probably in better physical condition than anybody on our team. I could play with the best, anybody in the country. I had developed a certain confidence in my body. Once I started dating Nancy, it sank in that maybe I was attractive to other women too, especially once I got my teeth fixed and felt I could smile. I realized when Nancy and I broke up that there were other women who thought I was cool. My senior year began at SMU, and I was dating Miss Texas!

Penny came to Dallas for the weekend, on a promo, and to see me. She purposely went to Nancy's sorority house just to rub it in her face. Penny was a little on the crazy side. She was dating me and a couple of other guys, though denying that she had these other relationships.

Nancy and I had not forgotten about each other. Nancy knew that I was seeing Penny. I was trying to figure out whether I could have a deep, meaningful relationship with Nancy, where she would be the only person. I thought yes, I could, but she was still keeping her distance. Then, about this time, in the fall of 1962, the Cuban Missile Crisis broke out. It was during football season of my senior year that Nancy called me.

"I don't want you to go to war."

"Well, I'm not sure I'm going to, but I'm glad you're concerned. Would you like to talk about it?" I asked.

We agreed to see each other, and she was really distraught, thinking that I was going to go to war, that I'd get killed. As we were talking, I was realizing how mad I still was for her.

Then, she told me she still loved me. We started dating again. And that was it.

Interracial dating was a big deal. Nancy's mother was from a small Southern family in Louisiana with land in Greenwood, a town of fewer than 200 people. All her sisters and brothers shared the property, with their homes backed up to each other. It was off of a main highway between Shreveport, Louisiana and Texas, steeped in the traditions of the South. They were segregationists, and they had Blacks who worked for them, but they were very respectful of everyone. That's where Nancy came from—a cultured, warm, and loving family, proud of their values. You treated all people correctly. They were never demeaning in any way. Southern but very respectful of everyone, both White and Black. They were not mean people.

Nancy's mother liked me, and when I came to see her after we got back together, she didn't object. Nancy's mother saw something in me. She was tolerant and let bygones be bygones. Nancy's father was another story. He was still angry because I had hurt his baby girl. Nancy's Aunt Hattie Ruth accepted me. Her husband, Uncle Ben, was a real stereotype—skinny, little, comical, friendly, very Southern. He had a grocery store, and he wore the Dallas Cowboy T-shirts I gave him. He served a lot of Blacks, but when I walked into the store, he hit the counter hard, and they moved back to let me in. This was common, even a hundred years after the Civil War. The races were separate and still segregated. However, Nancy's parents were more tolerant.

SPORTS VS. ACADEMICS: ACHIEVING A BALANCE

After my junior year, in 1961, I won All-Southwest All-Star Team honors. I also played at nose guard, tackle, guard, defensive end, and linebacker. My senior year, 1962, I also won All Southwest Conference and All-American.[30] But I was just as proud to receive Academic

---

[30] *Punahou Hall of Fame*. "Raymond E. 'Ray' Schoenke (1959)." *Punahou School*, 16 July 1959. https://www.punahou.edu/alumni/recognition/athletic-hall-of-fame?MonthNumber=&YearNumber=1959.

All-American honors as a senior from the conference. I had wanted to be a history major because I had always read history books. That was what I was into—maybe because I sat in the dunce's chair at Davenies in England, and I wanted to enlighten myself now that I was older. I got to SMU, and some of the seniors on the team asked me about my major.

"What do you wanna do that for? You should major in business. We've got all the exams. You can make straight A's."

"Well, I'm not gonna learn anything then," I said. They looked at me like I was stupid. I thought the idea was that when you went to college, you're supposed to learn something.

One professor taught Southern history, and word had it that he used racial slurs, and he was a very strong supporter of the Confederacy. I avoided him. Instead, I gravitated toward the two best professors in the department, Dr. Boller and Dr. Powers, who were both liberal and socialist in their teachings. They were tough.

On the first day of European History during my sophomore year, Dr. Powers said, "Mr. Schoenke, I understand that you're a football player on scholarship here. Is that correct?"

"Yes, sir."

"Would you please stand up and tell the class why the school should give you an athletic scholarship and what value that is to this university?"

What I thought he wanted to do embarrass me, and I thought to myself, *Are you frickin' nuts?*

But I kept my cool. I said, politely, "Well, I'm here to play football, and if I can offer a way in which the school can benefit, either income or prestige that brings students here, I'm glad to do that." I sat down.

"Thank you, Mr. Schoenke." From that point on, he called on me for his questions on the readings, and I was ready. He played a big part in helping me question orthodoxy.

Once I declared history as my major, all my history courses were with Dr. Boller and Dr. Powers. Dr. Boller was erudite. He taught Asian History and led heated discussions about Vietnam. Dr. Powers was exacting. He never gave me an A, just a lot of high B's. He taught about the development of socialist principles coming out of Russia, the turmoil and upheaval in England. They both questioned things that were sacred at the school, and not just football.

My teammates and many of my classmates viewed Dr. Powers and Dr. Boller as communists. They were outstanding teachers—not communists, but socialists. They shaped me intellectually and were articulating ideas that were in me, but still not fully formed or developed. And they let me know they saw me as more than just an athlete.

"I expect you to excel," Dr. Powers told me. "You're grad-school material."

Dallas was a very conservative community, and SMU was a very conservative school. John Birchers permeated Dallas and the student body, along with that hard-right ideology. The players on my team who were ardent conservatives badmouthed these professors all the time. I argued that their ideas had value. My teammates were all White and upper-middle class, professing their conservatism, and here I was, this liberal brown person, arguing that socialist principles have value.

"Schoenke, you're gonna turn out a communist!"

"That's bullshit. I'll set up a meeting, and if you guys have any balls, you can debate these professors." And I did.

Dr. Boller sat with them and questioned them, but the discussions tended to devolve into shouting matches. After one especially bad one, Dr. Boller excused himself.

"Ray, you don't need to do this," he said to me later.

Of course, some students were liberal, and a particular group loved to hang out with me because I was this big jock, and they were a bunch of nerds. I went to their rooms, and they were in classes with me, and they helped me with some of my papers. We sat and talked, and it gave me confidence in my intellectual side.

My thesis for my term paper as a senior was on the socialist principles of George Bernard Shaw. The head of the department, Dr. Gambrell, who taught South American History, gave me an A. Dr. Powers gave me a high B.

By this time, I thought of myself as a bona fide socialist, though really, I was just further left than the SMU crowd. If my teammates saw me as a communist, I wasn't fearful of the label; I was proud. I believed in equality and freedom and respect for all. These professors inspired me to study the socialistic advancement in Europe, Russia, and Southeast Asia and to think differently about what was then called the French Indochina War. As one of the few dark-skinned people at the undergraduate school, I was experiencing racism personally, and my feelings about race were evolving. By the time I graduated, I had my eyes on law school and, eventually, my unique form of social and political activism.

When I graduated, I was listed in *Who's Who in American Colleges*, and I had received coveted awards from Cycen Fjodr, a secret fraternity unique to SMU honoring scholarship and service for senior men, and Blue Key, a National Honor Society organization. The University honored me with the 1963 SMU "M" award, which recognized creative student activity and was given to "the most Distinguished Seniors to graduate." I felt that I had come into my own. I finally felt secure. Later, I was also named to SMU's 75th National Honor Society Anniversary All-Time Football Team and received the Silver Anniversary Mustang Award from the SMU Letterman's Association, which honors the character and achievements of former athletes.

THE PRESS IS NOT ALWAYS YOUR FRIEND

I was proud of all those honors, but at the time, I was extremely disappointed not to have made the SMU Hall of Fame. You never know about these things, but I have often thought about an interview I gave to reporter Dan Jenkins[31] just before my senior year on Press Day.

---

31 SI staff, *Sports Illustrated*. "The Best of Dan Jenkins." 08 Mar 2019; https://www.si.com/sports-illustrated/2019/03/08/dan-jenkins-stories-sports-illustrated.

"Tell me, did you ever try to hurt anybody?" he asked.

I told him about when I was a sophomore and I went into a game as a fullback. There was an All-American player named Danny LaRose on the Missouri team. When I hit him, I hit him right underneath his chin. I was protecting the passer, and I put him on his back, and I stood over him.

"I felt like the strongest man in the world." And then, when I was a junior, we played TCU. The quarterback was Sonny Gibbs, a six-foot-six quarterback and a very good athlete. "I'm coming to get him," I told Jenkins, "and he's stretched out as far as his arms would reach with the ball, and I put my helmet right in his ribs."

"Were you trying to hurt him?"

"Of course I was trying to hurt him!"

"If you broke his rib, would that be good?"

"Yeah, damned right!"

He titled the article in the paper, "*Schoenke Likes to Crack 'Em.*" I was young and naïve at the time. In truth, Jenkins set me up by the way he phrased the question.

Later in my career, I was savvy enough to be wary of the press. At this age, I was not. My job was to tackle, hit, and stop Sonny Gibbs in the most forceful way allowed. Injury to a player you tackle is collateral damage. You are not planning to hurt the other player, but this is a violent game. You have two powerful, highly trained people running at each other at high speed who are equipped with gear intended to both protect them and also function as weapons, who are trained to either block or tackle each other, which are violent acts in and of themselves.

If I had broken Gibbs's rib, and he had to come out of the game, this collateral injury would have been good for our team, and I would have been praised by my coaches and teammates for disabling him in a way that was perfectly legal in the game. However, Jenkins suggested that I liked to intentionally injure other players, and I was made to appear like an unsportsmanlike, out-of-control, violent football player.

All hell broke loose. Alums wrote in and said I should be kicked out of school. Nobody else was getting this kind of negative notoriety. I called Jenkins, and he said he understood that my response was honest and acknowledged that football is a tough game. Ironically, Jenkins got a lot of negative public backlash as well, and he wrote a retraction in which he said, "Schoenke knows he is a player who loves football and only likes to play it tough." He admitted in the retraction that there had been a negative public reaction to suggesting that I liked to hurt people, but by the time he retracted his comments, it was too late.

Hayden Fry had me stand up in front of the team and disparaged me for what I said in the interview. He basically accused me of being a dirty football player, someone who wanted to hurt people, and said he and SMU did not condone that type of behavior. I was already embarrassed and humiliated by the article, and my innocence about talking to the press was destroyed. I felt Fry was trying to motivate the team at my expense by singling me out and turning the team against me. He totally demeaned me after the article had already managed to do it quite successfully. He didn't want the team to feel they needed *my* talent to succeed. He decided to make an example of me in front of the team even though I was one of his best players. This wounded me at a very deep level.

On top of this, I was the only man of color on the team. What he couldn't understand was that his attack also felt racially motivated to me. He needed an excuse to elevate the team, so he humiliated me to do it. I lost a lot of respect. I have always blamed Jenkin's article and Fry's response to it for not getting inducted into the SMU Hall of Fame. With Jenkins's instigation, Fry ruined my relationship with the team, and players who already resented my notoriety used this as an excuse to block me from being team captain in spite of the fact that I was a first team All-American and All-Southwest Conference preseason pick. But by the end of the season, I made the preseason predictions stick.

THE NFL: NEGOTIATING BECOMING A COMMODITY

I had been on the SMU team at a time of change. When Hayden Fry took the job at SMU, he was promised that he would be allowed to recruit Black athletes. He grew up in a segregated atmosphere, but when he entered the military, it was integrated, and I remember him referring to a fellow soldier, who was Black.

"Even though I grew up in a Southern segregated community, I trusted that guy enough that I could go to sleep on his watch. The military changed my attitude," he said.

When I was on the team, we had no Blacks. Right after I left, the team became more integrated. Fry recruited Jerry LeVias, a great player, an exceptional student, and an All-American. I take my hat off to what Fry did, but he did also make *me*, a man of color who was also an All-American, an example in front of the team to humiliate me.

In December 1962, I was selected by the Dallas Cowboys in the 11th round of the 1963 NFL Draft and by the Oakland Raiders in the tenth round of the 1963 AFL Draft. It wasn't a high draft choice. I was very disappointed, but I had played a lot of different positions, so they had not had an opportunity to see me play one position for my entire football career, and I wasn't as heavy as your typical lineman. I only weighed 225, which was below average weight for a pro lineman, who at that time, typically weighed 240-270.

The Cowboys were then in transition from being a new team in the league to becoming contenders. The AFL was new and a bit unknown. The Dallas Texans (who later became the Kansas City Chiefs) had also drafted me. Lamar Hunt, the son of oil tycoon H.L. Hunt, was a founder of the AFL, which was a new league at the time, and he had played football for SMU. Even though I knew a lot of the players on the Dallas Texans, I was partial to the NFL—I had watched NFL games on TV as a kid with my father, and I had delighted in the great games between the NY Giants and the Baltimore Colts. And I still wanted to play with the best.

My dad was my lawyer, and we didn't know how to negotiate. Tex Schramm,[32] the general manager, offered me $10,000.

My dad encouraged me to take the offer. "That's more money than I've ever made in my life," my dad said.

"Well I need to figure this thing out," I replied. I negotiated with Tex, and I ended up agreeing to $11,500 as a salary with a $3,500 bonus, or $15,000. In 2022, that's about $107,204.[33] I could have gotten more, but I wasn't into high finance. I just wanted to pay off the fraternity debt of $500 to Phi Gamma Delta.

The personal highlight of my senior year was returning to Honolulu for the 1963 Hula Bowl. As a pre-season pick as well as an All-Conference and All-American, I was being approached to play in various postseason games—which offered money and all kinds of incentives. The big college competitions were the East-West Shriners game in San Francisco and the North-South game in Mobile, Alabama. I said, "Hey, guys, if I get invited to the Hula Bowl, I'm going." And I got the invite.

For the Hula Bowl, the top college players in the country were brought to Honolulu Stadium for one of the final games of the college football postseason. It was an honor. It was a big deal to me when I was a Buff 'n' Blue player in high school in Hawai'i, and it was a big deal to me as a college senior. So, in January 1963, I played the East-West game in San Francisco, then flew to Honolulu to play in the Hula Bowl. South lost to North, 20-14. I went out every night to connect with friends that I knew in Hawai'i, and I took two carloads of players to learn bodysurfing at Makapu'u Beach, where the players put their valuables underneath the seat of the cars that I was able to secure for free because of my local contacts. I totally forgot that the local boys would break the windows and steal everything because there are no police out there on the other side of the island. I should have known better. I felt terrible.

---

32 Dallas Cowboys. "Tex Schramm-General Manager, 1959-1989." https://www.dallascowboys.com/team/roh-tex-schramm.

33 *Inflation Tool*. "Inflation calculator – US Dollar." https://www.inflationtool.com/us-dollar/1969-to-present-value?amount=25000&year2=2022&frequency=yearly.

The guy in charge of relations with the players made sure that the players were reimbursed, including having their rings replaced. The workouts were only 30 minutes long, so I had lots of energy, and I went nonstop, but I did have to play a football game after not sleeping for a week. Marv Fleming, an offensive end, warned me that this wasn't going to be "nice" because of racial tension on the part of tourists, many of which were visiting Hawai'i from the South during the holiday season.

In the first play of the game, a White kid from Kentucky who was over Bobby Bell, a Black All-American from North Carolina playing college football at the University of Minnesota, approached me in the huddle and asked me to block Bobby Bell because he didn't want to. I figured out pretty quick just why. I set up, and he came right at me, and instead of hitting me with a forearm into the chest, he went for my face and elbowed me under the faceguard right in the face.

"Don't ever do that again," I said.

His response was basically, "Fuck you." So, for the rest of the game, we chased each other around on punts where I ran down the field. As we ran side-by-side, we tried to punch each other.

There was a couple in Honolulu who were tied to the ownership of the Cowboys. So before the game, they took me out to dinner, along with Sonny Gibbs, the TCU quarterback, the Dallas #1 draft pick. They were talking about everything they were gonna do for Sonny. Sonny was the #1 choice, and I was like #11. He was a big deal, and I wasn't.

I went to play for the Cowboys my rookie year, and Nancy and I got married on April 4, 1964, in my second year with the NFL. I know everyone cries at weddings, but at my wedding, walking down the aisle, I could see Nancy's parents and family crying, and as I approached the minister, even *he* was in tears. I was trying to figure out if anyone in the church wanted me to marry her. Many people at weddings cry because they are such emotional events or because they are saying goodbye to a family member as they leave for a new life. In my case, it seemed like it was more like they were watching Nancy go to the gallows.

RAY SCHOENKE

Everyone was crying, hopefully not because Nancy was marrying me

CHAPTER THREE

Cowboy Up (1963-1964)

In the summer of 1963, after I graduated from SMU, I worked as a youth counselor at a summer camp. It was a great place for me to train before reporting to the Dallas Cowboys' training camp. I was able to work out in the morning and evening and during breaks. There was a wrestling gym, swimming pools, a track—even a weight program. Two lakes offered chances to sail, and you could canoe on tributaries. Many camp counselors were college athletes, including some distance runners. We ran along the country roads, and in the morning, we ran barefoot on a golf course. When I reported for rookie camp in Dallas, I was in fantastic shape—I was built like a brick shithouse, and I ran the mile in 5:45.

I called Coach Tom Landry after I took the job and explained that the camp didn't break up until the day after the Dallas rookies started practice. Could I come in a day late? I always found Landry to be a bit of a cold fish, direct but terse.

True to form, he didn't say much, maybe just, "Fine."

I got there a little late on my first day of practice, after they'd done all the drills, so I went to run my mile. A lineman was expected to run a mile in six minutes, 30 seconds, and backs had to do it in six minutes. I was so confident, I just coasted in the second half, and I did 6:40, which means I was 10 seconds too slow. I crossed the finish, and the line coach, Jim Myers, grunted, "You ran it in 6:45."

Normally, every time you went by him, he called out your time. He hadn't called out the splits, and I was pissed.

"Why didn't you tell me what the goddamn time was?" I asked. He mumbled something. My penalty was extra running that day after practice.

I compensated by doing a lot more than extra running. I ended up being in great shape and looking like Mr. Universe. My picture was in the local paper with a caption that read, "Best Physical Specimen in Camp."

Getting ready for Cowboys rookie camp

I was feeling good about myself. I bought a 1963 Falcon convertible, purple, with a black top, black interior, bucket seats. It cost $1,500. Nancy loved it. I thought I was so cool—that was until I pulled up in the parking lot. The players for the Cowboys were all in their big cars. The veterans got out, looked at my car, and shook their heads. I could practically hear them thinking, "Rookie." Buddy Dial, an All-Pro out of Rice, who had come to the Cowboys from Pittsburgh and was a spectacular receiver, came into the lot in his Cadillac, which was about two blocks long.

He pulls right up next to me in the Falcon, and says, "What is *that?*"

JACK OF ALL TRADES, MASTER OF ALL OF THEM

In college, I had played guard, tackle, and center, as well as linebacker on defense. At the Cowboys, I was tried at tackle, guard, and center. I was on the suicide squads, all five special teams—the kickoff team, the kickoff-return team, the punt team, the punt-return team, and the field-goal team. When the game starts, at the kickoff, if you're on the defense's kickoff team, you run down, and your job is to make sure you have a lane; you try to make the tackle on the kick returner. Then, of course, they're setting up a play where they're lining up, and they're trying to block you. On the other side, when you're on the kickoff-return team, you're positioned to block, so they kick off, and your return-man catches the ball; then you run and try to block players you are assigned to.

A few times during training camp, a starting lineman was having difficulty, and I was put in to replace him. I was scared to death. I was a good athlete, but I really didn't know how to play the game, especially how to pass block, and nobody would teach me how. My senior season at SMU, our new coach, Hayden Fry, was all drive-block and four-point stance. But in the pros, you have a drop-back passer, and he usually holds the ball three to five seconds. The offensive team comes out of the huddle, runs to the line, and everybody gets down into a set position. The ball is hiked; the quarterback drops back to pass, and the linemen (who know how long the quarterback is going to take) then drop back to protect him. Meanwhile, the defensive linemen try to break that chain and get to the quarterback. As soon as the ball is hiked, BAM! The defensive line is coming. You drop back, and they come in and hit you, and they try to maneuver you in such a way as to get around you. They'll hit you right in your head, push you, slap you, pull you. Their job is to kill the quarterback. Your job is to make sure that they don't ever get to touch him.

For a short pass, the ball is typically released from the quarterback's hands in three seconds. That seems fast, but not against a good defensive lineman. You have to figure out how to beat someone strong as a mule and quick as a cat, before they hit you, stun you, and pull you down. But there are times when it's a five-second pass. That's an eternity, and a really good defensive lineman, or a mean one, can beat your ass every time. You have to know how to handle it, and I didn't. I didn't understand the whole theory behind pass blocking. It was a totally new technique to me—one I'd never learned in college. And no one on the team, particularly the veterans, who found it quite humorous to watch me, would help, including the one who was supposed to be training me, the offensive line coach Jim Myers.

Myers had arrived in Dallas in 1962 with a colorful reputation already established as the former head coach at Iowa State and Texas A&M, where he had replaced Paul "Bear" Bryant. He was described as having a "hard-nosed, no-nonsense style,"[34] which must have already been in evidence as a Marine because he had been promoted to instructor at Quantico during World War II. One story he told about himself involved contract negotiations at A&M. The school offered him a four-year contract extension, "but when he saw the salary, he told the school president that he'd 'just as soon be fired as to have a contract like this.'"

---

34 Buchanan, William T. 'Buck', *Glory Days: Life with the Dallas Cowboys. 1973-1998* (Taylor Trade Publishing, 2006), 101.

The reply was swift: "OK ... you're fired."[35] He was willing to stand on principle, even if it meant losing his job. Myers was organized, smart, and so weathered that *Los Angeles Times* writer Jim Murray wrote this about him in 1979:

> *His face looks as if he just went 10 hard rounds with Dempsey or as if he were the last guy out of a plane wreck. It would have to improve to be called 'craggy'. ... Life never dealt Jim Myers many aces. Every card he ever turned over broke the flush. It made him hard, and his face got the message.*[36]

Myers and I had a history: He had tried to recruit me to Texas A&M out of high school.

I arrived in Dallas, and I needed his help. But he didn't know anything about pass-blocking, either. It was a disaster. In practice, you've got guys like Bob Lilly, a defensive tackle, who was the key in Dallas's vaunted "Doomsday Defense."[37] He could go around you so fast you didn't know what just happened.

Coach Myers is screaming at me in his usual abrasive tone, "Schoenke, Goddamn you, you don't know how to pass block!"

"Right, I *don't* know how to pass block," I respond.

The veteran linemen thought it was really funny, and they laughed. In the end, I just grabbed Lilly's face mask and pulled him down, and we got into a fight.

Finally, a veteran guard, Jim Ray Smith, who had been an All-Pro with Cleveland, pulled me aside and said, "Come over here, kid; let me show you how to do this." He gave me some techniques, which took me a year to master before I could implement them in a game.

---

35 Williams, Charean. "Longtime Cowboys Assistant Myers Dies at 92." *Fort Worth Star-Telegram*, 12 Nov. 2014. www.star-telegram.com/sports/nfl/dallas-cowboys/article3865848.html.

36 Williams, Charean. *Fort Worth Star-Telegram*.

37 Golenbock, Peter. *Landry's Boys: An Oral History of a Team and an Era*, (Triumph Books, 2005).

Made the team, but YIKES! I don't know how to pass block

I became a student of pass blocking. I became a student of the offensive line. I became a technician. You study your opponent. You know what kind of student he is. You've watched the films. You know what he's going to do. If he comes up with something new, then the game gets tough. I really believed by the end of my career that you could put anyone in front of me, and I could hold him off for three seconds. If it was five seconds, it would be a close contest.

In the pros, I was never anything but an offensive lineman. When Ted Marchibroda left the Redskins to be the head coach for the Baltimore Colts, he asked me if I would come with him and be his line coach. At that time, I was about to leave the game, so I declined.

A good offensive player is typically taller than six feet, weighs somewhere between 240 and 285, is strong, agile, and values quickness over running speed, although speed is important. He has a mentality that makes it possible for him to receive a blow and also strike a blow—strike, counterpunch, strike, counterpunch. He has to have a low center of gravity and excellent upper-body strength. The defensive guy has to go through him to get to the quarterback. As a rookie, I was 230 pounds, but after a few years, I was 245 to 250. When pass blocking, my job was to make sure I stayed in the way. I had to keep my opponent within three yards of the line of scrimmage. That's as deep as I could let him go.

I'm only giving him the outside, or he has to go over me. When I deliver a blow, I quickly step back in a move that requires two steps but is so quick, it looks like one and occurs in an instant. He is charging into me at that point, and by my stance, he knows it's a pass block. I must fire out over a short distance, but I cannot lose control or give an advantage to my opponent because the counter punch is so vital. To sustain the block, I must maintain an offensive position for three seconds, or, on a long, deep pass, for five seconds. I must have toughness of spirit, and I must persevere. I can't let my opponents wear me down over the time it takes to do this many times over the course of a game, and I must have the intellectual capacity to handle all situations, both physical and mental.

Stance is extremely important because offensive guards and tackles have to be able to execute both a pass block and a run block. In a pass block, which constitutes typically 40 to 60 percent of the game, you have to find a neutral position that enables you to go forward *or* back so your opponent doesn't know it's a pass. Otherwise, you will tip the defensive tackle, end, or linebacker as to whether you are executing a pass block or a run block. I had to practice for hours to be able to assume a neutral position that did not overly compensate for a run or a pass that I could leave instantaneously to carry out either a run block straight ahead, to the right or left, or a pass block, where you typically move backward. My body could even give away information. So I also had to practice making my *body* neutral, as well as positioning it in such a way that I could instantaneously move in the direction I wanted to move. I practiced endlessly to ensure the positioning of my feet or body would not tip the play to my opponent.

Typically, the defensive guys grab you and pull you. What the veterans try to teach you is to block their hands. But you can't do that because it happens so quick. You can't knock a guy's hands off of you. It's incredibly difficult. And once these guys grab you, they can throw you. So you gotta figure out how to counter all that. Jim Ray Smith showed me that when they come to grab you at close quarters, you hold a balanced stance on both feet and hit them in the chest or face with your helmet to deaden their momentum, then slam your fists into their ribs. Players wear padded sponges on their hands that are taped. I wore a fiberglass cast underneath those pads to keep my wrists from buckling when I hit my opponent in the ribs. It was like having brass knuckles, and when I hit the defensive tackle in his ribs, I knew I could badly bruise his ribs, and I could tell I was successful by the way he gasped and groaned when I hit him. Hitting a player in the ribs hard enough can also potentially stop him if you are strong enough. I spent hours lifting 50-pound dumbbells to get strong enough, but my arm strength wasn't always enough against these huge, powerful guys.

The pressure on a player is enormous. You have to stop these guys, or you could lose your job. You can use your hand position on their ribs to pinch them, and you struggle against each other in a kind of counterbalanced dance. Because my hands are closed into fists, and

I am pinching him with my fists, the ref doesn't call holding. You're just trying to delay one, two seconds. By that time, the ball is gone.

The idea seems simple: You know the count, and your opponent doesn't. He weighs 20, 30, or 40 pounds more than you. You have literally half a second to get set up with your legs underneath you. You have to keep a guy from attempting to grab you, actually grabbing you, and headbutting you.

Even in the NFL, there are bullies. You would think that, with its highly respected image and the overall size and athleticism of the players, that bullies wouldn't exist in the NFL, but they do. Superior athletes can be intimidated even in the NFL. Most people are decent; they try to comply with the rules, but then there are people who don't go by the rules. Then what do you do? Most refs today just look the other way. It's really flagrant. You learn very early that the way you deal with it is to meet force with force, or with greater force, until they know that if you play that game, you're going to get hurt. But there are players who feel that they can't resort to such tactics to neutralize unsportsmanlike conduct.

We're playing the St. Louis Cardinals, and our defensive tackle comes to me and says that the offensive lineman is grabbing his facemask.

"All you have to do is to grab his wrist when he grabs your face mask, and pull straight down, and you will break his wrist," I tell him.

This giant six-foot-six monster says, "But that will hurt him!"

"That's the idea!" I reply.

"I can't do that!" he exclaims.

"Then he is going to keep pulling on your face mask. Welcome to the NFL."

It is possible to hit a player extremely hard with your helmet under the chin by springing forward and elongating your body like a spear. You literally lift off the ground as you launch toward him like that. But it has to be perfectly timed, and you absolutely *have* to surprise him. The helmet takes most of the blow, but when you hit someone under the chin like that, you stun him, jack him up in the air, shock him, and put him on his back. It's not like someone punching you. It is a game changer. It really HURTS. It's like taking a sledgehammer to the face. No player wants to go through it again. Another part of this process for me was screaming as I fired out and leapt toward my opponent. In practice, if my teammates heard that scream, they instantly froze to avoid my attack because they knew they were going to take one on the chin unless they were quick enough to avoid it, which was rarely the case.

In games, I only used this technique sparingly, because if you miss your opponent when you launch forward, he'll kill the quarterback. One time I used this technique was in an interesting encounter with defensive tackle Dave Butz, the first day he arrived at training camp in Carlisle, Pennsylvania. Butz, a six-foot-seven, 295-pound giant who later became an All-Pro legend with the Redskins, had just been traded to the Redskins, and the trainer had brought him out to morning practice, where we were engaged in pass blocking drills. There had been rain early in the morning before practice, so the ground was wet.

As we were beginning the drill, the trainer brought Dave out to join the linemen and to introduce us to him, at which point the coach asked Dave if he would like to take a turn.

"Sure!" he said.

"Who wants 'im?" the offensive line coach challenged. And everyone looked up at the sky or the ground.

The coach looked at me. "OK. I'll take 'im," I said.

So I get down. They call "set," snap the ball, and set up for the pass block. Just as his big arms are about to grab me, I fire out, and my helmet hits him right under the chin. He doesn't have any traction due to the rain that had fallen earlier. The hit jacks him up in the air, and he falls on the ground on his back.

As I'm taking a bow, Dave jumps up off the ground pissed off and screams at me, "Let's do it again!"

"He's all yours," I say, turning to my offensive teammates with a big grin on my face.

Of course, I was never able to do that to him again. You only get one shot like that with any good defensive tackle. They're looking for it after that. Dave and I developed a cordial relationship that extended into my post-football career. He later expressed his amazement that I could just walk away from football with no financial repercussions.

Run blocking, on the other hand, can constitute as much as 40 percent of a game. It can be a very effective part of the game because it can set up the pass. The central difference between a run block and a pass block is that on a run block, you fire straight out at the defensive lineman. You are trying to drive him backwards or to the side. It is a very aggressive block and requires great strength and balance. As you fire straight out at the defensive lineman, you slam your helmet into his face while keeping your own body from collapsing as the other player counters by pushing you and punching your head with his forearm. You are elongated out toward him, so your head may slide down his body as you collapse from his weight.

He will likely fall on top of you because you've thrown off *his* balance, and if you can't get your feet under yourself, which is usually the case, you may even end up crawling on the ground carrying a player who is typically heavier than you on your back with your back up while maintaining your stance and continuing to dig and push him backwards or to one side. You end up looking like two huge turtles in a battle, one on top of the other. All this happens in *four* seconds. It's *over*. If you keep him occupied and give room for the runner to pass by, your block is successful.

I played offensive guard and offensive tackle, both right and left, both of which require pass blocking and run blocking. When I played guard, I was typically at the point of attack on just about every play. I had to be proficient at blocking straight ahead as well as being able to pull from my position for quick blocks at the end of the line of scrimmage directly across from me or to lead a sweep where the ball is given to the half back, who then follows me and/or my teammate as we lead the runner to the outside of the line of scrimmage and head downfield.

When the regular season started, during my rookie year, I was primarily on the suicide squads the guys used in kickoffs. In the sixth week, playing in New York against the Giants, I was a reserve tackle. I got the call when New York's defensive end, Jim Katcavage, was beating our starting right tackle, Ed Nutting. Katcavage was only six foot, one inch or so, maybe 240 pounds, but All-Pro—he was later credited with 96.5 sacks with the Giants in his career. He's giving Nutting a lot of trouble.

Myers grabs me and says, "Schoenke, go out there and stop Katcavage."

I'm a rookie, maybe 220 or 230, and I think, "Oh great, I get to block Superman."

We got in the huddle, and our quarterback, Don Meredith, called a passing play; then Don called "Break." The way the Cowboys used to line up, the linemen would break to the line of scrimmage; we'd get to the line, and Meredith would say "Set!" and all of the linemen would stand up and then go down. The idea was to camouflage the positions of the running backs as they moved to set their positions in the backfield before the ball was snapped. So I went up, and I came down, and the defensive end should have been right in front of me. Well, Katcavage was not there.

"Where the hell is Katcavage?" I'm screaming. I look out, and he's split out, about 10 yards away, and I'm wondering why he's way the hell out there. He wasn't playing his position because he had the leeway to mess with me because he knew that I was a new substitute and from the program that I was a rookie.

The ball is snapped, and Katcavage is hauling ass by the time I figure it out. If I don't get this guy, he's gonna kill Meredith. So I turn around and catch him, and I hit him in the back and drive him right into Meredith. The ball goes up straight up in the air, and the Giants recover the fumble.

We come off the field, and Meredith, who graduated from SMU three years ahead of me, says, "What the hell are you doing out there, guy?" They took me out after that. That was my rookie christening.

My last year with the Cowboys, I played against Katcavage again and brought all my new techniques. I stopped him dead. He said, "You've figured it out, kid, haven't you?"

While all of these skills are essential, you occasionally meet defensive players whose skills may at times be superior to yours. There are two such players who fit in that category—Bob Lilly and Willie Lanier. Willie played middle linebacker for the Kansas City Chiefs, unlike Bob, who played defensive tackle for the Dallas Cowboys. On plays going to the outside on my side of the line or straight up the middle, the middle linebacker was my responsibility. On plays called on my side of the line to the outside, the center has the option to make a call that makes me block his man (Willie); he would be responsible for blocking *my* man, the defensive tackle. I tried every way possible to block Willie. As I chased him and then fired into him low into his legs, he hurdled me. Then, I tried to adjust by hitting him higher, only to have him duck and run behind me, causing me to miss him completely.

When a play was called straight up the middle, and the center blocked my man, Buck Buchanan, I was responsible for a fold block (coming around the center and going straight at Willie, who was stepping into the hole between the two guards.) Willie either jumped over me or went underneath me and, in either case, jammed up the hole, so we made no yardage. When I was chasing him to the outside, he simply outran me. The only way I could take him down was to outsmart him, making him think I was going to do one thing and doing something else. He was one of the most difficult middle linebackers I ever had to block. We were constantly trying to outsmart each other, and he won that guessing game more times than I did.

RAY SCHOENKE

Blocking against the Kansas City Chiefs

Willie recalls:

The middle linebackers of my period (Dick Butkus, Ray Nitschke, Tommy Nobis, and Bill Bergey) were all tremendously physical in their approach to the game. Since I was the first Black middle linebacker in the history of the game and the first Black middle linebacker to ever play the game full time for Kansas City, I had to craft a different approach. The reality is that football requires physical skills that most people do not have and mental skills that are much more sophisticated than one would imagine. Football is more than mass and muscle colliding. When the Redskins played the Kansas City Chiefs, Ray Schoenke and I became combative from the opposite side of the line of scrimmage. Ray was an intelligent, quick, athletic offensive guard who had to block me on certain plays, which became a cat and mouse exercise because I had to constantly outthink him.

Offensive linemen were typically 25–30 pounds larger than me. The physics is irrefutable. You will automatically lose against a person who outweighs you by 30 pounds because you spend so much time engaging and then disengaging. My strategy was to avoid that contact. Ray had great difficulty determining the proper angle or the structural reality it would take to block me. I played at an extremely high intellectual level before the game became physical. Because I had so little contact as a result of this strategy, I had very few injuries. I had to quickly process each step and half step, and I had to have an exceptional understanding of the weight distribution an offensive lineman would take to attempt to execute his block. My execution couldn't allow his angle to benefit him.

I told Ray recently that because offensive linemen had to have their hand on the field for one second before they could move, I could use that time to adjust my position to take a half step back and a half step to the side or to take a half step forward, which would create the need for a longer single step by Ray or a quick two step to be in position for the change. All of my movements were designed so the offensive lineman could not gather himself to thrust because he wouldn't quite know where he would have to be. I can only imagine the frustration that this created for my opponents. The time that I played against the Redskins was especially joyous because they were the last team in professional football history to integrate. Black players were thought to be inferior in terms of their ability play the middle linebacker position or the offensive guard position that Ray played. What we did on the field was clearly a wonderful expression of two men plying their trade in different spheres, but our intellectual and mental approach to the game was what allowed us to truly appreciate each other.[38]

---

38 Personal communication with Willie Lanier, Kansas City Chiefs middle linebacker NFL Hall of Famer, March 18, 2023.

Regardless of all their physical attributes, offensive linemen have to be sold on playing in the line. Their dedication, or lack of it, will often determine the success of the team. In short, they must like to hit. My strength is that I could play any one of these positions. I could also play center, although I never did. The Packers, the Redskins, and the Cowboys had me at guard and tackle. The Browns put me at guard.

THE ANSWER TO THE QUESTION EVERYONE ASKS

People often ask me, "What happens in the huddle?" I've been asked this question by neighbors, by CEOs and members of the board of directors, by close personal friends, by fans, by people I meet at social events, on the golf course, and by a president of the United States. They always have this look on their face like they think I have a key to some mystical, secret communication that takes place in the huddle. It *is* secret, and it is sort of mystical, but the code is simple because it has to be interpreted quickly and correctly and then executed flawlessly. As a player, I honed my ability to understand and execute this secret language through hours and hours of physical and mental repetition. I think what fans don't understand is the immense amount of practice and study that goes into understanding that language and turning it into the play they see executed on the field. That is the part that seems mystical. The other part is sweat and blood.

I think what people really want to know is what happens in the huddle *and* in the seven to 10 seconds that take place after it breaks that make a play either a success or a failure. When I was playing, most of the plays were called directly by the quarterback. We typically didn't talk in the huddle, and if we did, we made damn sure we knew what we were talking about. This information might be something you are seeing that the quarterback wouldn't know about that would be helpful to him. But we had to be careful when we told the quarterback that information because he could be overloaded and could get angry. What takes place in the huddle is choreographed by the quarterback to evoke an interesting display of controlled violence, which is what the fans see taking place on the field after the huddle breaks. The secret code is actually the play, the formation, and the count.

During my time as a football player, the quarterback spent hours with the offensive coach and the quarterback coach, and sometimes the head coach, after the coaches had reviewed films of offensive and defensive plays for several games and categorized them, a process that could take hours to lead to the development of a single play. A game plan was developed for as many as 30 to 60 plays, and they sat down with the quarterbacks and went over what was expected. During the game, the quarterback pretty much had autonomy other than when plays were sent down from the press box to the sidelines, and a player was sent out with a play, or a time-out was called to inform the quarterback of a suggested play. The process was very cumbersome, and the pressure was mostly on the quarterback. Nowadays, the process is much more efficient and almost instantaneous. The same grueling planning process takes place, and the quarterback still determines most of the plays, but coaches can now send information directly to the quarterback by talking directly to him on his helmet earpiece and suggesting a play that could be a gamechanger.

In the huddle, an example of this 'secret code' would be a situation where the quarterback has called a red right 28 on 1. He is communicating a code that tells me that our backfield line is strong on the right, based on the game plan for both the running play and the passing play against this team on this down, where it is assumed this play will more than likely work because he is familiar with the tendencies of the opposing team. So, red right 28 means we're running a sweep to the right, and 1 is the count for the play to begin, when, as a guard, I have to pull out and get in front of the running back, who has been handed the ball by the quarterback.

My job is to lead the runner around the line of scrimmage and then look for a defensive back, who by this time, has figured out what we are doing and is coming forward to fill the hole and plans to take me and the running back out. The game plan is based on studying films of the opponent. It is assumed that your opponents have also studied *your* tendencies. Superior teams with exceptional players don't change a lot because they are so strong. They can use the same strategy game after game and be successful. The quarterback is taking into account the tendencies of the opponent's defense based on where the ball is located on the field, the yardage to be gained to get a first down, and the defense that is expected, where, based on what he actually encounters on the line and whether or not the play he calls is sufficient to meet that defense, he may call a change of play (an audible).

All of this happens within less than 10 seconds after the huddle breaks. Everybody on the offensive team has to be ready to execute the play called in the huddle, but if the quarterback decides to change the play and calls an audible at the line of scrimmage by repeating the count called in the huddle, the number he calls after that is the new play. Everyone must be alert that an audible has been called and that a new play has to be executed, and there can be no mistakes. This goes on 60 to 70 times in a game.

What's in my mind as I leave the huddle is how to execute the play that has just been called because I am also familiar with the tendencies of the *defensive* players on that particular team. At the line of scrimmage, I'm listening for an audible while at the same time assessing the defensive alignment that I will be blocking against and the strategies that I need to use to make that block. I have a good idea if the play that is called is going to work against the defense; if not, I can anticipate an audible.

I also have to be careful when I'm looking around and assessing the situation that I don't tip the defense what direction I'm going to block or what kind of play it is by how my feet are positioned. If an audible is called, I have to immediately completely revamp my approach to fit the new play, an adjustment that has to take place within maybe a couple of seconds. What I have to be concerned with is whether the quarterback has changed to a new play, whether I hear it called, and, if it is called, whether I have to change my blocking assignment to fit the new play.

I have to determine how to execute a block within a matter of seconds. I go to the line thinking one way, and within maybe two seconds, I'm totally adjusting, and I have to determine what kind of new block I'm going to have to make…and then the ball is hiked or snapped. When the play is determined, and I know the count, I then have to execute based on the defense in front of me. You have to be perfect, and you *can't* be perfect. You have to get as close to perfection as you can, but it is incredibly difficult because the goal of the defense is to mess you up in that short period of time by causing you to make poor decisions on either the run play or the pass play. If you make a poor decision, and it costs the team a loss of yardage, or the runner or the quarterback is hit, there's hell to pay. Physical mistakes will often be overlooked. Mental mistakes will not be overlooked and can cost you your job.

You constantly live with the fear of losing your job. You have to dedicate yourself to being perfect in a situation where each time you walk onto the field may be your last. The stress is overwhelming, but you are more likely to make mental mistakes if you let that stress affect you. I dealt with this situation like a Hawaiian warrior. I mentally dug a hole, picked up my spear, and said silently to my opponent, "I'm willing to die out here. Are you?" My mind was so focused, I intimidated my opponent both physically and mentally, and most of the time, this was effective. When I encountered someone whose mindset was mentally and physically equal to me or even superior, it was brutal, but exhilarating, when I was victorious. The rush I got from the encounter was glorious.

So, the huddle is the stage on which the quarterback lays out the dance to take place on the field, but the other dancers who will appear on that stage are not your partners, but rather are your adversaries. We are performing at a level at which we are expected to be flawless, which is only possible maybe 70-80 percent of the time. If the attempt is acceptable, and I slow the blocker down the other 20-30 percent of the time, I won't lose my job. If not, I'm history. The dance is violent and combative, and we risk injury, being yelled at by a coach, or even losing our job every time we go back out on that stage, and we do it many, many times each game.

You have to be able to memorize plays; be incredibly physically fit and conditioned; able to handle an opponent who is an All-Pro who can take advantage of your inexperience; avoid confusion when under stress (the play is on a count of two, and you leave on one); make mistakes and deal with the consequences of those mistakes and overcome them knowing you might have cost the team a touchdown or the game; being demoted to backup and having to struggle to regain your starting position; and most of all, handle the mental pressure associated with all of these. This is why so few players last more than three years in the NFL.

STARTING MORE THAN JUST THE GAME: DRUGS IN THE NFL

In my second year with the Cowboys, 1964, I became a starter, but I still wasn't confident in pass blocking. You're coming in as a kid and playing against superior athletes with experience and knowledge. You have to be strong—with enough foundation in your feet and enough force in your hands to stop a 280-pound guy coming at you at full speed. I just didn't believe I could do it. I actually hoped something would happen—a car accident or a plane crash, so I wouldn't have to play.

We were facing the Cleveland Browns, and Dick Modzelewski, who played at Maryland, was their defensive tackle and a former Giant All-Pro. He kept setting me up by going to the outside—so I set up for that move, and he faked to the outside, and then went inside, and BOOM, he sacked Meredith. I was a little shocked. I had embraced the new techniques, but they weren't working. Modzelewski kept double-cutting me. He then switched, and faked going inside and then went to the outside, hitting Meredith. They took me out of the game. I was upset about that. But I kept practicing the techniques I'd learned from Jim Ray Smith, and I continued working with 50-pound dumbbells to strengthen my arms. I had two seconds to counter before the ball was gone. I got beat less and less until I finally perfected the pass block, and, consequently, I hardly ever got beat again. Once I had mastered all the techniques, you could put a goddamn gorilla in front of me, and in that three seconds, he wasn't gonna get there. I knew how to do it.

The older veterans showed me the techniques, and they showed what people did to make life miserable for you—what a defensive lineman would do to you and what you'd need to do to counter that.

In my second year, we were playing in New Orleans, where it was incredibly hot and humid, and it rained on and off during the game. I couldn't get off the bench. I was so exhausted in the third quarter because I was starting *and* playing on all of the suicide squads.

When the offensive team ran out, everybody yelled, "Where's Schoenke?" They ran over and said, "Get out here!"

"I can't stand up," I said.

"What do you mean?" They're screaming at me.

Then the trainer takes me back into the locker room and says, "Don't you ever, *ever* do that to me again. From now on, you take these," he says, handing me pills.

Using amphetamines was a practice; it was common. Most players took amphetamines (Dexedrine) to overcome fatigue and to reduce pain, and when I played for the Cowboys, they were dispersed by the trainers. It was against the rules, but nobody was testing in those days. And when you got hurt, you hardly felt any pain. Walt Sweeney famously wrote, "Amphetamines and painkillers were passed out like candy."[39]

You couldn't get exhausted. If you couldn't go out there and play, you were in trouble. I thought I was responsible for myself. But in the trainer's view, he's responsible for my being on the field. So that introduced me to the drug part of the game. And then, of course, you had to learn how to deal with those drugs—to take just enough to get you through the game, but not so much you had to drink your way to sleep. Most of the guys took such big doses that they couldn't sleep for days. After the

---

39 Sweeney, Walt with Swank, Bill. *Off Guard*, (Silver Cat, 2012), 3.

game, they'd say, "See you Wednesday." I took one five-milligram pill at warmup, two before kickoff, and one at halftime. 20 milligrams. There were guys who literally took handfuls. On my very last game with the Redskins, when I retired, I took the bottle and flushed the remaining pills down the toilet. Robert Kerlan, former team doctor of the Los Angeles Dodgers and the Los Angeles Rams football team, summed it up:[40]

> *"Excessive and mysterious doping use is likely to be a major athletic scandal that will damage public confidence in many sports, just as the gambling scandal tarnished the reputation of basketball."*

The history of drug use in professional American football covers at least 60 years and included the use of stimulants (amphetamines and cocaine), anabolic steroids (anabolic steroids and growth hormones), and painkillers (narcotic analgesics and codeine). Shortly after World War II, amphetamine use emerged in the National Football League (NFL). A research report on drug use noted that

> *"within the great American sports, the use of amphetamines was the highest in football."*

Amphetamines were used in contact sports such as football. Not so much to mask the fatigue, [but] rather to overcome the pain and to give a 'spiritual boost.' The eminent psychiatrist Arnold Mandell (1934-), who was team doctor of the San Diego Chargers from 1972 to 1974, illustrated this with a quote from a former player:

> *"Doc, I am not prepared to stand in front of a man who charges at me growling, drooling, and with large dilated pupils, unless I am in the same condition!"*

---

[40] *Medico Sport*. "Doping and Sports – 1969." 2016. https://www.medicosport.eu/en/doping-and-sports/doping-and-sports1969.html.

Mandell continued:

"A football player uses amphetamines once a week, as a truck driver takes them to grind a long ride or as a student swallows them to finish his final work or to cram for his exam, Usually he hates that feeling and he looks forward to never having to do this again, it's just a way to get the job done."

Late in my career, because I felt guilty about taking drugs, I tried to go cold turkey at a Monday night game against the Oakland Raiders. They were in a line, and I was in a line facing them about 10 to 15 yards away on the end zone at the end of the stadium. As I was enthusiastically singing "OH, SAY CAN YOU SEE," I was looking into the distant faces of what could only be described as zombies—cursing, growling, yelling, their pupils dilated and foamy saliva running out of the corners of their mouths like rabid dogs as they screamed with wide-open mouths, "I'M GOING TO *KILL* YOU, MOTHERFUCKER!"

I raced to the bench and said, "Who's got drugs? Anybody got drugs?"

I gave up the idea of *not* taking drugs, but I was determined to figure out how to equalize myself with defensive guys who were on drugs while making sure I could sleep after the game, function, and not become addicted, so I could give them up at the end of my career.

I kept having trouble with Jim Myers, the Cowboys line coach who didn't like me. I was a bit of an anomaly in that I was going to law school at SMU at night; after practice, when I had free time, I studied. Myers didn't like that.

One day at practice, Landry blew the whistle. "Schoenke, what's going on here? Why are you doing that?"

"Because that's the way it's drawn up. My guy is going this way," I say.

Myers goes crazy, saying, "No, it isn't drawn up that way." (It was—I checked later.) Then, Myers says to Landry, "Schoenke is more interested in his law books than he is in his playbook."

He made a big scene out of that in practice, using law school against me. But I held the position for the season, and Myers didn't appreciate that I was a starter. I couldn't stand the guy. I was a starter because I was that good, but I didn't understand how quickly I could be demoted.

Before I played for the Cowboys, I met Landry at the time of the draft. I was at the Cowboys office a lot that spring, partly because I had talked the secretary into typing up my senior thesis on George Bernard Shaw. Landry was one of those men of few words. Very direct, very matter-of-fact. But he was so unapproachable that after practice, when we were sitting on the bench still in our practice uniforms, and he came out of the locker room because he had showered and was heading to the office, just as he got to us, he turned and looked the other way so he wouldn't have to say anything.

Usually, a coach would say, "Hey, Ray, good work out there today, good to see ya."

I guess I was impudent. I told the guy next to me, "Watch this."

And as Landry got near me and looked away, I said, "Hi, Coach!"

He had to turn around and say, "Oh, hi." I thought I was being real cute, which probably didn't endear me to him. In 1973, Tex Maule, writing for VAULT, quoted me as saying:[41]

> *On a blackboard, Tom Landry's teams would always win, but the human element is hard for him to deal with. He tells a man exactly what to do, but he forgets what motivates a man to do it. With robots he'd be undefeated.*

Notwithstanding his personality, Landry commanded my respect. He wanted everything by the book. He had these crazy ideas—like his own evaluation algorithms, or very specific, odd plays that weren't

---

[41] Maule, Tex. "WHEN YOU'RE AS OLD AS A LOT OF US, YOU LEARN THE SHORTCUTS." *Vault* 08 Jan 1973. https://vault.si.com/vault/1973/01/08/when-youre-as-old-as-a-lot-of-us-you-learn-the-shortcuts.

traditional in football but ended up working. The Cowboys eventually became wildly popular, even gaining the nickname "America's Team."

I'M THE ONLY "OTHER"

In my first year with the Cowboys, I shared an apartment with my college roommate, Orville Jones, and one of my Cowboys teammates, Lance Poimboeuf. Nancy lived in a one-bedroom apartment in North Dallas, in a complex with a pool. After we got married, I moved in with her. In the apartment complex, one of our neighbors was Leroy Jordan, a Dallas Cowboy who had played for the University of Alabama, a great middle linebacker, and everything you'd expect of a White guy from the deep South, a Southern conservative. His wife Biddie was as gracious a Southern lady as you could ask for, like Nancy. Another of our neighbors, also on the team, was a tolerant guy, but his wife was a real segregationist. We tried to be friendly to everyone, but we knew we were in a situation that eventually could become problematic.

Dallas was known as a politically conservative city. As soon as I had gotten on the Cowboys, I realized that the team was steeped in prejudice and that racism would be something I would have to contend with in a new way. The small slights and large frustrations I had endured at SMU made me alert to racism but didn't prevent me from being appalled by what I saw at the Cowboys. First of all, the league was mostly White and Black, with few other brown-skinned players. There weren't many Mexicans, and there weren't any Polynesians. For a while, I'm sure I was the only Hawaiian playing, though there had been a few ahead of me and would be many more to follow.

I may not have felt that prejudice was directed overtly my way, but the attitude I sensed was not reassuring. "You may not be White, but you're not Black. We accept you because you're not Black." The real problem, though, was between White and Black players. The team was loaded with White guys from teams in the Southeastern Conference, which was totally segregated. We often got into discussions that would, when I was around, escalate into arguments. The team was about 60:40 White to Black, and the pay was not always equal. It was an explosive situation. The Black guys liked me, and they knew that I was supportive of them.

Things happened in the locker room that were impossible to ignore. Leaders on the team openly called teammates n*****s. And there were incidents I couldn't forget, like those I experienced in the showers, where we washed each other's backs. In practices, you are in the dirt and mud a lot, and you typically have a short t-shirt on under your pads so the pads don't rub. You get really sweaty and dirty. The trainer even brings you fresh shirts periodically, but your back gets really dirty, and you can't really clean your back yourself when it is that dirty. Even in games, you change your shirt during halftime. In the showers, sometimes a Black guy would ask me to wash his back. Then I'd ask him to wash *my* back.

Once a Black guy asked a White guy, "Hey, you wanna wash my back?"

"No," he replied.

"But you washed Schoenke's back," the Black guy said.

"But he's not Black," the White player replied.

We were a team, but guys drew lines. I was neither Black nor White. I couldn't be easily labeled—like in the forms where you have to fill in your race. I couldn't check White or Black, so I wrote in "Other." Guys on the team, particularly the Black guys, called me "Other" in jest.

Nancy and I were trying to figure out how we were gonna deal with all this. She supported my views and also saw that racism existed on the team. We went to parties with the players, and I often ended up in a political argument. And there was another source of anxiety: there was always a chance that some of the Northern guys would ask one of the Black wives to dance, and if that happened, everybody was afraid the Black guys would wanna go dance with the Southern wives. There was enormous tension at these parties.

INSURED

I was trying to navigate how to establish myself as an NFL player and, at the same time, figure out how to support my family in the off-season. I hadn't forgotten the faith my SMU professors had placed in me. As I had planned, I had started law school at night, but that was proving to be really grueling. And it got me in hot water with my line coach.

I was also dabbling in insurance. The year before, I had worked at a men's store in Dallas that provided discounts to football players at SMU. As a favor to the owner, I had offered to work for nothing during the holidays after the SMU season ended in 1963.

While I was there, my boss from one of my summer jobs came in, saw me, and said, "I have someone I want you to meet. He's an insurance executive."

I met the guy, and he suggested I come work for him and sell insurance. I didn't think insurance would be my thing.

"We can guarantee you a salary," he said, "but let's first do a test to get a sense of whether it's a good fit." The test was at American Security Life, which had a big office in Dallas that was part of American Security Bank.

I took the aptitude test to see if I was suited to sell life insurance. The results said, "Do not hire. This individual has thin skin." But it also said I was "highly disciplined"—a trait necessary to be a life insurance salesman.

So they hired me despite my "thin skin." (My skin always seemed to be an issue). I was selling life insurance to college seniors who had to pay $10 of the first year payment of $180 and finance the balance. The graduates started paying the premiums a year after graduation. The company reasoned that because I was calling on seniors at SMU, people would know who I was, and I would at least get appointments. My first 10 appointments, I think I sold 9 policies. You could make $200 or $300 every time you sold a policy. By the time I started my rookie year, I had one foot on the field and another in business. I traded on my school connections and whatever celebrity I could muster as an offensive lineman.

I had entered a conservative business world, where, in contrast, I was a strong liberal. Dallas was a hotbed for conservatism. I got into huge arguments with some Cowboys teammates who were arch-conservatives. When John F. Kennedy got killed, and the word came into the locker room, some of the guys were cheering. I went running at these guys and started screaming at them. It still bothers me today—it's hard for me to talk about it without getting choked up.

I said to the guys who had voiced their opinions against the president, "What the hell are you doing here? Shouldn't you be up in a tree somewhere, getting ready to kill the rest of the Kennedy entourage?"

Nancy and I sat in front of the television for three days, dealing with the aftermath. Nancy was working right across the street from where Kennedy got shot. It was a dark, dark time.

And it wasn't just hard being on a team with conservatives. I was calling on businessmen and some very successful people in Dallas, who opened their doors to me because I was a well-known football player, but didn't like my politics. And they would tell me that outright.[42]

Tolerance was important to me, and I tried to "agree to disagree," but Kennedy's assassination, right there in the town I was part of, pushed me to find a way to get more politically involved. I began to look for a way to do something that gave my political ideas an on-the-ground expression.

But it would not be through law school. By the last game of the first season, I told Landry I had dropped out. I had hoped that that would solidify my position with the team despite my problems with Myers. I wanted Landry to know that I was committed.

FAMILY FIRST

Then, we played Pittsburgh in that final game of the '64 season, and one of their guys, John Baker, who bloodied the Giants' quarterback, Y. A. Tittle, when he hit him in the head, came after me. We went at it a

---

[42] Joyce. "The Game Beyond the Game."

little. We were just going through the motions, trying to finish the season (5-8-1), and neither team was in the playoffs, but I had done something to piss off Baker, and he came after me. I came off the field, and Myers started shouting at me. I think he called me a fucking asshole. We got into a shoving match, and I was getting ready to hit him. I knew better.

We won the game. After the season ended, I told Landry I didn't want to play for Myers anymore. The Cowboys had drafted me to potentially play both offense and defense, and I had worked a little with the defensive line in my two years with them. I told Landry I'd take my chances on defense. I didn't know that you don't do things like that after being a starter. I just felt with my experience on defense in college, I could play defense for the Cowboys. Landry agreed to give me a shot. But he said I would have to go to camp early.

I did go to camp early, and I pulled a hamstring. The trainer said there was a new theory from Canada that if you stretch out your hamstring after you pull it, it will help with healing. They stretched it out and ripped the muscle, so it went from bad to worse to awful. I went to a private doctor later, the guy who took care of me at SMU. He said it was one of the worst tears he'd ever seen. He could literally reach in and put his hand between the two sides of the muscle.

Landry called me in and told me they were going to try to trade me and to come back that afternoon. I did, and Landry said they couldn't trade me; they were just releasing me.

"What about my injury?" I challenged. I knew you couldn't be cut while injured, and I went to plead my case to the trainer. He didn't respond to me. I did not realize I had a legal position to get my money from the Cowboys.

I was devastated. I was learning what the NFL's about, that you're just a commodity. In hindsight, there was a silver lining. I realized that football was such a short-term part of life that you needed to prepare yourself for when it was over.

Still, every day, I got on the phone and called around to see if anyone wanted me. Nancy and I were living in a one-bedroom apartment in North Dallas and expecting our first child. I slipped into the bedroom to make my calls because Nancy wanted me to give up football. She wanted me to focus on insurance.

I was surprised no one picked me up. My only response was from Andy Robustelli, a former New York Giant great, who was at that time coaching the Springfield Acorns in Massachusetts, a team in the (semi-pro) Atlantic Coast Football League.

He called and said, "Come up here and play with us. We'll pay you $250 a week. You only have to practice three days a week, and you'll be able to get another job."

"What kind of job?" I asked.

"Well, you could pump gas."

So I came out of the bedroom after a week of trying to cut deals with different teams, including the AFL. (Oakland had my rights but wasn't interested.) I told Nancy I got a job with the Springfield Acorns for $250 a week, and after practice, I'll be pumping gas.

"Springfield? Are you nuts? We're expecting a baby. You are not going to Massachusetts. You are going to go work."

"What work am I going to do?" I responded.

"You're going to sell insurance."

"I hate selling insurance."

"I don't care. That's life. We *are* going to make it. You are *not* going to play football. We have to live," she said.

I had to listen to her. I had no choice. I called Mercantile Security Life, and they offered to pay me $500 a month, which is something like $4,500 today.[43] I would be doing what I had done before: selling to college seniors, then to young professionals. I came out of the bedroom and told Nancy about the offer. I had to accept the fact that that's what

---

43 What cost $500 in 1964 would cost $4532.34 in 2022. *Inflation Tool.* "Inflation Calculator." https://www.inflationtool.com.

I had to do. I hadn't been out of the apartment in a week, so when I stepped out, many of the neighbors were around the pool and applauded.

"He *lives*," they shouted. I was so embarrassed.

I wasn't playing, and I was selling insurance because I had to. I had to pay the bills, cover the apartment rent, and I had a baby on the way, so I'm not sure I *was* really living. With Mercantile Security Life, I focused on students, but I was watching some of the highly successful agents, who were telling me how much they were making selling insurance to a wider swath of adults, professionals, and business owners.

There was some happy news on October 17, 1965. My son Eric was born at Baylor Hospital. Nancy and I were blown away when Leroy Jordan, the All-Pro linebacker and #1 draft choice for the Dallas Cowboys, and his wife Biddie came to visit us in the hospital. We were neighbors in the same apartment complex, but I was still very surprised. I knew he viewed me as "different" and liberal, and he was a conservative Southerner. And I had been cut. And yet here they were, and on a Sunday, after a game! After a football game, you are exhausted, and the last thing you want to do is go to a hospital to be nice to a neighbor and welcome their new baby. The last person I would have expected to show up was Leroy Jordan. I was dumbfounded and shocked. I wasn't expecting to see *any* Cowboys, and I certainly wasn't expecting to see this one. I wasn't exactly on his "most popular" list because our political views were on opposite spectrums, and I had been cut from the team.

I have a job I hate and a new baby boy. I'm up at night changing diapers and handing Eric off to Nancy. I stay with her until she finishes breastfeeding him, and if he starts fussing after she feeds him, I get up again and walk and comfort him. In the daytime, groggy and suffering from a lack of sleep, I am still thinking about football, and I am unhappy.

I couldn't stand to watch Dallas Cowboys games on television, so on Sundays, I drove around, and when I saw guys playing touch football in the park, I asked if I could play. They generally would let me, not having any clue who I was. One of my former SMU teammates had a touch football team, and I played for them. Everyone was out to get me because I was a former All-American and former pro football player. When we played the Baylor Hospital team, the crowd all started chanting, taunting, and making fun of me.

When I walked up to the chanting crowd, I said, "Who wants a piece of me?" They all froze.

I was doing well in the insurance business but was disappointed not to be playing. I wrote several teams in the league looking for a job in the next season, 1966. I asked the defensive secondary coach from when I was playing for the Cowboys, Dick Nolan, if he would provide a reference for me. He said he would. He knew me, and he liked my style. I started writing all the teams, saying I'd played against them and all they'd had to do is look at a film of me playing in those games. I wrote every team the Cowboys played against and then started calling them all.

One of the guys I'd become close to in the insurance business, Bud Nichols, told me I was "doing very well" in the insurance business, and I needed to ask for a guaranteed contract with football teams.

"Believe in yourself," he said.

Although I knew it could make it more difficult, I took what he said to heart. I resumed calling teams, telling them I played right tackle or right guard, and letting them know there's a film on me playing against them the year before. Some said they were not interested, or some said they were interested and asked how much money I wanted. I was saying $20,000 (I had made $15,000 with the Cowboys), and I wanted it guaranteed.

I knew I had had good games against certain teams, so they had film on me and could assess my ability. There was interest from the Baltimore Colts and the Green Bay Packers. Green Bay was the best team in the league. I called and talked to Pat Peppler, director of Green Bay's player personnel.

"We'll call you and talk about it. Let me take a look at the film," he said.

He called back and said, "OK, we want to sign you, and we'll give you a guaranteed contract. How much do you want and how much up front?"

"$15,000 guaranteed and a $5,000 signing bonus," I said.

Peppler said they were flying to Dallas and would see me the next day. I felt I had died and gone to heaven. I was back in the league. The best franchise and the best team in the league and they just agreed to a guaranteed contract with me, with a signing bonus of $5,000. Back then, $5,000 was like $43,966 today.[44] And $15,000 would be $131,990. I could have bought a Cadillac!

---

[44] What cost $5,000 in 1964 would cost $43,966 in 2022. *Inflation Tool.* "Inflation Calculator." https://www.inflationtool.com.

CHAPTER FOUR

Wisconsin Cheese to Ohio Buckeye Trees—Packers and Browns (1966)

I didn't buy a Cadillac. I traded in my purple 1963 Falcon and bought a used Thunderbird convertible. Coral pink, with a white top and a horizontal row of massive taillights, so that when you hit the turn signal, the lights lit up one at a time, flashing from inside to outside—t-toong-t-toong-t-toong.

"You're playing in the pros; you can't be driving that damn Falcon," the guy who owned the convertible said. So he offered me a deal.

When I went to finance it, the banker looked at me like, "Are you crazy?" He knew my employment history and financial history, so he thought this was a risky purchase and that I was being foolish.

Nancy and Eric and I drove in that car to the camp where I had worked the summer before my rookie year with the Cowboys, where I was going to work for a second summer before heading to Green Bay. It was a wonderful way for me to get in shape as I did when I went to Cowboy rookie camp. Nancy and Eric were given their own cabin since I was in a cabin where I was the counselor to a group of boys, and Eric was just eight months old. But the heat was devastating. Eric got sick, and it seemed like Nancy was on the verge of a heatstroke, so her parents drove up and picked up the two of them and took them back to Bonham.

I tried to concentrate on training, but I strained my Achilles running. I wanted it to heal quickly, so I went to a local hospital to get physical therapy every day after dinner at the camp.

"You gotta pay for some of this. You're screwing up my group health insurance!" the owner of the camp told me.

The net result was that when I got to the Packers' training camp at St. Norbert College in De Pere, Wisconsin, I was not in the shape I was when I joined the Cowboys. But I was really excited. Vince Lombardi, a former Fordham University player who was one of the group of linemen known as the "Seven Blocks of Granite,"[45] was already a legend as a coach.

But I was asking myself, *"How am I going to fit in?"* The previous year, the Packers had won the NFL championship, and all the greats were at training camp that summer: Bart Starr, Jerry Kramer, Fuzzy Thurston, Forrest Gregg, Bob Skoronski, Willie Wood, Ken Bowman, Bill Curry, Ray Nitschke, Jim Taylor, Paul Hornung, Bob Jeter. They had the coach, the players, and the system.

NO ONE IS READY FOR VINCE LOMBARDI

Everybody, for the most part, was gracious and friendly. They loved that I sang Hawaiian songs at dinnertime when the rookies were made to perform. Since I was new, I volunteered to perform even though I wasn't a rookie. But there was also fierce competition. Lionel Aldridge was a defensive end and a bit of a nemesis. This surprised me because when we played together in the East-West College All-Star game, and at the Hula Bowl, he had asked me if the way he was being treated was racially motivated—he was Black and thought he would be treated better in Hawai'i. But I told him the issue, if there was one, had to be with tourists. Aldridge had married a White woman and had received a lot of criticism from players and fans. Lombardi, on the other hand,

---

[45] MacCauley, Kevin. "Lombardi's "'Seven Blocks of Granite to Success'." *Upper hand, 2019.* https://upperhand.com/lombardis-seven-blocks-of-granite-to-success/.

FAT GIRL SINGS

This is the only thing I played for the Packers and Browns

supported him, which at the time, was a big deal, and spoke well of Lombardi. There was camaraderie then, but not on the Packers when I faced him in scrimmages.

Despite my summer injury and my uncertainty about key players, I thought I was prepared. What I was not prepared for was Vince Lombardi.

As soon as the veterans came into camp and started drills, Lombardi started being Lombardi, and I got a taste of what life was going to be like. He started screaming at me, and he didn't stop.

"Don't worry about it, Schoenke. It's gonna be OK," the veteran players told me.

The first time it happens is during a blocking drill. I'm blocking this guy, a rookie, continuously on the same play several times, and finally, after the fourth or fifth time, he spins out and makes the tackle five yards down the field. I'm thinking it's no big deal; it's a five-yard gain, but I thought it was still a good block on my part. I go back to the huddle, and I hear a loud voice screaming.

"WHOSE MAN IS THIS? WHOSE MAN IS THIS?" It's Lombardi. I turn around and go, "It's me, Coach."

"GODDAMMIT, SCHOENKE! WHAT THE GODDAMN HELL ARE YOU DOING OUT HERE?!" And he runs up to me and starts pounding on my chest. "YOU'RE NOTHING BUT A GODDAMN NUMBNUT!"

He's banging on my shoulder pads, and I'm looking at him like, Whoa. I look over at Ray Nitschke, who's a tough son of a bitch. He's standing right behind Lombardi, shaking his head and mouthing, "Don't hit him; don't hit him."

I'm looking at Nitschke, and I'm looking down at Lombardi, who's shorter than me, barely six feet tall. He's just *BOOM*, pounding on my shoulder pads, and I'm thinking, "This is crazy. This is sheer madness." I don't know what to do.

A little later, I block someone, and Lombardi runs up, saying, "SCHOENKE, GODDAMMIT, THATTA WAY TO BLOCK!" Talk about extremes.

One minute, I hated him, and the next, I loved him. He was very predictable. I'll give him that.

Nitschke was a middle linebacker, bald, mean. When I had to block him on a play, I flew down the line of scrimmage, and as I reached him, he stayed firm in the hole, and I blasted him with my helmet and shoulder and drove him right out of the hole. I came in from the side and decked his ass.

He jumped up and instead of being pissed, he grabbed me, and said, "Schoenke, I love you! You're good. Don't worry, you're gonna make the team." Then he added, "Just don't let the old man get to you."

I asked Forrest Gregg, who was from SMU, how long they had put up with Lombardi screaming at them.

He yelled to Nitschke, "How long has Coach been here? Seven years?" Then he turned back to me and said, "Seven years."

A few days later, Pat Peppler, the personnel director, comes into my dorm room at St. Norbert and says, "I'm sorry, but we just traded you to Cleveland."

I guess he thought I'd be sad, but I jump up, grab my bags, and start packing right there in front of him.

He says, "You don't have to be so excited."

I say, "I'm ready to get the hell out of here."

CLEVELAND

It wasn't supposed to be this way. I believed I was an asset. After a year out of the game, I had gotten on with the No. 1 team in the NFL, with a guaranteed contract. But the Browns were the second-best franchise in the country, so I had gone from the best to the second best. Nevertheless, I thought I had a great deal to escape from Lombardi. I left right after practice and drove all the way from Green Bay to Hiram, Ohio, where the Browns had training camp. Blanton Collier was the coach. I went from Green Bay with a hard-ass coach to Cleveland with a soft-spoken, laid-back one. I went from a practice session with a hardcore coach screaming at me to a practice that was very short with absolutely no screaming. The silence was almost deafening.

Innovator Paul Brown, who cofounded and served as coach for the Cleveland Browns, had hired Blanton Collier as his assistant coach, who later was promoted to head coach by Art Modell, the team owner, after Modell fired Brown.[46] When Collier was promoted to head coach, he basically just stuck with Brown's system. Cleveland reached the NFL championship game four times and won once, in 1964. Collier coached the team until 1970.

I was happy to be at Cleveland and was aware of the team's legacy.

My very first impression of the team involved another Brown, the legendary running back Jim Brown. After practice, I walked into

---

46 *Hopewell Museum.* "A Gentle Man and a Gentleman: Blanton Collier." May 2020. https://www.hopewellmuseum.org/2020/03/31/a-gentle-man-and-a-gentleman-blanton-collier/.

the training room cafeteria, and at the first table I came to, there were a bunch of Black guys I knew sitting and eating. I headed over there to sit down.

Monte Clark, a White veteran tackle who'd been recently traded to the Browns the year before from the Cowboys, grabbed me and said, "No, you just go over here."

"What?" I said.

"They sit there; we sit here."

"Really? Where'd that all come from?"

"Jim Brown," he answered. "Jim Brown said that the Blacks are as good as the White boys, and they'll do their own thing. So we ride one bus; they ride another. We sit over here; they sit over there."

I wasn't surprised that there was a racial distinction: I was just surprised that it was driven by Jim Brown, who set the tone and drew the lines. Jim Brown felt the Blacks were equal to the Whites and didn't need to kiss ass.

"Wow. How does that work?" I asked.

"Well, it works," Clark said.

Jim Brown wasn't there at that moment. He was off in London making *The Dirty Dozen*. The 228-pounder was the 1965 MVP after rushing for 1,544 yards in a 14-game season, and he led the sport in single-season and career rushing yards, rushing touchdowns, and total touchdowns.[47] But that wasn't enough to keep him from getting bored, so he started acting in the off-season. But when his first movie was delayed in filming, he told Art Modell that he couldn't be back until September, after the season started. Modell answered by telling Brown he expected him to be in Hiram when the veteran players reported and that he would fine him $100 a day for each day he was not in camp. It was a showdown. Finally, Jim Brown, the Pro Football Hall

---

47 Cortez, Ryan. "Jim Brown Retires While on the Set of The Dirty Dozen." *ANDSCAPE*, 13 Jul 2016. https://andscape.com/features/jim-brown-retires-while-on-the-set-of-the-dirty-dozen/.

of Famer considered one of the all-time great running backs, retired in mid-July. I missed playing with him.[48]

Even without Jim Brown, we had a great team: quarterback Frank Ryan; as well as John Wooten, a guard; Paul Warfield, a receiver; Leroy Kelly, a halfback; Gary Collins, a tight end; and Monte Clark, an offensive tackle. We could dominate. But some of the guys on the defensive line were tough—some of them were quite dismissive of me, somewhat rough, and not so much into Collier's "Dick Schafrath training your mind" approach, which was introduced to me later by Collier.

Jim Kanicki, a big defensive tackle from Michigan State, was one of the players that I felt didn't respect me because I was new on the team. In practice, where we typically go half speed with the offense against the defense, against me, he didn't just go through the motions like he was supposed to. He wanted to embarrass me and wanted to put me down in front of the team. When I fired out to block him, instead of trying to simulate his defensive actions, he went full speed. He grabbed my shoulder pad and forearmed me in the face with enormous force, knocking my head back, which is actually illegal and a 15-yard penalty in a game but is rarely called because it happens so fast, you can't see it.

When a player hits you like that, you are sort of in shock and on the verge of blacking out. But you have to quickly recover and be prepared to counter with equal force.

"What the fuck are you doing?" I said as I recovered.

"Take a flying fuck."

The next play, I went full speed at him, at which point he started a fight with me. I then countered very quickly with forearms to his face, knocking him back as I told him, "You wanna do this? We'll do it every time."

Later, when we played each other in regular NFL games, we had ballbuster games against each other. On the day of the worst fight I had

---

48 *The New York Times*. "Jim Brown Quits Football for the Movies." 13 July 1966. https://archive.nytimes.com/www.nytimes.com/packages/html/sports/year_in_sports/07.13.html.

with him between the Redskins and the Browns, we were walking off the field, me at one end and him at the other, and, amazingly, we both turned toward each other at the same time. He waved at me, and I waved back, like we were saying to each other, "Hey, man, good fight." It was really cool.

ALOHA NFL!

I had to fit into that whole scheme. I should say that at the time, I was starting to look at race and my Hawaiianness in a new way. I had been back to Hawai'i a few times, but my awareness was still very private, internal. In my many years in the NFL, there were only a couple of other Hawaiians. Mel Tom was with the Eagles. He was my nemesis from Maryknoll in Honolulu. The story of how I learned he was in the Eagles makes me laugh to this day. The Redskins were playing the Philadelphia Eagles in 1967, and at the time, in addition to being a regular, I was also a back-up center. We went out early to snap the ball and practice punting before the whole team came out for the game.

Someone said to me, "Hey, they've got a Hawaiian on their team." I looked over, and I saw a dark-complected guy.

This was late in the year, and there'd been a snowstorm in Philly, so there was snow stacked up along the sidelines. I was a regular, but I was also on special teams.

So, I'm running down to cover a punt. All of a sudden, this guy comes out of nowhere, puts a hit on me, and slams me right into a big snowdrift.

He bends over me and says, "You don't remember me, do you?"

"No," I say.

"I'm Mel Tom. We were in a big fight at a basketball game when I was at Maryknoll."

I jump up and hug him. "Where in the hell you been?"

"I was in the service for four years."

Melvyn Maile Tom was a rookie that year. He was a defensive lineman, and we ended up playing against each other more than once. He had a style where he could come around the tackle very fast because of his speed, and then, as he came up on the quarterback, rather than tackle him, he chopped the quarterback on the back of the neck with his arm like he had a tomahawk, which was illegal even though they very seldom threw the flag on him. He knocked the hell out of the quarterbacks.

When Lombardi, who was at that time my coach with the Redskins, reviewed the films, he screamed, "WE'VE GOTTA GET THAT GODDAMN HAWAIIAN!"

I yelled back, "Wait a minute, Coach. *I'm* Hawaiian."

"You don't count," Lombardi said.

For years before I entered the NFL, there were scattered Polynesians on league rosters, mostly playing linemen. For the most part, we were known for being big, strong, fast—huge guys who could knock anyone down. Slowly, that began to change. Players started to play other positions—running backs, quarterbacks, and defensive backs. Mosiula "Mosi" Tatupu, a 1974 Buff 'n' Blue star, was a special teamer and running back during a 14-year professional career with the Los Angeles Rams and the New England Patriots. He made the Pro Bowl. Troy Polamalu was inducted into the Pro Football Hall of Fame in 2020, and before him, Junior Seau, a linebacker, was the first Polynesian to be inducted.

Great Polynesian players had come before me. My personal hero was Hawaiian Charlie Ane because I had learned about him in high school and continued to draw inspiration from him my entire life. He paved the way for other Hawaiians in the NFL—including his son Charles, Jr., known as Kale. Charlie was elected to the Pro Bowl during my years on the Buff 'n' Blue team, and he was the early role model who made me believe I could play football on the national stage.

My goal had been to make it to the NFL and be like Charlie Ane. At the time, Polynesians in the NFL were all linemen, all warriors. Haloti Moala, in an interview for *USA Today*[49] described Polynesian

---

[49] Corbett, Jim. "Polynesian players bring passion, power." *USA Today Sports*, 03 Feb 2013. http://www.usatoday.com/story/sports/nfl/2013/02/03/polynesian-super-bowl/1882001/.

players as "built for football." "Throwin' Samoan" Jack Thompson was the first Polynesian quarterback. Samoan quarterback Marcus Ardel Taulauniu won a Heisman Trophy. Another Samoan quarterback, Tuanigamanuolepola "Tua" Tagovailoa of the Miami Dolphins, is from the same community where my extended family in Lāʻie live. His brother, Taulia, is a quarterback for the University of Maryland who is often compared with Jack Thompson.

Guys I used to hunt with call me and say, "Tell me about Tua."

The story is quite different when it comes to coaching—football has some catching up to do. The NFL has *never* had a Polynesian head coach.

The Polynesian Hall of Fame was founded in 2013 by former NFL players and Super Bowl Champions Jesse Sapolu and Maʻa Tanuvasa. This organization specifically honors the greatest players, coaches, and contributors of Polynesian descent in American football, many of whom are not well known. One of the greatest honors I've ever received was being inducted in 2015. I have always been aware of how much football had opened up to us and how much we have contributed to the game, and I tried to address that in my acceptance speech:

> *One of the greatest compliments I ever had is when I met Junior Ah You, a great, great athlete and football player. He said to me that I was his hero. And then Vai Sikahema was telling me last night, "Guess what? Junior was my hero." Then Reno Mahe said, "Guess who was my hero? It was Vai." And guess what? It goes on and on and on. And this is the legacy that…we built. Can you imagine? 60 years, and now we have Marcus, who's gonna influence thousands of young men to follow in his footsteps, as well as our inductees. So we don't always know who we're influencing, but it's important that we have and recognize that responsibility. Ko mākou makua o ka lani a me nā akua o Hawaiʻi. (Our heavenly father and gods of Hawaiʻi, thank you for this blessing.)*

FAT GIRL SINGS

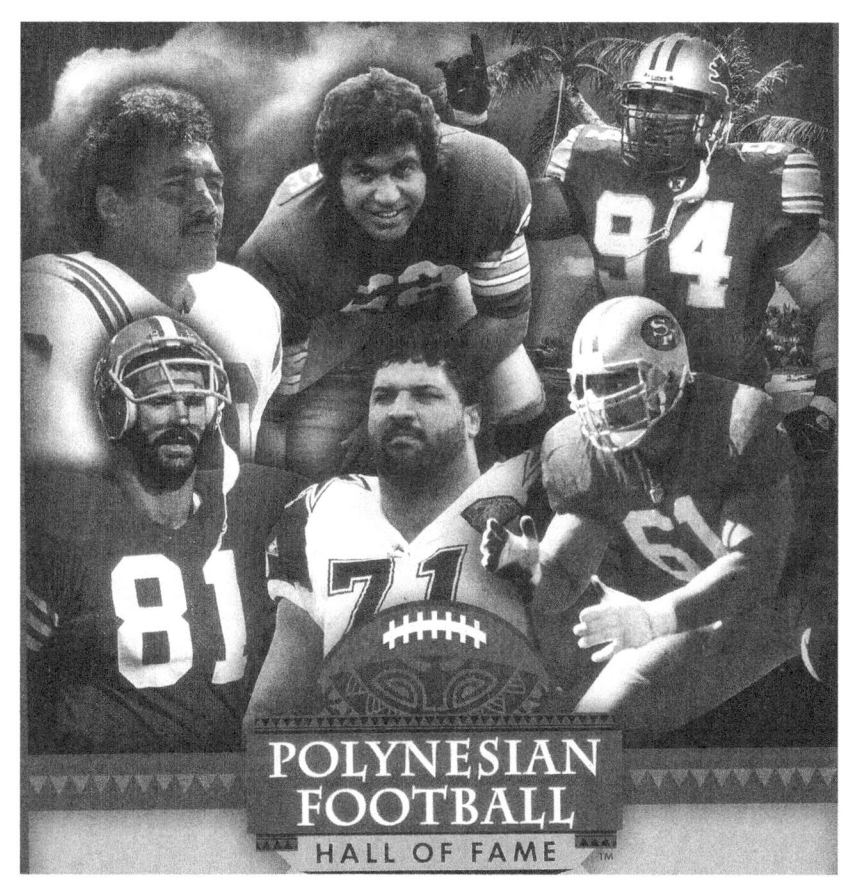

Program for the Polynesian Football Hall of Fame induction ceremony

I cannot tell you how much it gave me goosebumps, or "chicken skin" as we say in Hawai'i, to one year later see Charlie Ane—the man who by his example had enabled me to be a part of that chain of football players—inducted into the Polynesian Football Hall of Fame. Interestingly, the hall is located at the Polynesian Cultural Center in Lā'ie, the seat of my mother's family.

RAY SCHOENKE

Those who inspired me got me here

THE POWER OF THE MIND

Blanton Collier was nothing like coaches I'd had before that. He was very confident, very assured, and content to work the system he'd inherited from Paul Brown. He was kind of distant—he stayed above the fray. Even when there were new plays for an upcoming game, we didn't practice them.

There was a chalkboard on the practice field, and Coach said, "Let me draw this defense up. Here are the plays we run, who you block."

"Are we going to practice the plays?" I asked Collier.

"No," he said. "You're a pro. Do you have a problem with that?" He drew different defenses on the board and asked me what I'd do in each case. Satisfied with my answers, he said, "Why do we need to run that in practice?"

Another time he said, "Have you ever heard of psychocybernetics?" I said I hadn't. "That's when you mentally prepare yourself," Collier said. "You envision everything that's going to happen. We don't think it's necessary to practice everything."

That was Collier—he didn't want to expend all our energy in practice and risk accruing injuries. He wanted to save us for the game. And he wanted us to prepare mentally, not physically. The Browns had some really smart players. It was the combination of the mental and physical strength of the players along with an executable system that made them a winning team.

Later, Monte Clarke explained how psychocybernetics works. They gave me a book to read about it. During the week and before the game, I literally envisioned the possible plays and defenses that I would encounter and visualized how I would react to each one as to who I would block and how I would block on each given play. I used this method throughout my entire career. Dick Schafrath was captain of the team at the time, and he shared with me his approach, which was not envisioning what I would encounter in the game, but how I would handle fatigue, pain, and the idea of giving up by challenging my mind to endure whatever

I faced. Schafrath, who, after a stellar football career, became an Ohio State Senator, was a big proponent of eliminating negative thinking and never quitting. In his book, *Heart of a Mule*, Schafrath said:

> *Although there comes a point when your body says, "I quit," you can train your mind to say, "I'm not dead yet. I can still go on." …It's up to you to overcome the pain of those negative thoughts and never quit. Most professional athletes have learned to do it…. My dad always said, "As long as you can feel the pain, you know you're not dead!"*[50]

Then comes the first meeting with the line coach, Fritz Heisler. Most coaches are coherent; you can understand what they're saying, and they pause and allow for questions. He was a small, skinny guy in a baseball cap and a T-shirt, coaches' pants, and black sneakers. He stood in front of a chalkboard and talked nonstop while constantly drawing a myriad of plays on the board that made no sense. His words all slurred together, so he was, as least to me, totally unintelligible. I raised my hand to ask a question, and Monte Clark next to me reached out, touched my arm, and pulled it down. All the veterans just wanted to get the hell out of there. Heisler talked non-stop for 30, 40 minutes, and I couldn't understand a damn thing he said. It was like listening to one of those radio ads where the speaker vomits disclaimers as fast as is humanly possible at the end of the ad. Heisler pointed at what appeared to be random spots on the chalkboard while drawing up plays:

> *K…here's the play I'm drawing here now this is the trap play where the guard comes across and we have a variety of defenses and the guard will have the option of blocking the guy here and here's another play here and we are going to be facing a variety*

---

50 Schafrath, Dick. *Heart of a Mule: The Dick Schafrath Stories*. Gray & Company, 2006, 38.

of defenses and choices by the pulling guard and here's another play where we are actually pulling the guard and the tackle so it's easier for the running back to pick a hole and the guard and tackle depending on who's leading and the first guy will hit the defensive end or the linebacker or the safety or the cornerback… Are there any questions?[51]

When I walk outta there with Monte, who by this time is taking me under his wing, I'm shaking my head.

"Ray, don't worry. We know exactly what to do. We've been doing it for years. Just sit there and smile, and we'll tell you what to do out on the field. Just make sure you know the plays," he says.

"That's how you guys do it here?"

Monte Clark was matter-of-fact about it all. "We've been doing it for so long, we all know how to do it," he said. "Paul Brown put in the system many years ago, and nothing has changed. Everybody knows what to do. The coaches do very little coaching, and the practices are just a little longer than one hour."

I couldn't believe it. I wanted to make sure I knew what I was doing. I was used to guys staying around after practice and working on plays and techniques. I believed in self-motivation. So as the guys were heading off the field, I asked Clark if I could stay out longer.

"We don't do that here," he said.

At practice the next day, they called a sweep, where the linemen get out in front of the running back, sweep around outside of the line of scrimmage, and open a lane for the running back. In Green Bay, they had what they called the Green Bay Sweep, a well-known signature play. It was a delayed power move. After we broke from the huddle, we lined up on the line of scrimmage. After the ball was hiked, the guards pulled back deep, and the halfback delayed and got right behind

---

51 Note: An approximation of a typical offensive line meeting led by Fritz Heisler.

them, letting the guards lead him around, through, and past the line of scrimmage into the secondary (the area behind the line of scrimmage). The guards were like a convoy in front of him, shielding him. They'd knock people down, and he'd skirt around them in whatever lane they created for him.

So the Browns' quarterback called a sweep, and I pulled out to go back deep, as I would have with Green Bay. With the Browns, however, everything was very fast; the lineman's job was to run like hell outside the line of scrimmage and to be only focused on getting in people's way to make a lane for the running back. If he could block them, so be it. I was just expected to get in the face of the defensive back coming at me and distract him in the short window the running back needed to go by us. So Leroy Kelly, the running back, ran right over me because I had pulled back deep and was in his way. I heard the whistle, and everyone started screaming and yelling. Heisler screamed directly at me and made it clear that I was the problem with the play.

"What are you doing? You're in the way of the running back! Where'd you learn that? You need to RUN! Block somebody and get out of his way!"

"That's the way we did it in Green Bay," I replied.

He was publicly degrading me because I had come from the Packers. Heisler, the Browns' line coach, didn't like me because I was from Green Bay. The Browns hated Green Bay—there was a longstanding rivalry, and the Browns always lost.

Clark grabs me and says, "Just get your ass out and run. We don't actually block anyone. You just touch them and occupy them while the running back goes by you."

I try to keep my head down, but I just don't gel with Heisler. Then, I look up about two weeks before the season begins, and there's a guy from the Cowboys, a guard named Joe Bob Isbell, walking around camp. I'm playing backup guard behind starters Gene Hickerson and John Wooten.

"What's going on here?" I ask the coach. Apparently, I was not as secure as I thought I was.

"Don't worry about it. It's no big deal. Joe Bob was available, so we wanna take a look at him, but we wanna take a look at you, too," he said.

I intuitively know there is trouble. But I have this no-cut contract. The guys tell me not to worry, go ahead, bring my wife and baby to Cleveland; I have a guaranteed contract. So I send for Nancy to come to Cleveland with Eric. She shows up the week before the season starts, and we get an apartment.

IF YOU WANT A GUARANTEE, ALWAYS CARRY AN UMBRELLA

After the last exhibition game, there was a movement initiated by leaders among both the White players and the Black players to get together and go out as a team. And we did: we went to a couple of clubs together, and there was a lot of drinking and camaraderie. I felt good about it and was ready for the season.

The next morning, I got cut. I went to Art Modell, who had been friendly to me when I arrived, and told him I thought I had a guaranteed contract. He said,

"That agreement only applied if you made the team, so we're not going to honor that agreement. You have to go back to Green Bay." They had no real obligation to me. Because Green Bay held my contract, I had to go back to them to get paid.

"You know goddamn well that Lombardi's not going to give me any money! He'll run me out of town!" I saw that I would not get anything from Modell—Joe Bob was cheaper for the Browns and that was that. Years later, after the Redskins had played the Browns twice, in Cleveland, including a game in which I had gone against Jerry Sherk, defensive lineman of the year, Modell graciously came into our locker room after both games, congratulated me, and told me he had underestimated me, and that they had made a wrong decision (a little late!). That was one of two times Modell told me that he had made a mistake cutting me from the team. My last season on the Redskins, we played the Browns, and Modell came into the locker room and told me that he had been wrong about me.

I got cut on a Monday, and the season opened the following Sunday. I went back to the apartment on Monday and told Nancy I had been cut. Nancy looked at me and said, "You've been cut. That's two times cut, traded once. We need to go home."

I told her to give me a week. I did not want to face Lombardi's wrath. So I called all the teams, just like I'd done in Dallas when I got cut, to see if I could get a job. The Kansas City Chiefs owned the rights to me, but they were mad at me because I didn't sign with them originally.

That whole week, I lived in a phone booth. The Browns had paid me a stipend for my time with them in the exhibition season, but not my salary. Nancy and I didn't even have a phone. We went to a park where Nancy could sit on a blanket with Eric, and I got in the phone booth and called teams that had expressed an interest in me. I called the Oakland Raiders, who had drafted me.

"We gave your rights to the Dallas Texans (now the Kansas City Chiefs). They're gonna have to give us a draft choice," they said.

I said to myself, *"Goddamn, I'm not even worth a draft choice! I'm a has-been. I've been cut twice!"*

I called everybody, but I couldn't get a deal. Nobody had any sympathy for me. None. So Nancy said, "We need to go home. Mom and Dad are looking for us because they know you've been cut." It had been in the Dallas papers.

The season opened on Sunday, and the Browns played the Redskins. I watched the game. Some players had reminded me that Redskins coach Otto Graham had been a Brown.

My week without a team or job was just about up. On Monday, after the first NFL Sunday game, the last day Nancy had given me to try to get a job in football, I decided to call Tim Timerario, the Redskins' director of player personnel. There was film on me from when the Cowboys played the Redskins in 1964, and I suggested that they could call the Browns' coaching staff.

He said, "Let me check it out. Call me later today."

So I call him that afternoon, around 5 p.m.

"Well if you're half as good as your recommendations, you'll make our team. I want you at the Mayflower Hotel tomorrow at 9 a.m.," he says. I gesture to Nancy to give her an idea of what's going on and to tell her to come over.

"Well, my wife and child are here," I say.

"Leave 'em."

"Nooo," Nancy says.

So I just say, "We're coming!"

We ran down and got a U-Haul trailer, threw everything in the trailer, and hitched it to the coral-pink Thunderbird. I drove all night to Washington, DC. Nancy nursed Eric and drove while I napped. I was very tired. Outside Washington, I woke up, and the trailer was fishtailing behind the Thunderbird, and Nancy was trying to drive the car while nursing Eric. I panicked and told her to pull over. We got to the Beltway outside of DC, and I went right when I should have gone left. That wasn't the only mistake I made. We barely made it to the Mayflower by 9. Of course, they wouldn't let us park in front of the hotel with a U-Haul trailer. But Tim Timerario picked me up and brought me back at 4 that afternoon. Nancy spent the day in the Mayflower, washing diapers.

In two weeks, I'm on the team. And in four weeks, I'm starting.

CHAPTER FIVE

Fear, Trust, Service—Lombardi, Allen, and Special Olympics (1966-1975)

I kept the U-Haul trailer hitched to the Thunderbird for what seemed like weeks.

"When are you going to get rid of that thing?" the guys would ask.

"When I know I'm on the team, man," I say.

That first day in Washington, after I got to the Mayflower, head scout Tim Timerario picked me up and took me to DC Stadium. They showed me films and went over some plays and grabbed a couple of rookie linemen and took us to a football field. We started going one-on-one. We were just hitting each other and hitting each other again. Then, we went back to the locker room and went through more films. Finally, it was almost 4 o'clock in the afternoon, and I couldn't keep up the front. I hadn't eaten; I hadn't slept.

"Hey guys, do you mind if I stop and get something to eat or drink? I haven't eaten today," I said.

"You haven't eaten? OK, let's stop."

And I said, sheepishly, "Well, uh, the other problem I have is—I don't have any money."

They went to Coach Graham and told him.

"You don't have any money?" Graham asked. He was surprised first that I hadn't eaten or slept and also that I was penniless. He went into his wallet and pulled out 50 bucks and handed it to me and said in a very kind way, "Think that's enough?" He was a sweetheart—such a contrast to Lombardi.

I go back to Nancy and say, "Hey, I just got 50 dollars; we're going to go out on the town tonight and eat at a fancy restaurant." That was a lot of money at the time, so we went to the best place we were able to find in town.

STRADDLING THE FENCE

For the next several weeks, with only the rookies, we basically scrimmaged. For hours. Every day. It appeared that they might be looking to replace Fran O'Brien, a popular veteran on the team. Then, suddenly, veterans started showing up. The starting defensive line arrived, and they went one-on-one with me. I knew my stock was going up because they were worried about their friend, Fran, who was well-liked by the team.

Finally, Otto came to me and said, "OK, we're going to activate you." They released Fran; he was picked up by Pittsburgh, and I started playing.

Pass blocking was one of my strengths. I had built a reputation on that and very seldom got beat. I knew I had just needed someone to give me a chance to show it.

Still, I kept one foot in Washington and one in Dallas. Over the next three years, when we were in Washington, we rented Fran O'Brien's house. He went to Pittsburgh, and we moved in. Then, he came back at the end of the season, and we hitched up a U-Haul again and drove back to Dallas, where I sold insurance from the moment one season ended to the moment the next one started. By now, we had two kids, Eric, who was three at the time, and Page, who was a year and a half, who referred to O'Brien's as "Tina's house" in deference to Fran's wife. Fran had a restaurant in DC, Fran O'Brien's, and later opened one in Ocean City, Maryland. Both were popular and hugely successful.

I was happy to be with a team, but there were reasons to be less excited about joining the Redskins than I had been about joining the

Browns or Packers. The Redskins in 1966 were in a historic decline. They had not had a winning season since 1955.

The previous year, Washington lawyer Edward Bennett Williams had gone from being a minority stockholder in the franchise to being its president. He had graduated first in his class at Holy Cross, first in his class at Georgetown Law, and was building a legal practice that was second to none. Yet on Sundays, Williams took his friends out to DC Stadium and suffered utter embarrassment. As longtime *Sports Illustrated* writer Joe Marshall recounts, Williams's friends watched his players "run into each other, miss tackles, botch blocks, drop passes, fumble handoffs and lose, lose, lose." After what Marshall described as some "brooding over the fate of the team in his offices," Williams decided to fire Coach Bill McPeak and hire Otto Graham.[52] Although Graham had frequently publicly announced that he would never coach in the pros, he took the job Williams offered him as head coach in 1966.

On opening night of Redskins training camp in Carlisle, Pennsylvania, Graham made clear his zero-tolerance policy for the lax ways of the past. Football training camp is a notoriously wild institution. You have a lot of players in one place, some who are single and some who are married—but separated from their wives and families for the summer. The temptations are rampant: groupies flock to camp to meet the players, and they aren't there to talk game strategy. There are probably a hundred women there determined to go to bed with half the team. Graham laid out new rules and warned that they applied to everyone, from the lowliest rookie to the biggest star.

The biggest star, and probably the biggest misbehaver, was Sonny Jurgensen. Sonny was a playboy, known for drinking and not taking things seriously. He would not conform. But he was incredibly talented. Bobby Mitchell was the other star. He was a halfback and flanker who

---

52 Marshall, Joe. "YOU WON'T HAVE WASHINGTON TO KICK AROUND ANYMORE." *Sports Illustrated* Vault, 15 Jan 1973. https://vault.si.com/vault/1973/01/15/you-wont-have-washington-to-kick-around-anymore.

had been traded from the Browns to the Redskins in 1962, when they became the last NFL team to integrate. He was a sensational player.

Otto Graham was a Hall of Fame quarterback with the Browns, but he was not a Hall of Fame coach. Graham didn't cuss at you. Instead, when he was frustrated, he'd bang his clipboard against his leg. We had players who would ridicule Otto, even betting how often he would do that clipboard thing during practice.

Despite Sonny Jurgensen, we were 7-7-0 in 1966, with the third-best scoring average in the league (25.1). Sonny led the league in passing, with 3,209 yards and 28 touchdowns. Charley Taylor caught 72 passes, Bobby Mitchell 58, and Jerry Smith 54. But we couldn't stop anyone. We allowed 25.4 points a game.

One memorable game was against the Giants, whom we beat 72-41.[53] I experienced what a gracious guy Otto Graham really was. One of my cousins, who was a union official in Minneapolis, came to DC for a union meeting and called me at the stadium before the game when I was in the locker room suiting up. He wanted to watch the game. Otto overheard me talking to him and told me to tell him to come on down, and we would find a place for him. Otto had a chair brought out and put it next to the players' bench. My cousin watched the whole thing from that chair on the field.

It was the highest-scoring game ever. One factor in the game was the middle linebacker Sam Huff, who was nursing a serious grudge against the Giants. He just kept wanting to run the score up. Huff was from West Virginia and one of the great NFL players. He had played in four consecutive Pro Bowls with the Giants (from 1959 through 1963), and he was named most valuable player of the 1961 Pro Bowl.[54] Giants coach Allie Sherman had tried to improve what he thought was

---

53 Katzowitz, Josh. "Remember When: Redskins, Giants score record 113 points in 1966." *CBS/NFL*, 24 Sep 2014. https://www.cbssports.com/nfl/news/remember-when-redskins-giants-score-record-113-points-in-1966/.

54 Antonik, John. "Profile: Sam Huff." *Western University Varsity Club*, n.d., https://web.archive.org/web/20021209174513/http:/www.wvuvarsityclub.com/profiles/huff_sam.html.

a defensive problem by trading many defensive players, but the owner had assured Huff he would keep his job. But then in 1964, Sherman traded Huff to the Redskins for a defensive tackle and a running back. The trade made front-page news in New York City and was greeted with jeers from Giants fans, who jammed Yankee Stadium yelling, "Huff-Huff-Huff-Huff."[55] Huff played like hell against his former team and was undeniably part of our success that day. With the time running out, the score 69-41, Huff on his own sent Charlie Gogolak, our field goal kicker, onto the field to kick a field goal, making the score 72-41, just to rub it into the New York Giants for trading him.[56]

In spite of Sam Huff, defense was not our forte. Otto's focus was on a passing game. And we had an incredible passing game. We had the top receivers in the league, and Sonny just lit up the place. He was a natural. And we had a good offensive line, with pass blocking of utmost importance because they didn't want Sonny to get hurt. But we had no defense. So even if we scored 30 points, they would score 35 points. There'd be some shootouts. We would win half our games, but we wouldn't make the playoffs.

NOT SITTING ON THE SIDELINES

My ideas about race and society have evolved very slowly. During my childhood in Weatherford, Texas, I had been acutely aware of being "different." At SMU, I had enjoyed being Hawaiian, but I was also aware that it marked me socially. It made me "less than" in the eyes of some people, and I was overtly discriminated against.

Then, I became acutely aware of the racism permeating the Cowboys team and the Dallas community. Since studying history at SMU, I had become aware of the haves and have-nots in our society, and I developed

---

[55] Katzowitz, Josh. "Remember when: Redskins, Giants score record 113 points in 1966." *CBS/NFL*, 24 Sep 2014. https://www.cbssports.com/nfl/news/remember-when-redskins-giants-score-record-113-points-in-1966/.

[56] Richman, Mike. "Huff Had His Revenge vs. Giants." *TAKE W COMMAND*, 13 Jun 2015. https://www.commanders.com/news/flashback-huff-had-his-revenge-vs-giants.

a strong conviction that economic inequality must be opposed. I had affiliated myself with the political left, and Nancy's sympathies lay there, too. We were being affected by the tide change occurring in the 1960s. President John F. Kennedy was killed right in our hometown. I was greatly influenced by Martin Luther King, Jr. and the civil rights efforts in the South. We opposed the war in Vietnam, and Nancy was becoming quite passionate about women's issues.

When we returned to Dallas in the off-seasons, I worked in the insurance business, but I became active in supporting and working in programs that focused on the urban poor in African American communities. But in the meantime, I continued with my professional focus: making a mark in the NFL.

When Nancy and I returned to Dallas after the 1967 season, change was in the air, and Washington was having an effect on us. I was taking tentative steps to becoming more engaged in causes I believed in—and Nancy backed me completely. I had made a commitment to myself after JFK's assassination in 1963, and I hadn't forgotten it. I heard about the Better Boys Foundation in Chicago, which had a relationship with the NFL Players Association, and I flew to Chicago for a lunch to try to support that effort and to see whether the organization could be brought to Washington, DC. The speaker was Alex Karras, a defensive tackle who had been All-American at the University of Iowa[57] before joining the Detroit Lions. Karras had become an actor, and he was a great off-the-cuff speaker.

In the meantime, I was dismayed to see racism in the ranks of the Redskins, as it had been at the Cowboys. Our team was over 30 percent Black, but some of the other guys actually formed a group, calling themselves the WUF Pack—the White United Front.

There was a confrontation later between me and some of the members of the WUF pack. I had invited a bunch of Redskins to an event for Senator Ted Kennedy. I had started to get to know his sister-in-law, Ethel,

---

57 *Hawkeye Sports, General*. "Former Hawkeye Alex Karras Passes Away." *Hawkeye Sports*, 10 Oct 2012. https://hawkeyesports.com/news/2012/10/10/former-hawkeye-alex-karras-passes-away/.

who liked to have Redskins at her events. She asked me to invite some players to attend his announcements, but I didn't invite the members of the WUF Pack. One of the WUFs came and sat next to me with the others.

"What's going on?" I said.

The ringleader said, "What is this event?"

I must have looked at him like, "You fuckin' racist. Get the fuck outta my face!" I don't remember what I actually said, but the WUFs got up and left. The whole thing really, really surprised me, and it led to some bad blood. I thought they were snakes although, over time, I rebuilt a close relationship with some of them because I felt they had evolved. Back then, they became more vocal at meetings, and I wasn't afraid to voice my opinion about things. These guys hated me because off the field, I had a lot of clout. I was a regular invitee to the Kennedy compound at Hickory Hill. I was our backup player rep. The next year, the guys who resented me worked very hard to get me voted out, which they did.

In 1968, when Martin Luther King, Jr., got assassinated in April in Memphis, I felt sucker-punched. He stood for everything that mattered to me, and he put words to my feelings. Then, Bobby Kennedy was shot in June, and I was devastated. These were people I deeply admired because they were committed to ending racism and classism in our country. They represented values I believed in; they called attention to things I felt were unjust in our society—I felt strongly that disadvantaged people should be given some support, that racism was wrong. I lived in a very rich community, and there was little sympathy and understanding for the disadvantaged. I knew that I had to have the balls to put myself on the line. I couldn't sit on the sidelines. Sometimes my teammates appreciated it, and other times they didn't. But in that whole mix of things, I wasn't afraid to stand up. I was taking a big risk—both in sports and in the business world. The extreme rage I felt when members of my team celebrated JFK's death was triggered again, and my faith that others shared my ideals about justice and equality was undermined. I realized I could no longer stand on the sidelines. I needed to be visible, and I had to stand up publicly, not just privately in conversations with Nancy.

I called Reverend Ship, the minister of our church in Dallas, Lover's Lane United Methodist Church, and said that I wanted to do some work in the Black community. He told me that our church sponsored a Bethlehem Center and suggested I make contact with them. I had to voice my opinion. RFK and MLK were the catalysts that drove me to walk into the Bethlehem Center in south Dallas. So I marched into the Bethlehem Center, which is predominantly Black. There were two women, one White woman who was maybe my age (late 20s), and an older woman who was Black.

"I wanna help you," I said.

"You're welcome to help, but what's your skill? We're a center for kids who come here after school."

"I don't know, but I'll try to figure out how to be of help."

I became a fixture. I went there a couple of afternoons every week, just trying to be active and to figure out how to support them. I started helping the kids with sports, and I decided to put on a football clinic for them. It had been more than three years since I'd been cut by the Cowboys, and I wasn't still in touch with a lot of the guys, but Tom Landry was still coach.

I went and met with him and said, "I'd like to put on a football clinic. Would it be possible if some of the Cowboys came out to help?"

"Sure," he said, but I was skeptical about how many players would actually show up. The day the clinic was to start, a bunch of kids showed up with their parents. I had invited a couple of friends who played amateur football because I didn't know if the Cowboys would show up.

I look up, and here comes 20 guys, all Cowboys football players. About half are White, and half are Black. I'm stunned. They all showed up! It was a huge success, and there were even pictures in the paper. That was the beginning of me stepping into the world and advocating for others.

One day after that, I was walking down the street in Dallas, and a successful oil executive who was an acquaintance of mine saw me and said, "I saw that article about you helping those kids in south Dallas. I hate those fucking n******s."

"Well, I'm sorry you feel that way, but these kids really need help. You think you could give me a check to help them?" I ask.

So he writes me a check for $500, and says, "But Ray, just take it easy, will you?" Whatever that means.

I didn't "take it easy." I started going into the offices of more businessmen—White conservatives who welcomed me because of my role in football but who were not shy about lambasting me for my politics.

I asked them for financial support anyway, saying, "I understand our differences of opinion, but I need you to help me with this program in south Dallas." And many would turn around and give me money! So I learned that people might disagree with you, but if you have the courage to stand up, they might support you. Not every time, but many times. That carried me over, and I never stopped asking people for donations on projects even if I knew they might not politically support the idea.

WHAT IT'S REALLY LIKE PLAYING AGAINST THE BEST

In my first year with the Redskins, I made the team. I was on the Suicide Squad (the team involved in punts, kick-offs, and field goals), and by the third game, I made the starting lineup when we were playing the Dallas Cowboys, which was just becoming a powerhouse team. I was put up against Bob Lilly, who was undeniably great—quick, fast, and strong.

Before that game, I worked all week with Jake Kupp, who had been traded by the Cowboys. He had played guard for the Cowboys and had blocked Lilly a lot in practice. For the Redskins, he was a blocking tight end. He and I worked on blocking Bob Lilly. Peter Golenbock[58] described

---

58 Golenbock, Peter. *Landry's Boys: An Oral History of a Team and an Era.* (Triumph Books, 2005).

Lilly in this way—"…he was so quick for five or 10 yards, and brother, once he got his hands on you, he was strong, too. You couldn't get away."

I knew Lilly would come at me with enormous speed and strength in his upper arms. He probably weighed somewhere around 265-270. He'd be in a four-point stance, with both hands on the field, and he would crowd right up to the line of scrimmage, so he was practically touching you, which allowed him to generate his full force while leaping toward you when rushing straight ahead. If you even flinched, he'd spring like a cat and grab your jersey and shoulder pads and then throw you to his outside. Then he'd shoot inside, and the quarterback became easy prey in the mayhem that ensued. He could dominate a game because of his unique defensive style, which led to many accolades over the course of his career.[59]

The game comes, and I want Lilly to know he can't pull that stunt on me. The first time I set up on a pass block, and I'm left guard, I step back a half yard to set up, which forces him to have to reach farther than the length of his arms to grab me, and Lilly makes that incredibly quick move to grab me, throw me, and propel himself to the inside. Just as he makes the move to grab and throw me, I hit him with my full force and block and drive him all the way over to the other side of the line.

The coaches can't believe I did that. It blows everybody away. Like, how did Ray figure that out? Well, here's the secret: What I did is to carefully create just enough distance between us by setting back and increasing the distance between us at the line of scrimmage while being careful to avoid a penalty.

As a result, he had to lunge toward me, which took away some of his catlike speed and force and caused him to be slightly off balance as he leaned forward to grab me. For a brief moment, he became vulnerable, so he couldn't knock me to one side. In that small window of opportunity, I was able to slam my helmet into his body and drive him

---

[59] SI Staff. "Ten Most Revolutionary Defensive Players." *Sports Illustrated*, 21 Nov 2006. https://www.si.com/uncategorized/2006/11/21/21ten-most-revolutionary-defensive-players#gid=ci0255ca63301d2515&pid=lawrence-taylor-lb..

to the other side of the line, where often, my center, Len Hauss, who was open because he had no blitz to cover, was waiting. He dropped down and hit Lilly in the knees, sending Lilly straight into the air. It was quite a sight to see this huge man floating briefly above the field. In that first game, his force was so overwhelming that when I hit him, his own momentum carried him. Five yards down the line! *The New York Times* said I "neutralized Bob Lilly."[60] He was so powerful and athletic that most players couldn't handle his move. They didn't break it down and couldn't counter, so they typically double-teamed him or even triple-teamed him. I outsmarted him for a while.

Another technique I used was to get so close I was up in his face. This made it possible for me to counter his move by hitting him first by putting my helmet right into his face. I had to make sure I didn't miss. If I was slightly off in my attack or slightly off balance, he could shove me to the side, skate right by me, and kill the quarterback. For several years, Len and I were able to neutralize him. It didn't last. He decided to change his approach and faked going in but then went out, and then faked going out but then went in. I loved it. He didn't have an edge on me anymore. He was forced to try other methods. We were equals. That's when the game becomes really smart and tough.[61] This press incentivized Lilly and made me a target in the future.

In the same game, in a key play early in the game, I had to pull out and block Chuck Howley, who was an outside linebacker who had great disdain for me when I was with the Cowboys. The game was in Dallas, and it was overcast and raining hard. As I pulled out and went to hit him, I went low. In the films, it looks like I tackled him, but I actually hit him low in the ankles, lifting him up in the air by the force of my block as Charley Harraway sailed around us for a 57-yard

---

60 Wallace, William N. "About Pro Football." *The New York Times*, 06 Oct 1971.

61 *Note:* Years later, in 1971, when Ken Denlinger with *The Washington Post* said to him, "You know, Ray got a game ball against you in that first game in 1966." Lilly replied, "Be sure you tell Ray: No more game balls."

McFarland, John, editor. *Facing America's Team: Players Recall the Glory Years of the Dallas Cowboys.* (Sports Publishing, 2015).

touchdown.[62] I saw Chuck Howley later in Santa Fe with his wife and said hello to him, only to receive a dirty look and no response. He was a pain in the ass when I played for the Cowboys, and he was a pain in the ass when I didn't. At least he was consistent.

I was so successful in that first confrontation with Lilly and Chuck Howley, it elevated my position on the team. From that point on, I was known as a solid lineman as a starting left guard. Then, they learned I could play other positions on either side of the line (tackle and guard). In many games, I was the first substitute for right guard and either right or left tackle, and in dire situations, where both the center and the backup were disabled. My versatility added to my strength, particularly when I had to go into these positions in the middle of a game, and I delivered. My reputation shot up. *The Redskins Encyclopedia* described my skill set like this:

> *...another king of versatility battled for the Redskins in the trenches: Ray Schoenke. Schoenke floated from position to position on the O-line in his 10 seasons in Washington, starting or substituting wherever needed. He spent much time at the guard positions but also played tackle and center. Adaptability was his middle name.*[63]

MY FUTURE IS NOT IN TEXAS

My roommate for the last two years I was on the Redskins was Walt Sweeney, who was an All-Pro guard traded from the San Diego Chargers. He had a reputation for heavy drinking and drug use that I was unaware of when I first met him. I only knew of his reputation as a football player. Sweeney demonstrated to me that you could seriously

---

62 *YouTube*, 19 Oct 2018; https://www.bing.com/videos/search?q=%22Charlie+harraway%22&&view=detail&mid=08D4F4B2EC1593D0C3CC08D4F4B2EC1593D0C3CC&rvsmid=A4EE4BC47E77229C144CA4EE-4BC47E77229C144C&FORM=VDQVAP.

63 Richman, Michael. *Redskins Encyclopedia*. (Philadelphia: Temple University Press, 2008). https://vdoc.pub/documents/redskins-encyclopedia-5b7a8kg9f0q0.

abuse your body with heavy drinking, abusing drugs, partying, going without sleep, and missing practices. In spite of his antics, he performed as well as I did or better on the field.

He made fun of me because, in contrast to him, I was a goody-two-shoes. Every week, he came up with some excuse or faked some pain in his gut and ran to the locker room to get out of practice, and George Allen let him do it. He told me that he was saving his legs and encouraged me to do the same. He mentions in his book, *Off Guard*, how freaked out I was when I went through his shaving kit to look for something mild to help me sleep one night. There were so many different kinds of drugs in there (all given to him by the Chargers, according to him) that I became confused and was afraid to take anything. When we discussed his drug use and my concerns about it, he indicated that he had control of his dosages and assured me that it wouldn't affect his performance, which it didn't.

However, he didn't take into account what affects his depraved lifestyle would have on him after his football career. While he indicated that he was impressed that I was preparing for a life outside of the game at the time, he apparently was not impressed enough to do it himself. He writes about his post-football life stating that by his second year away from the game, he was broke:

> *I couldn't get a decent job, because I couldn't hold a thought. ... another old drinking buddy, had a small paving company and gave me a job as a laborer. There's nothing wrong with being a laborer, but I felt there must be something better out there for me. Anything. I had a BA with a history major. I had a successful NFL career with years of making All-Pro teams and winning numerous awards. You know what? That didn't mean shit in the real world.*[64]

---

64 Sweeney and Swank, *Off Guard*, 2012.

I had to learn how to compartmentalize football and continue to grow other parts of my life. I learned that I needed to control what I could.

"You walked in, and you acted so confident," a lot of guys told me. I'm not sure if I was confident, but I was certainly determined. I knew I could block. I knew I could play. But I also knew I couldn't depend on the game because at an early age, I was cut twice and traded once in less than three years. I knew it could happen again. I never again trusted the league. I had kept up with the insurance business in the off-season in Dallas, and I was starting to look at it as a way to walk away from the game when I needed to. That gave me an inner strength—I had that drive to build a life outside of football. I realized that the only one who controls his destiny is an owner, not a coach or a player. I aspired to control my own destiny, so I determined I had to own my own business. This was a belief that would alter my life forever.

My professional aspirations didn't always sit well with the team members. Some guys wanted to go to local bars and drink on their days off. They partied Sunday night, all day Monday, and on Tuesday night while I was home sleeping at night and working on my business during the day. They went to bars and invited women to join them. They didn't spend any time preparing for a future outside of football. They were too busy enjoying the adulation of fans, not realizing, as I knew from experience, that their career could be very short.

They'd say, "Ah, Schoenke, you're full of shit," which was pretty true since I was no saint. I faced all the same temptations and challenges they did. Being critical of them made me appear to feel as if I felt I was better than they were, which was not the case. However, because I had experienced being fired more than once in the NFL, I did feel that my experience had actually made me wiser and had given me greater foresight. I was certainly equal to them as a member of the team because I had worked hard to maintain this career. But what separated me from most of my teammates was my effort to also create a life for myself outside of football where I would be able to sustain my economic lifestyle, which also gave me the ability to help humanity in meaningful ways. I had the vision to understand that their NFL 'lifestyle' was going to lead most of them to fail to obtain a college degree, and many of them would unfortunately ultimately end up unemployed and/or bankrupt.

Being a professional football player *and* a businessman involves a strange balancing act. I'm at heart a nice guy, but I guess a heart can have layers—or chambers. I became an aggressive football player in Texas during my freshman year of high school because of the bullies coming after me. I responded by becoming very aggressive on the football field. I was praised for it. When I got to Hawai'i, there was a constant need to prove myself. In Texas, it wasn't bullies, exactly. It was, "This is our territory, and you better not challenge us, or we'll kick your ass." There is a classic tough local guy in Hawai'i we call a "moke," with loads of a certain kind of machismo. Polynesians get a lot of strokes for this behavior—always being ready for a fight.

I learned to switch off the layer of me that's the nice guy. I had to hold my own with the best athletes on the team, some of whom were very tough. The nice guy thing just hadn't worked for me in high school. The problem with that switch is that, over time, turning it on and off can become increasingly problematic. Both on and off the field, any kind of perceived threat can cause you to flip the switch. The problem is that off the field, it may not be a legitimate threat, and it is exhausting to always be looking over your shoulder or preparing to react.

The nice guy thing didn't work in the NFL, either. You can't be a nice guy on the line of scrimmage. You don't have to hate the guy you're playing against; you don't have to want to kill him, but your job is to push him back, knock him down. If you wanna make an impression, you pick it up a couple notches. You summon some incentive that has some anger to it. I had to figure out a way to put myself in a state of mind that would allow me to take on a monster for two and a half hours and defeat him.

He's bigger than me. He's typically stronger than me. He's coming at me with everything he has. He pushes, pulls, grabs, slaps, forearms me in the chest, headbutts me, and tries to drive his helmet into my face or body. I get across to him that he is simply *not* going to defeat me, or if he does, it will be over my dead body. When I counter all those moves and stalemate him, he may become frustrated and angry and belligerent. He might grab my facemask and try to punch me or forearm me in the face. The challenge is to elevate myself mentally over him to the extent that I am physically willing to die.

When it's all over, you let it go, although you rarely say anything to the other guy. There are a few players where the battle gets picked up a few *more* notches. You try not just to outhit the guy, but to outsmart him. If it's a player like Jerry Sherk, afterwards you hug, and agree, "Jesus, that was so much fun." It is the ultimate challenge, both physically *and* mentally.

My awareness of the power of my body and my mindset carried over into business. For the most part, when I talked to a client or even a competitor, we had a nice conversation. But the minute a guy came in and said, "Hey, you motherfucker" or did something to undercut me, boom! I changed. Then I slipped into another persona because I was dealing with someone who wanted to attack me or hurt me, and in football, I had developed an almost instinctual response: "Kill or be killed."

Up until the 1968 season, I was back and forth—Washington, Dallas, Washington, Dallas, Washington. Once the season started, Nancy came up with the kids. She had her life with the wives and dealt with all the struggles of being the wife of an NFL player. We went through the trials and tribulations of teammates being cut, or hurt, or traded. We watched friends leave.

By the end of the first year with the Redskins, I'd established myself on the team. I felt more secure. And I wondered whether I could do better selling insurance where I was playing. After the 1968 season, when we went back to Dallas, I said to Nancy, "This going back and forth doesn't cut it. We need to move to Washington."

EVERYBODY WINS

I started to look for a way to establish myself in insurance in the DC metropolitan area. I found an agency in Georgetown—Raymond A. DuFour & Co. Raymond DuFour was a successful local businessman, and a powerful trustee at his alma mater, Catholic University. He was a committed and active supporter of the Republican Party. I started with him in the early spring of 1969.

DuFour wanted a presence in Maryland and wanted me to live in Montgomery County, Maryland, which has a population that is one of the most highly educated in the country and numbers among counties with the highest income per capita. We first looked at the closest community to the district, which was Chevy Chase. It was too expensive. Then we looked at Bethesda, which was also too expensive. Nancy and I kept going till we got to Gaithersburg, where we found a house in a new development, for $33,000. We were putting down roots. Eric by then was three, and our daughter Page was one.

I was to handle the life insurance division; DuFour had a guy who handled the casualty side, Stan De Rizzo.

There was a hitch: when I went into the office and asked the secretary for all the files on the life insurance, she said, "I can't give them to you. You'll have to talk to Mr. DuFour."

"You don't have to worry about that. You'll get to that later," DuFour said. It was a struggle for him to let go.

Shortly after that, in the spring, at a party that De Rizzo invited Nancy and me to, I met Wally Duncan, the lawyer for the Joseph P. Kennedy Foundation. The foundation, headed by Eunice Kennedy

Shriver, had been, for more than a decade, a leading advocate for research and athletic programs for people with intellectual disabilities. In a joint venture with the Chicago Park District, the foundation launched the first International Special Olympics Summer Games in 1968. There were more than 20 events, including broad jump, softball throw, 25-yard swim, 100-yard swim, high jump, 50-yard dash, and water polo.

I was impressed with the project, and Duncan described the plan for the coming summer when there would be eight regional Special Olympics. In addition to providing a fantastic program to kids, the entire event was a way to change perceptions about kids with mental disabilities and to shift the language used to describe them, from "retarded" to "special."

Duncan introduced me to some key people, including Eunice Kennedy Shriver. They asked if I'd be interested in running the mid-Atlantic region. The idea was to bring in 1,000 kids for a track and swim meet at the University of Maryland in College Park in the summer of 1969. I saw this as an opportunity to network and to garner publicity—for DuFour, for myself as a businessman, and also for the Special Olympics since my profile in the NFL might bring attention to the games. Things started running in my mind, like, "This could be really good. This would be my pro bono work."

I cleared it with the folks at DuFour, arguing that it would help establish me in the DC metropolitan area. I already had some notoriety as a football player, but this would get me more because I sensed there was going to be a lot of publicity.

I was getting $1,000 a month from DuFour, but I soon realized that trying to get this thing off the ground in a few months—bringing kids from eight states into the Mid-Atlantic region—would mean I would have very little time to sell insurance. Eventually, Raymond DuFour balked at continuing to pay my salary. I took a leave of absence.

THE "GENTLE GIANT"

I began to work full-time at the Special Olympics and drew a modest salary. I started going around town telling people about it, trying to raise money, and also going to schools with special-ed student populations and telling them about the program. I went to schools in DC and Baltimore. Then, I started going out further, to West Virginia, North Carolina, South Carolina, and Pennsylvania. I loved that. I made the pitch that this would be a chance for special-ed kids to go out and do something publicly. At the time, children with these mental disabilities were stigmatized, and people were quiet about revealing that they existed. In fact, it was only in September 1962 that Eunice Kennedy Shriver revealed that her sister Rosemary had a mental disability, the first such public acknowledgment by the Kennedy family, 44 years after Rosemary's birth. One of the Kennedys' goals was to reframe the way it was viewed: to put these kids in the sun so that everybody could see and celebrate them.

We needed funds, food, housing, and transportation. We needed $100,000. I went to every organization I could think of for financial help. I went to the Washington Redskins Alumni Association, which donated $10,000. I decided to go to the Mid-Atlantic supermarket chain, Giant Food, and met with the Executive Director of Advertising, Al Miller.

"Come with me," he said, and we walked into the office of the CEO, Joe Danzansky.

Danzansky thought the idea was fantastic. He said, "I think we should lock into this and give Ray some of our staff. Let me talk to Izzy Cohen, Chairman of the Board."

Izzy agreed, and Giant committed staff and financial support. They assigned an employee, Mel Pfefferstein, to be my right-hand man. Mel was phenomenal. Anything I needed, he somehow came up with it. The support of Giant Foods was over the top. But along with that came other supporters, one being Leonard Rodman—the founder of a chain of discount food and drug stores that attracted an international clientele—which helped give us credibility and assured us that the games would be successful.

Separately, that May, in 1969, I was invited out to Ethel Kennedy's house with a group of Redskins for a charity benefit pet show. It was an annual thing, the Hickory Hill Pet Show. *Washington Post* columnist Art Buchwald was ringmaster; various athletes umpired baseball games, and Redskins, led by Sam Huff, set up the obstacle course. Congressional legislators and others willing to wear white played "Celebrity Tennis," and there was a Diplomats Soccer team, known for playing with whoever wanted to play.[65] Nancy and I were invited to bring the kids.

Ethel had attended the first Special Olympics with Ted Kennedy in 1968, and in the spring of 1969, I asked her at the pet show if she would help me promote the Mid-Atlantic Regional Special Olympics event. She agreed to do so. In late spring 1969, Lombardi started holding workouts at a park next to Georgetown University, and I asked him if Ethel could come to a Redskins football practice for a picture to promote the Special Olympics. By this time, she and Senator Ted Kennedy had promised to attend. He agreed. Lombardi and his wife, Marie, also accepted Ethel Kennedy's invitation to visit Hickory Hill. I saw her again at a big event when the name of the downtown stadium was changed to RFK Stadium in homage to her late husband, who had been such an inspiration to me as an activist.

At the stadium event, she came over and asked whether I'd like to come to a party with Lombardi.

"No," I said.

Then she asked if I could get some guys together to come out to McLean that afternoon to play touch football with her kids.

I said, "Yes," not realizing that touch football was a big Kennedy thing.

---

65 Martin, Judith. "A Pet Project Unleashed at Hickory Hill." *The Washington Post*, 16 May 1977. www.washingtonpost.com/archive/lifestyle/1977/05/16/a-pet-project-unleashed-at-hickory-hill/1527fcae-097a-4333-9777-327e14fab254/.

FAT GIRL SINGS

Coach Lombardi telling special needs children about football

    I had spent my life being yelled at, betrayed, and left on my own to deal with adversaries—and I had learned to be tough as a result, but Special Olympics was a chance to be who I was before I had been called "Fat Girl" in elementary and junior high school in Texas and bullied for being Hawaiian. As Executive Director of the Mid-Atlantic Region, running the Special Olympics gave me a chance to put my softer, Hawaiian self into athletics and to coach kids in an entirely different way than I had been coached. I identified with these kids. I knew they had gone through some things. I knew they had struggled to be loved. I wanted to give them a chance to participate and to win something for the first time—to get a medal! It was a beautiful thing.

Myra MacPherson wrote a piece about the Special Olympics in *The Washington Post* Style section.[66] The headline was "Gentle Giant Bends for Children," and the story focused on my involvement in the regional event. I was somewhat amused by the way she described me ("245 pounds of hulking gentleness"), but I was honored that she grasped what I was trying to do and put it into words. "To the ones who did it the worst, he gave the most encouragement," she wrote, and "He handles them, not with pity, but kindness, something the children instinctively seem to appreciate." In 1974, I received the Kennedy Family Award for service to the mentally retarded through Special Olympics.[67] In 1973, I testified before the US Senate on Education for the Handicapped in support of Senate Bills 896, 6, 34, and 808, which would provide financial assistance to the states for improved educational services for handicapped children, support research and development in the care and treatment of autistic children, and authorize a screening program to identify children with specific learning disabilities.[68]

MacPherson's article put me on the map, but it also put me in the sights of Raymond DuFour. MacPherson wrote of the Kennedy Foundation's sponsorship and mentioned that I played tennis with Ethel Kennedy. DuFour, apparently, read the article.

He called me into the office. He hated the Kennedys. He told me he wanted me to quit my involvement with the Kennedy Foundation.

"What? I've got 1,000 kids coming up here!"

His response was, "Screw 'em." I turned around and walked out.

By the time of the event in June of 1969, I had invited the Baltimore Colts and the Redskins to the opening ceremony. What was incredible

---

66 MacPherson, Myra. "A GENTLE GIANT: GENTLE GIANT BENDS FOR CHILDREN." *The Washington Post, Times Herald* (1959-1973). https://www.proquest.com/docview/147638174/CDC46F683224AA2PQ/1?accountid=189667&forcedol=true.

67 Rosen, Ron. *The Washington Post*, "NFL Players Union Lifts Retarded." *The Washington Post*, 03 Mar 1978. https://www.washingtonpost.com/archive/sports/1978/03/01/nfl-players-union-lifts-retarded/305d5ec9-73f1-4799-ad12-b3099125e6af/; https://www.washingtonpost.com/archive/sports/1978/03/01/nfl-players-union-lifts-retarded/305d5ec9-73f1-4799-ad12-b3099125e6af/.

68 *The Subcommittee on Handicapped of the Committee on Labor and Public Welfare United States Senate - Ninety-Third Congress, First Session*; 03 1973. https://files.eric.ed.gov/fulltext/ED081129.pdf.

FAT GIRL SINGS

Plaques sold in Rodman's Drug Store to benefit the DC Special Olympics

was that most of them showed up. The event itself was held at the University of Maryland, and the kids stayed in the dorms. There were 1,000 kids from eight states. In the opening parade, Senator Jennings Randolph from West Virginia marched with the kids from his state. It was a two-day affair, with a swim meet and a track meet. It was a huge success. Parents sat watching their kids and cried because this was the first time their kids had ever done anything so publicly.

One story makes me cry almost every time I tell it. We had planned a mile race, but we didn't know if it'd be too much. We decided to do it, though, and there were two kids we knew would be contenders. One was a Black kid who was a fabulous athlete and had won all the sprints. And one was this long, gangly White kid. He often came up and talked to me. Anyway, in this race, the kids took off, and the Black kid was way ahead. He just sprinted around and around, and the entire pack was farther and farther behind him, with this one White kid lumbering along in the middle of the pack. They get to the final lap, and suddenly the White kid breaks out of the group and begins to chase the Black kid.

As they come around the second turn, he gets closer and closer. They come around the final turn, and the White kid comes up to the Black kid. They start to sprint, and the White kid passes him. Everybody's going crazy. As he's coming toward the finish line, he slows down. We are all watching. He puts his hand back, angled behind him, slows down more, and waits till the Black kid catches up with him and grabs his hand. They cross the finish line together.[69]

We gave them both gold medals. It was so inspirational. It was mind-boggling. That experience has stayed with me ever since. I tell it often, and I tear up every time I tell it. Winning isn't just about *you*. It's better if you can share it.

The Special Olympics event was in June 1969, and Redskins training camp started in July. Because I had had six weeks with Lombardi in Green Bay with the Packers—and even though I was now a starter—I tried to warn everybody, "Get ready. This guy is a madman. He's gonna be tough."

Joe Marshall of *Sports Illustrated* described our first meeting:

Lombardi stands at a lectern in front of his squad, hand held upward so that the three diamonds in the championship ring sparkle toward the players. The lips part and the big square teeth flash in a feral expression. "Let's be winners; there's nothing like it.[70]

"If You're Going Through Hell, Keep Going" ~Winston Churchill

---

69 Ryan, Joan. "Special Games Offer Rewards for Everyone." *The Washington Post*, 22 April 1977. https://www.washingtonpost.com/archive/sports/1977/04/22/special-games-offer-rewards-for-everyone/bcbc597b-677e-4cd4-9877-ab4e09aeb832/.

70 Marshall, Joe. "YOU WON'T HAVE WASHINGTON TO KICK AROUND ANYMORE – *Sports Illustrated* Vault.

We returned to Washington in the fall for the 1968 season, and things didn't improve on the team. Sonny got hurt; I got hurt, and our top draft pick, defensive back Jim "Yazoo" Smith, sustained a serious neck injury. I was in and out all the time, but I played most of the season.

A note from the Redskins Archive about our October 8 game against the Cowboys gives a sense of the dismal picture of the team at the time:

An unfunny thing happened to the Redskins yesterday on their way to a 14-10 victory over the Dallas Cowboys with 18 seconds remaining on the clock at D.C. Stadium. They lost, 17-14.[71]

We ended the season with a record of 5-9-0. That was all Edward Bennett Williams could take. He fired Graham, who returned to the Coast Guard Academy to serve as athletic director. He pulled all of his experience as a persuasive lawyer together and attempted to lure Vince Lombardi to Washington.

Lombardi had left the sidelines in Green Bay in January 1968 to run the Packers' operation as General Manager, but it was publicly known that he was missing the challenge of coaching,[72] and it was rumored at Washington parties I attended that his wife, Marie, missed the sophistication of New York and wanted to be on the East Coast. Williams offered Lombardi the job of Head Coach and also that of Executive Vice President, with a 5 percent share of ownership. His hiring in Washington was a major story. It became an exciting time for sports in DC.[73]

I wasn't thrilled with the news about Lombardi, but I was in a different place than I had been when I was with Green Bay. By the time I entered the Redskins locker room in 1966, I was a different

---

[71] Brady, Dave. "Redskins Fall in Last 10 Seconds." *The Washington Post*, WP Company, 9 Oct. 1967, D1. https://www.washingtonpost.com/wp-srv/sports/redskins/longterm/1997/history/allart/dw1967a.htm.

[72] *NFL* Network. "A Football Life: Vince Lombardi returns to coaching in Washington." https://www.nfl.com/videos/a-football-life-vince-lombardi-returns-to-coaching-in-washington-279281.

[73] Note: Williams's offer put Lombardi in the same ownership group with Williams (5 percent), Milton King (5 percent), C. Leo DeOrsey (13 percent), and Jack Kent Cooke, who had purchased 25 percent of the team in 1960 from George Preston Marshall.

man. I'd been a starter for the Cowboys, and while my time with the Packers and the Browns was short, that experience had taught me that I could compete with the best. I knew I was good. I could play. I knew that people had been wrong about me. I had been playing against the very best in the league. I knew that it wasn't a game of chance, that you've got to deliver. I wanted to show everybody that they were dead wrong about me.

Lombardi's training camp was brutal. He had us do these grass drills where on command, "Up!" or "Down!" you had to hit the ground flat on your stomach, catch yourself, and spring back to a standing position continuously while running in place between the commands, maybe 50 to 60 times. Guys who were not in good shape just flopped like big seals. He also liked to have the captains take the team "around the field." What this meant is that the entire team would be led sprinting to a goal post maybe 200 yards away and back. When they returned to Lombardi, I warned them not to pant, because, if they showed any indication of being out of shape, I knew from my experience at Green Bay, he would do grass drills every day until we were in shape. In Green Bay, it was Bart Star. With the Redskins, he yelled at Sonny Jurgensen, the quarterback, and Sam Huff, who had come out of retirement to play for Lombardi, to take the team around the goal post at the end of the grass drills, but they were not quite prepared to do this, and the team ran right over them because they were so exhausted from the grass drill. But with time, they were able to take us around the field.

Coming off a knee injury from the previous year and knee surgery, I wasn't starting at first. Again. When my knee began feeling better, I thought I'd impressed Lombardi. I could play guard, tackle, or center. That helped. As we got through camp, I wasn't in the starting lineup, but I was having outstanding practices.

Lombardi finally said, "Schoenke's our man. We've found our starting guard."

Then, in the last exhibition game, I have a play where I pull through the line to lead the runner, and they have a safety blitz. The defensive back comes sprinting through the hole, and I come around the other side. He's lean and much smaller than I am and spears me right in the chest with his helmet and separates my rib cage from my sternum. It feels like someone hit me in the chest with Thor's hammer. Needless to say, I'm a little shaken up. I leave the field, and they ask me if I'm OK and let me rest. At halftime, I'm in the training room, and the doctor tells me I can't play anymore that day. Lombardi isn't aware of this.

The coach in charge of personnel called me over the weekend and asked if I was OK. They were just about to release some other offensive linemen because they knew I could play several positions on the line and didn't need the backup. They could get other people in other positions they wanted to fill.

I said, "Yeah, I think I'm OK," even though I was beginning to have trouble breathing. But I could walk. But Tuesday morning in the stadium, it hurt, and hurt bad.

Joe Kuzco, the trainer, looked at me and said, "Ray, you're in trouble. You're not going to be able to play this week. Let me go tell them."

Later, I'm in the weight room in the back, lifting weights, when Lombardi walks in.

He approaches me, points at my chest, and says, "GODDAMN YOU, SCHOENKE! THIS IS NOTHING BUT A GODDAMN PUSSY INJURY! DO YOU HEAR ME, MISTER? JERRY KRAMER PLAYED WITH BROKEN RIBS. PUSSY INJURY! IF YOU'RE NOT READY SUNDAY, I'M GETTING RID OF YOU. YOU HEAR ME, MISTER? I'M GETTING *RID* OF YOU!" And he storms out of the room. I grab my playbook and throw it at him. Luckily, it misses him.

I am so angry. We had just moved up from Dallas and had just bought a house, and I'm thinking to myself, *"How am I going to pay the mortgage?"*

I run into the training room and say, "Joe, you gotta do something. He's gonna get rid of me!"

Kuzco says, "We can't do anything for a separated rib cage. I can't tape it up."

So I throw on my uniform and go out to practice. For the first drill, all of us get up on a sled, and Lombardi gets on, and says, "Hike!" and then we fire at the blocking dummies on the sled.

I fire into the sled, and it feels like somebody has taken a knife and cut me wide open. I collapse. The trainers run over to help me, and Lombardi screams, "LEAVE HIM ALONE! NOBODY TOUCH HIM! MOVE THE DRILL OVER!" So they move the whole drill over.

I am lying on the ground, and all the guys are saying, "Get up, Schoenke. He's gonna get rid of you!" I get up, but I figure I'm toast.

I didn't start in the first game of the season. I didn't play. The second game came around, and I was still in the same boat. But then there were some injuries on the Suicide Squad, so I ran to the coach for the special teams, grabbed him, and said, "Put me in!"

Lombardi was standing right next to him. He looked at my chest and started poking at it. He sarcastically said, "You're the guy with the pussy injury."

"Put me in!" I said to the coach. I was furious. This was my general attitude the entire time I played for Lombardi. I always had something to prove, and I intended to do just that.

My position is left guard, but they put me on the punt-return team, and I start killing people. Then, the right guard gets hurt, and they put me in that position, even though my regular position is left guard. I'm really kicking ass. Then, a right tackle gets hurt, and they put me in that position. At some point, I get back to right guard. You have to lock into each position without missing a beat. I do it. I am determined to prove I can play any position. I am determined to prove Lombardi wrong. I want to spit in his face.

This goes on, and I'm having outstanding games. Later in the season, he comes up to me before practice. I'm sitting in front of my locker, and he comes up behind me and starts rubbing my shoulders.

"Ray, I'm really proud of you," he says.

I want to say, "Get your fuckin' hands off me." I know he knows how angry I am at him for insulting me in the training room.

With some guys, Lombardi didn't yell because he knew they couldn't handle it, and he needed them. Apparently, he thought I *could* handle it. He never spared *me*. With Sonny, Lombardi played that game. He knew he couldn't get rid of such a great quarterback, so he didn't criticize Sonny.

Lombardi and I clashed, but I had started to figure out how to deal with him. On Tuesdays, after a Sunday game, on most teams, the coaches review the game films with all the players. The team is broken into offensive and defensive groups in their special categories, and they watch the films separately. The offense has four groups: the offensive line, the receivers, the backs, and the quarterbacks. Each group goes with its respective coach and watches the films. Not with Lombardi. Everybody on the offensive team was in one room.

He went through every play 11 times, one time for each player. He started at one end. He screamed, "WHO'S 74?! WORST BLOCK I'VE EVER SEEN!" When it was really bad, he yelled, "WHERE'S 74? TURN ON THE LIGHTS!" The coaches turned on the lights and pointed to the player.

Lombardi ran over, got in his face at close range, and screamed at him, and when he was finished, he yelled, "TURN OFF THE LIGHTS!"

He went down the line critiquing everybody on the team. We were there for hours. He finally came around to me. Most of the time I was doing great. I rarely missed a block. But when I did miss one, I was prepared to hear him scream. When it was my turn, and my block was average-to-bad, I just plugged my ears there in the dark until the screaming stopped. I literally put my fingers in my ears. I knew when

175

I had a good block, so I didn't plug up my ears. I knew when I'd done well, and I knew when it was bad.

If I'd made a good block, he'd still yell. "62—WHO'S THAT? SCHOENKE? GODDAMN GREAT BLOCK!"

Then, the next time, "GODDAMMIT, WHAT A PISS-POOR BLOCK!"

He put so much pressure on you that you did not want to make a mistake. I played well often, and those times, he'd yell praise more than criticism. I just waited for the good moments when I wanted to unplug my ears.

If he can't find you, he can't yell at you

I became a starter in 1966, so by the time Lombardi got there, I was in my fourth season with the Redskins and my sixth season in the NFL. I had been able to more than handle myself against just about anybody. And I was versatile, which made me valuable. I apparently even impressed the owner, Edward Bennett Williams, who once called me "the most intelligent football player he'd ever met."

If I was confident, that helped. If I was intelligent, that helped. But working under Lombardi required something more because he was such a tyrant. You didn't want to make a mistake. You didn't want him to explode at you. In response to Lombardi, some guys said, "I don't give a fuck." Other guys became basket cases.

I had something else going on. Because he let me go when I was with the Packers, I was driven to prove I was as good, if not better, than anything he'd ever seen before. I was graded out as his top lineman. By the end of the season, I had figured him out. I knew when to counter him. I would do something, and he'd blow the whistle, and I'd hear, "GODDAMMIT, SCHOENKE!"

I'd turn to him and say, "That's the way it's drawn up, coach."

He'd turn to the line coach and ask, "Is that right?"

And when the guy nodded, he'd just growl, "OK, Schoenke." Then he would cuss under his breath. I loved proving him wrong.

He knew that I knew what I was doing, that I was good. He liked that, and he liked me. So I just had to learn how to deal with his anger. If I did something wrong, he was going to scream at me. That's just the way it was. But he could scream, and then he could *really* scream. If you got the scream two or three times, he'd go, "STOP EVERYTHING!" and then get in a player's face. He didn't do it to me, but he did do it to some of the guys and got up in their face. He was awful, totally hostile and extremely aggressive toward these players.

Lombardi really made it difficult to achieve a Zen attitude and to be able to reconcile yourself with your mistakes. If the team lost, he just reamed our asses out.

We're playing the Los Angeles Rams, and I'm playing against a guy named Merlin Olsen, an All-Pro defensive tackle, six foot, five inches, pushing close to 300.

Typically, in football, you are facing a defensive line of four down linemen on the line of scrimmage and three linebackers off the line, one over the center and two on the outside. When you have a pass play where the offensive linebackers rush forward toward the quarterback (who is falling back and setting up for a pass), usually, your offensive backs, one of which is a rookie in this case, blocks the linebacker assigned to him, which in this situation, was the middle linebacker over the center, who he expected would rush toward the quarterback. This time, that linebacker instead went to the outside around the line of scrimmage instead of rushing straight forward as he typically would do, so the rookie, Larry Brown, chased after him toward the outside of the line of scrimmage in order to meet him and block him, opening up the center of the line of scrimmage. The linebacker on the outside then went around the line of scrimmage and into the hole over the center that opened up. The quarterback was now being pressured and had to release the ball in a second and a half before a receiver had been opened up or had to pull the ball down and "take a sack" and lose yardage on the play.

I've got this big guy, defensive tackle, who breaks to my left shoulder on the outside, and I'm watching *him* while I'm trying to figure out if the middle linebacker is opening up a hole, and my guy is helping him do that. I see the middle linebacker head around the line of scrimmage. Consequently, there's nobody covering the middle, and the outside linebacker comes in and just kills the quarterback. Larry does that a couple of times—he is so intent on doing the job assigned to him that he doesn't anticipate the linebacker coming around from the other side and going down through the hole. He's thinking he's supposed to block the middle linebacker because that is his assignment. He doesn't have the experience to know to let the guy go to the outside because there might be somebody else coming through the hole he inadvertently helped create by chasing his man.

I'm aware that they're sending their outside linebacker around and into the gap, and we need to figure out who's gonna block him. We realize that Larry, the rookie running back, doesn't know what's happening. As someone who is a backup on everything, I try to anticipate things on each play, and I can see what's going wrong here.

We are unable to make the first down, and as we trot off the field, Lombardi runs out and confronts us, screaming, "YOU GUYS ARE SHIT! SHIT! THE FALCONS (the worst team in the league at the time) ARE BETTER THAN YOU GUYS! YOU GUYS ARE SHIT!"

Leading the charge for Larry Brown

Each one of us got that in our face as we ran by him. So I run right by him, trying to ignore him because he's such a distraction. I go down and grab the assistant coaches to let them know what's happening, that we gotta figure something out, but Lombardi is chasing after us getting in our faces. "YOU GUYS ARE SHIT! YOU GUYS ARE SHIT!"

We fixed the situation although we eventually lost the game and got our asses reamed out as usual both on the field and in the locker room. Larry had a hearing problem, which may have saved him that day in the locker room. Lombardi eventually bought him a hearing aid, probably just so he could hear him scream.[74]

LOMBARDI'S GHOST

Lombardi was the first to scream at you and the first to praise. Of course, we lived for the praise. The intensity was overwhelming. All the time. The screaming never stopped. He just drove you all the time. He never changed.

The second-to-last game of the season, we're playing the Philadelphia Eagles, and we win. We secure a winning season, although we have one more game. Everybody's ecstatic; Lombardi's ecstatic. Then, we have our last game of the season, and it's with Dallas. The game is in Dallas, and they beat us.

"Last game, surely he won't chew our asses out in the locker room," I say to myself.

We had finished the season 7-5-2, the team's first winning season since 1955. It was a joyous season. Larry Brown was a rookie sensation. Sonny was very good to outstanding. But anytime we lost, Lombardi was a madman. He was consistent as usual with this last game. He couldn't help himself. He went crazy.

"YOU GUYS ARE AWFUL," he told us. I couldn't believe he still chewed our asses out.

Then, on the plane back from Dallas, I look back, and he is at the back of the plane walking up, talking to each guy, telling each one how much he appreciates them. He gets to me and says, "Ray, I really

---

[74] Note: Larry Brown eventually became an All-Pro running back.

appreciate everything you've done. You had a really great season. I'm really proud of you. I can't wait for next year to be with you again."

Talk about a paradox.

Then, he got sick. The spring of 1970, I saw Sonny at a function; he said, "We have to go to camp early. Coach is sick."

Lombardi had been suffering from digestive tract problems for a while, but he had refused his doctor's request to undergo a colonoscopy. He refused to have somebody sticking something up his ass. On June 24, tests revealed that he had colon cancer.

The cancer got really bad. He didn't come to training camp often; he went into the hospital. We had some practices, and the guys said, "We gotta go see Coach."

"No fuckin' way. I want to remember him screaming at me. I don't want to see him weak. I'm not gonna do it," I said.

And I didn't. He died on September 3. The service was at St. Patrick's Cathedral in New York. We went in, and the place was packed with people. The Green Bay Packers were there; the Redskins were there.

We sit down, and the doors are thrown open, and all of a sudden, this beam of sunlight goes racing down the middle aisle.

The hair on the back of my neck stands up. I say, "Coach is coming in."

The guy in front of me is Willie Banks, a guy from Alcorn A&M in Alabama. He got all this great praise at the beginning of the season because he knew how to block. But he was a rookie, and before it was all over, he was on Lombardi's shitlist. Lombardi screamed at him every day. The game was too much for him.

I say to myself, *"He's gotta hate Lombardi, so I'm just gonna watch Willie. I am not gonna cry."* But Willie doesn't get through it. Tears start rolling down Willie's cheeks, and then I break down. I'm a basket case.

Lombardi was a giant. If you want to pick a winner, you go with him. Because you are going to win. Lombardi knew a lot about the game, and he used fear as a means to motivate people. The problem with fear is that people play when they shouldn't be playing. Young men who feared for their jobs went out and played, and he ruined their careers. He did that to a lot of players. Young men tested their ability to handle his grueling drills and failed. For the most part, he treated everybody the same and was the same tyrant with everyone, but he knew that there was a certain point where he could break somebody. Sometimes he *wanted* to break a man. And sometimes he just wanted to test him, to find out if a man could play hurt. A lot of guys played hurt, and he ruined their careers, too. That was the price you paid for playing for him. But if you could get through the injuries and play hurt and survive, you were going to win.

In my case, I found out I could play hurt; I could play with injuries. I could play with my rib cage ripped open. You learn to deal with those injuries and ignore the things that would typically make you take a few days or weeks off. Because you knew that if you didn't play, he'd go after you.

I was determined to kill everybody in front of me and look him in the eye and say, "Ya see that, boss man?" I played angry. I played to spite him, to show him he was wrong about me, that he was wrong to have ever questioned me. At the end, when he was rubbing my shoulders and telling me how proud he was of me, I didn't let him seduce me. I didn't bend.

He was a tyrant, but he was also an inspiration. I had played some of my best football under Vince Lombardi. I wasn't afraid of him because by the time I was on the Redskins, I knew everything I needed to know, and he knew I knew it.

NEW LEADERSHIP

After Vince Lombardi's death, Bill Austin, our line coach, took over. But the team couldn't muster what it took to win. *The Washington Post* called the team "less than savage" on November 22, 1970, against the Cowboys. Two weeks later, the paper accused the Redskins of sinking "to one of the lowest points in their history." We ended the season with a 6-8 record.[75]

Edward Bennett Williams was not happy. He was ready to get the best coach that money could buy. He liked big names, and George Herbert Allen was available. Allen was an established NFL name, a former Coach of the Year with the Los Angeles Rams, a man with a career-long run of winning seasons. At Los Angeles, he had been successful in his five seasons but was fired because he didn't get along with the owner, Dan Reeve.

So, for $875,000, living expenses, travel expenses, a house, a chauffeured car, and other frills, Williams got George Allen. A couple of months after that deal, Williams said, "I gave Allen an unlimited expense account, and he has already exceeded it."[76]

Most coaches build their roster from the ground up and instill their system in new players. They believe in the draft. They pick young, pliable, highly talented athletes that they expect to be very successful within three to five years. Allen flipped the draft playbook. He wanted to get experienced players who could win immediately, experienced players he didn't have to train, teach, or motivate. He was giving veteran outstanding All-Pro players opportunities to "go out" as champions, which was highly motivating for men coming from a losing team who were aging out of football. He felt that if he put these players on a team with a good system, he could make these "reject" players successful, and he did just that. He also picked off great, respected players from winning teams who were being replaced by younger players.

He didn't stop there. Even though Allen had the passing wonder and future Hall of Famer Sonny Jurgensen as quarterback, he signed Billy Kilmer, who had been a running quarterback for the

---

[75] Gildea, William. "The Rivalry: 1970-79." *The Washington Post*, WP Company, 7 Dec 1970. https://www.washingtonpost.com/wp-srv/sports/redskins/history/rivalry/articles/1970sdec.htm.

[76] Marshall, Joe. "YOU WON'T HAVE WASHINGTON TO KICK AROUND ANYMORE - *Sports Illustrated* Vault."

49ers and the Saints. Billy Kilmer challenged Sonny for the starting quarterback job over the next four seasons. Kilmer's passes were not tight spirals like Jurgensen's and weren't picture perfect. But he got the job done.

One of the reporters who wrote about the competition between Sonny and Billy was George Solomon, a reporter with *The Washington Post*. I had been following George's column since 1966. While Solomon was the local sports reporter for *The Daily News*, he was not shy about criticizing the team if we had done poorly, but he was also the first to praise us. In 1971, when he was with *The Washington Post*, he started the Billy vs. Sonny quarterback controversy. It was an issue that whipped up fans, who tended to be loyal to one quarterback or the other and sported buttons at games that read "I like Billy" or "I like Sonny."

Solomon ran a column asking fans to write in about which quarterback they preferred. This dismayed Nancy, who felt that this campaign was dividing the team and community. She might have been a Southern belle, but Nancy was *not* a shrinking violet. She expressed her views to Solomon and his newspaper, writing a long letter airing her opinion, and she called Solomon on the telephone. In addition to negative public attention, Solomon was also being put through the player gauntlet because of George Allen's lack of trust in the press. There was an incident when a defensive tackle went after Solomon while he was walking through the locker room. Picture a player six foot, four inches, probably weighing 275, standing over a small, slim guy, five foot, six inches tall, while threatening to kill George and screaming at him. George was standing with his hands raised protectively in front of his face and was backing away. I put my considerable frame between them and said "Leave 'im alone." During Solomon's tenure as a reporter for the team, some players, empowered by management to have a lack of trust in the press, referred to him as a "fuckin Jew" as he walked through the locker room. Our relationship, which started as an uneasy alliance between a reporter and a player, became more than just jock and journalist. I trusted him, and I wanted to protect him.

Allen had brought several players from the Los Angeles Rams who bought his attitude—that the press was not their friend. He wanted the team to view the press as the enemy. I, on the other hand, viewed Solomon as my friend. I was very comfortable with Solomon, and I had a lot of respect for him. A lot of guys followed the coach's lead when it came to the press. If they said anything critical to Solomon, I'd jump them. It didn't improve the situation. After George Allen arrived in 1971, Solomon and I started seeing each other frequently. In my first years with the Redskins, I came off the practice field, showered, and started making calls from the locker room to set up appointments later in the day for my insurance business.

Allen didn't trust players to be able to do two things at one time or to have an outside line of work during the season. He definitely didn't like me doing business from the locker room. However, while I was still doing business in the locker room, I watched to make sure that my teammates didn't yell ethnic slurs at George Solomon as he passed by their lockers. Eventually, Allen told me to shower and change and use the phone upstairs. So, I started coming upstairs from the locker room to the media office on the second floor, where Solomon was writing and filing his story for the next day's newspaper. I found a quiet corner and did business alongside him.

PRESSURE COOKER

Training camp combines the pressures of marriage, children, and being the breadwinner with the tremendous stress for family men encountered in football—the pressure from coaches, the pressure you put on yourself, the competitive nature of players, the way that injuries can take you out, the reality that you might be replaced, not to mention worries about the future because a football career is very short-lived. So when players arrive at camp in early July, it's a combustible situation. To top it off, there are groupies vying for attention.

Meanwhile, on the home front, it is also very stressful for the wives of players. Nancy and I had children, with one still in diapers. She naturally was also under a lot of stress herself, albeit self-imposed. Nancy viewed herself as a pioneer woman, and she was prepared to sacrifice everyone else's comfort to prove that we could survive under difficult circumstances. Her attitude was every man for himself.

"I have my own problems, and you have yours," she'd say, "I got a home here; I got three kids, and I got a dog and all her puppies shitting on the front porch. Where are you? You're up in Carlisle getting fed, with people waiting on you, and I'm here dying. If you don't like it in Carlisle, quit and come on home. I need you here."

She wasn't interested in my complaints. However, at the time, she was refusing to use air conditioning and making the family live in the basement in the heat of the summer and was trying to "live off the land."

In addition to her concerns about the environment and trying to save money, Nancy was very principled. When we found out that our local country club refused to admit Blacks, she insisted that we withdraw our membership. Which we did. However, prior to my leaving for football summer training camp, this translated into my having to clear a level area on a hill and purchase an above-ground pool for the children to play in, where when I was at camp, they ended up paddling amongst the local wildlife, including snakes, frogs, water spiders, algae, and god knows what else. But they loved it.

When I was in summer camp, the kids had a ball, but Nancy was extremely busy, and she certainly wasn't hanging out by the pool getting a suntan. Nancy and I had a traditional marriage in that I worked long hours and made the money, and Nancy raised the kids and managed our home and five acres in Laytonsville. But Nancy was hardly a traditional homemaker. I gave her an allowance to run the house. She ran a tight ship, and she knew what she wanted. She allowed me to be free to do my thing, knowing the home front was covered, but she was traditional in that she demanded that I be there for dinner. It was the one time that the whole family was together.

At one such dinner, I came home from a workout, tired, exhausted, and voraciously hungry. I had worked out for many hours, and I was so ravenous, I could barely speak. All I was thinking about was food.

The serving platter for the family had only rice and beans, at which point, I exclaimed, "Where's the *meat*?"

"There's protein in the rice and beans, and this meal feeds 50 million Mexicans."

"How many of them are playing in the NFL?" I retorted.

I also gave her an allowance for the property, and she managed it all so well that she secretly put away some of the money.

One day, our bank officer called me and said, "Your annuity is ready now."

"What's this?" I ask Nancy. "Did you purchase a $100,000 annuity?"

She nodded.

"Where in the hell did you get the money?"

"From the allowance. I was very efficient," she said. I still have the annuity today. It's worth $300,000 and still growing.

Nancy was a certified Master Gardener and converted our five acres from barren fields into a paradise with a stunning contemporary home filled with art, as well as a guest house, patios, a swimming pool, and a tennis court. She did not like ornamental gardens, so the property was planted with trees—oak, pine, sycamore, maple, birch, elm, and magnolia. Cherry and apple trees bloom in spring. There are azaleas, daffodils, roses, ferns, gardenias, wisteria. She also had me plant giant bamboo to hide the house, the swimming pool, and the tennis court from the view of neighbors. I had to drive around all over the place digging bamboo off county property or asking people if I could take some from their property where it was leaving their property line.

I planted small pine trees between our property and our nearest neighbor, whose house was visible, and now those trees are heading toward being 100 feet tall and, with the bamboo, give the house almost complete privacy. She added a greenhouse, which was later converted into a sunroom and was filled for the winter months with all her plants and flowers. She was composting and recycling before most even knew the terms.

But that wasn't all. She studied Spanish, cultural anthropology, acting, and modern dance, and earned a Master's of Family Counseling. She ran a weekly women's support group for victims of domestic violence and volunteered for Gaithersburg HELP and as a children's Court Appointed Special Advocate for Montgomery County. As a young mother, she was involved in La Leche League and held classes for expectant and breastfeeding mothers. She belonged to the Brady organization and was passionate about gun control. She also donated to female politicians and advocated for women in politics. She donated to Emily's List and was good friends with Ellen Malcolm, its founder.

Our third child, Holly, was born in 1972, and my business was growing along with my family. One of my favorite personal memories of that period was when, to give Nancy a break, I took my kids with me to Redskins Park, driving the backroads and crossing the Potomac River on White's Ferry. I worked out in the weight room, and they ran around all over the place. This was late June; Holly was still in diapers. They had the place all to themselves, including the training room. To them it was like a playground, with a super cool jungle gym.

On Saturday mornings, at home games, it was a tradition for players to bring their children to the practices. Eric's hair was long and blonde, and he sometimes brought a friend, whose hair was also long. The football players on the team called them girls, chased them, taped them up, and threw them in the laundry basket. Tim Timerario's kid cried when they did that, and Tim, who was the team's head player scout, got quite upset, but Eric thought it was fun, so I didn't care. By the time we pulled into the driveway at home, the kids were sound asleep in the backseat of the car.

I worked on keeping a foot in the game while transforming my insurance business into something larger than just a broker's agency. I wasn't shy about linking my football world and my business world. Ray Schoenke's Montgomery County Business Redskins Luncheon, every Monday at the Washingtonian Motel and Country Club in Gaithersburg, had gained a reputation of its own. Len Hauss and Ron McDole were the weekly featured host players and were responsible for bringing a guest player. Hauss was the straight man; Ron, who was known as The Dancing Bear because of his fancy footwork on the field, was the funny guy. They yinned and yanged.

Each week there were drawings where we gave away tickets and autographed footballs. The attendees enjoyed it. I gave all the money from the luncheons to Hauss and McDole and to the ladies who helped out, including my secretary, Nancy Thompson. I took no compensation. What I got was the names, addresses, and phone numbers of the people who attended when they filled out the drawing tickets with their business and personal contact information. My return was great business contacts. We consistently had 125-250 attendees, and after a big win, we could have as many as 500 people.

TAKING A STAND

In camp, on the field, I was proving my mettle. Away from the field, I was developing a different persona, with my insurance business, political activities, and opposition to the Vietnam War. I had started out in Dallas selling life insurance, but I viewed that as a kind of bottom-feeder business. So I began to move into corporate insurance, targeting privately owned companies with anywhere from 20 to 200 employees. And I was starting to think about how to best offer coverage to the people who *owned* the companies. Did they want to buy a mutual fund or an insurance policy? I had gotten good at convincing them of the latter and was starting to develop instruments that treated insurance more as an investment vehicle for large corporations. My clients were not as conservative as they had been in Dallas, but they were businessmen and solid Republicans.

Being immersed in the corporate world didn't temper my own leftist inclinations, and in this, I had a partner in Nancy. In the late '60s, we joined some of the constant marches and demonstrations against the war downtown, even taking the kids. We all held hands and marched with everyone else.

In Dallas, I had learned that some people have built-in anger and that they may not share your views, but they also respect you if you stand up for what you believe in. When I moved up to Washington, I continued with this approach. I developed a certain comfort with dealing with conservative businessmen.

As the seasons wore on, I became more politically involved. I don't know how conscious I was of it at the time, but I was evolving my own identity as both a citizen and an athlete. I kept up volunteering with inner-city youth football teams and supporting the Special Olympics.[77] I joined the county Democratic Party organization, and first thing you know, I'm chairing a county committee to try to figure out which Democratic candidate to run against the incumbent, who's a liberal Republican. The committee members suggested that I run.

I said, "No, I can't do that." We put up somebody else. But I started meeting people, and my network expanded.

After first meeting Ethel Kennedy during the inception of the Special Olympics, Nancy and I became regular guests at Hickory Hill. Ethel had a dinner party almost every Friday or Saturday night in the spring, to which we were frequently invited. She liked me because I was a big-time football player. But Ethel *loved* Nancy. Most guests were

---

[77] Argetsinger, Amy, "Against Long Odds, Ex-Redskin Is Ready to Challenge Glendening." *The Washington Post*, 19 Jan 1998, B01. https://www.washingtonpost.com/archive/local/1998/01/19/against-long-odds-ex-redskin-is-ready-to-challenge-glendening/0e2f7cc0-2099-47ab-ae7e-4b81aab8a388/.

very nervous at those parties because, first of all, Ethel was flamboyant and intense, and she was able to use her last name and the appeal of Hickory Hill to attract VIPs. Her parties were legendary. Because Nancy wasn't intimidated by the celebrities, was never nervous, and enjoyed the banter, Ethel always seated her at her table, whereas I was seated elsewhere, typically with people I was less excited about engaging in conversation with. This was probably because I wasn't as interesting as Nancy even though I was the celebrity of the two of us.

For the next 10 years, we were out there practically every weekend. The place was loaded with congressmen, senators, ambassadors, members of the cabinet—the liberal political elite. Ethel also included movie stars, Broadway stars, actors, all kinds of celebrities. You never knew who was gonna walk through the front door. If they came into town, she invited them over. You'd be sitting there, and next thing you know, there'd be a movie star sitting next to you.

One night we're playing charades, and my team is huddled trying to come up with a comic, or an actor, or some marquee name. Then, Henry Mancini walks through the door. The crowd was in the dining room, so nobody saw him, and we say, "Let's do Henry Mancini." We'll do "man" (I would come out and pound my chest), then "see" (Judith Hackett would put her hand over her eyes like a sailor looking for land), and then someone would hit his knee. We get Mancini to play along, and after we give our clues, and they guess right, he walks out. That was what it was like at Ethel's.

My interaction with the people at Ethel Kennedy's parties propelled me to be more involved in things away from football and more willing to be open about my strong political feelings. Some of the guests encouraged me. Some even invited me to luncheons and up to their offices.

I made a point to go to the Capitol whenever I could. When I was in town, I called on Senator Ralph W. Yarborough and Congressman Jim Wright, both Democrats from Texas. I also introduced myself to the senators and the representatives from Hawaiʻi. Senator Daniel Inouye was already a giant in the Senate. When Representative Daniel Akaka was elected in 1976, I made sure to meet him. He later became the first Native Hawaiian US Senator in history.

Early in 1971, I'd earned a starting role on the team and was keeping my political convictions off the field. However, I wanted to do more, but I wasn't sure how. Gare Joyce wrote on Sportsnet:

> *George McGovern had announced his intention to enter the race to be the Democratic candidate for the presidency, but the polls showed that he was an uninspiring fifth in the race. The senator had an image issue—too reasonable, too conciliatory, too soft. He wanted to end the war in Vietnam, but to voters, he seemed incapable of stirring up enough emotion to fight for a peaceful withdrawal.*[78]

After a small bit of deliberation and a conversation with Nancy, I decided to call McGovern's Senate office and introduce myself and ask if I could talk with the senator. A meeting was set up.

As a football player, you usually don't do things like this. I put on my best suit, summoned my inner salesman, and drove up to the Hill. I was ushered into McGovern's inner office, and the senator stood up from behind his desk, came out to shake my hand, and then motioned for me to sit down. I figured I had five minutes to make an impression.

I introduced myself as a football player with the Redskins, told McGovern that I was impressed by how he was standing up against the war, and said I wanted to help. I followed with the uncomfortable truth: "You have this reputation of being soft, a liberal, a socialist, but I know you're a decorated military hero," I said. "You were a fighter pilot in World War II. You were awarded the Distinguished Flying Cross. You're a tough guy. You're brave. I'd like to see you put your war experience front and center. Your story would be an asset for making

---

[78] Joyce. "The Game Beyond the Game."

your case against the war. Saying that you prefer peace doesn't mean you're not a warrior."

I don't know quite how I could have been so full of myself, but I was. That was the lineman in me, but I was trying to do the right thing. My SMU professors might have been sitting on my shoulders. I did feel knowledgeable and strong in my views.

McGovern was listening, and I had the impression he was trying to figure out, "Who is this Ray Schoenke?"

It was a risky gambit, but I followed it with an offer to help. "I'd like to put you beside some big pro football players," I said. I felt it would really help his image.

I knew that Bobby Kennedy had used former Rams lineman Rosey Grier as a bodyguard and had also relied on Rafer Johnson, an Olympic decathlon champion and former starter for the UCLA basketball team. They were both backstage at the California primary victory party when Sirhan shot and killed RFK.[79] It wasn't uncommon for political consultants to send their candidates to football games, seek endorsements from players and coaches, and talk athletes into running for office. It is not unusual for politicians to compare their skill set to football. Gary Hart, McGovern's campaign manager, even referred to "the Kennedy/Lombardi school" of politics.[80]

"May I try to find some football players to travel with you?" I asked. I offered to find as many athletes as I could to endorse him.

McGovern was a deliberate, caring man, not aggressive at all, even in the face of the kind of bravado I was exhibiting. "Great," he finally said.

He told me to go to the campaign office and meet the people there. Someone told me I had to go to New Hampshire for the first primary and try to bring some athletes up there. I flew up to Manchester early. I went into the office, and nobody knew what to do with me.

---

[79] Bembry, Jerry. "How Rosey Grier and Rafer Johnson became friends with Robert Kennedy." *ANDSCAPE*, 05 Jun 2018. https://andscape.com/features/how-rosey-grier-and-rafer-johnson-became-friends-with-robert-kennedy/.

[80] Quoted in Berrett, Jesse. "A Political Education." *Victory Journal.* https://victoryjournal.com/stories/a-political-education/.

Campaigning for McGovern

"I'll sweep the floors," I said.

The campaign was loaded with young people who were against the war. I started pushing it hard, befriending people who referred me from one person to another. And I started using the office to call players.

I became the national chairman of the Athletes for McGovern Committee. The first two players I recruited were physically impressive defensive linemen: Kansas City's Buck Buchanan, who was six foot, seven inches and 270, and Chicago's George Seals, who was six foot, three inches and 280. McGovern was also tall, and with me in the mix, we were a big, beefy, winning group. The McGovern team loved it.[81]

In a matter of weeks, and still months out from the first primaries, I became a one-man political operation. I handed out campaign literature at training camp. I recruited several hundred players, a group that included 20 Redskins players. Lionel Aldridge, who clashed with me on the field, along with other Packers friends, like Bill Curry and Marv Fleming, who also signed up to help me.

I didn't think of my teammates as celebrities. I described them in interviews as "citizens with convictions." I traveled the entire Eastern part of the US and was present at all the early primaries until I had to slow down for training camp. I helped kick off McGovern's efforts in Maryland, calling him "a man who will make changes, end the war, and fill the spiritual void left by the loss of King and Kennedy." Then, I went door to door helping register voters. I auctioned off autographed footballs, and I posed endlessly for photos with kids, charging them a dollar a shot. Even during the season, I got my teammate John Wilbur to go with me along with Lady Bird Johnson's former press secretary to look for votes in Southern states just four days before we played Dallas.[82]

I was also working with a number of celebrities who backed the candidate and supported the withdrawal of US troops from Vietnam, including Warren Beatty and Shirley MacLaine and "That Girl" Marlo Thomas. It was a sort of parade of stars. Our role was to go to an event and be able to talk about why McGovern was the best candidate.

But my role wasn't to be starstruck; it was to find NFL players wherever I could who would join the campaign trail. I convinced some of my Washington teammates to make appearances or at least sign a petition for the withdrawal from Vietnam. Eventually, I got hundreds of players to endorse McGovern and travel all over the country for him. When there

---

[81] Joyce, SPORTSNET.

[82] Berrett, "A Political Education."

was a key event, Gary Hart, McGovern's campaign manager, would say, "Show up and bring some athletes," or "Meet McGovern in Manchester and walk around with him when he says hello to everybody in the factories."

I was moved around accompanied by a group of football players. Jan Stenerud was a field goal kicker for the Kansas City Chiefs who was also a ski jumper from Norway. I got him in New Hampshire where the first primary in the country was held since skiing and ski jumping are a big deal there.

The guys I recruited tended to be enthusiastic about talking to voters. They were naturals. They could relate to voters with whom they shared basic values or experiences. They made McGovern relatable by ensuring that he was known for representing small farmers and blue-collar workers. The Chiefs' Ed Podolak, who put in more than 10,000 miles on McGovern's behalf, knew how to fit in with voters who frequented bars or worked in construction.[83]

McGovern was a really decent guy, and his wife Eleanor was equally thoughtful and decent. He was just a nice, kind person. Very smart, thoughtful. I liked him.

My activism had always made me a little controversial among my teammates. I had gotten into huge arguments with Cowboys teammates who were arch-conservatives, but I hadn't considered that my politics might make waves with a new coach. I took a break from the campaign to go to Redskins training camp in 1971, which is where I met Coach George Allen, a staunch conservative and friend of President Richard Nixon.

In a 2017 article titled "How Nixon Turned Football into a Political Weapon," writer Jesse Berrett aptly describes Nixon's relationship to Allen:

> *Nixon was so obsessed with football that he showed up at Redskins practices and huddled with the players. He sent Redskins coach George Allen a shoebox full of encouraging notes, had his top*

---

83 Ibid.

assistants Bob Haldeman and John Ehrlichman help Etty Allen find the family a place to live when Allen was hired, and even invited Allen and his family to a state dinner. At least twice, he phoned NFL coaches to recommend they call certain plays— famously, he urged Redskins quarterback Billy Kilmer to try a risky double reverse in the upcoming playoff game against the San Francisco 49ers. In the second quarter, with the ball on the 8-yard line, Allen told Kilmer to go for it. The trick play backfired miserably, ending in a 13-yard loss, followed by a blocked field goal on the next down. The 49ers won the game 24-20— and many Redskins fans blamed Nixon.[84]

Allen was an alumnus of Whittier College, where Nixon had attended and played on the college football team.[85] Allen had even coached for six years there in the 1950s.[86] The two supported each other's endeavors for years. Allen campaigned for Nixon and appeared on the cover of an Athletes for Nixon brochure.[87] Dave Kindred with *The Washington Post* referred to Allen as "Nixon with a whistle."[88]

IF YOU WANT TO CUT ME, CUT ME

Politics aside, things on the team were starting to gel. Allen brought his personality to bear. His priorities were defense, special teams, and offense. The main thing he wanted from the offense was for us not to screw up his system. He liked veteran players because they didn't make mistakes and knew how to avoid injuries.

---

84 Berrett, Jesse. "How Nixon Turned Football into a Political Weapon." *POLITICO*, Oct 2017. https://www.politico.com/magazine/story/2017/10/14/richard-nixon-politics-football-presidents-215708/.

85 Klein, Christopher. "10 Things You May Not Know About Richard Nixon." *HISTORY*, Jan 2013; https://www.history.com/news/10-things-you-may-not-know-about-richard-nixon.

86 *Hall of Fame*. "George Allen." n.d.; https://www.profootballhof.com/players/george-allen/.

87 Berrett. "A Political Education."

88 *The Washington Post*, "Say What You Will About Allen, He Was Definitely a Winner", n.d.; https://www.washingtonpost.com/archive/sports/1980/12/21/say-what-you-will-about-allen-he-was-defintely-a-winner/bcbed210-cfce-4d59-8f80-ea4bac469e3a/.

We tended to lean on Sonny Jurgensen, who could pull a rabbit out of a hat and throw a 40- to 50-yard touchdown pass for us to win a game. But we hadn't been playing as a team. That's why Billy Kilmer was the perfect quarterback for Allen; Sonny Jurgensen just wanted to score.

Kilmer had a chance to prove himself sooner than we thought. In the last exhibition game of the summer, I went to Sonny before the game.

"Offensively, we haven't been doing that well, and this game is really important," I said. This game was very critical for the offense to make a statement.

"I hate his offensive plans, and I'm taking a dive," Sonny said to me. I didn't take this seriously. He was just complaining. This was somewhat fortuitous because if he had been serious, he didn't have to take a dive. He injured his shoulder trying to make a tackle after he threw an interception. That gave Billy the opportunity to start the season at quarterback. The night before the first game in St. Louis, Billy came into the offensive team meeting drunk, which upset everyone. Charley Taylor, an outstanding wide receiver, walked out.

I called a straight-arrow friend, Jake Kupp, who didn't drink and played with Kilmer in New Orleans and asked, "What's with this guy?"

"Don't worry," my friend said, "he'll be sober tomorrow, and he'll be ready for the game."

The next morning, the day of the game, I saw that Kilmer was indeed ready to play when he and I entered the locker room. We were not favored to win. In our first offensive series, it's third and long, which Sonny would have considered ripe for a passing play; Billy called a sweep for Larry Brown and said to us linemen, "You guys get the first down."

Sonny never asked us to get the first down; he tried to get the first down himself, using his arm to throw a pass. Sonny had a reputation for winning the games by himself. While Billy could pass, he never relied just on himself.

In this first third and long situation, we throw blocks; Brown goes for a first down; Richie Petitbon intercepts three passes, and we win the game going away. Kilmer keeps it up, and we continue to win.

I had an interesting relationship with Billy Kilmer. Once, when we were running offensive drills against the defense in practice, the defensive tackle told me that our rookie running back, Mike Thomas, was tipping by leaning to the right or left, giving away the direction of the play.

So, the next time we are in the huddle, I lean over to Mike and tell him that he is tipping.

Our All-Pro wide receiver, Charley Taylor, stands up and says, "Guess who's coaching the backs?" in a really loud voice. "Ray Schoenke."

"What the fuck are you doing?" Billy says.

"Go fuck yourself!" I say, as I make sure my helmet is buckled. Billy was the one who would determine if we were going to fight.

But we never came to blows. My captain, Len Hauss, kept telling me to quit pissing Billy off. Anyway, in that Eagles game, he had wanted me in, and I didn't forget that.

Joe Marshall, of *Sports Illustrated*, describes where we were by mid-October, where he mentions my roommate, Maxie Baughan:

The Redskins are 4-0, the only undefeated team in the league. They practice now in the seclusion of Redskin Park, a development near Dulles Airport that set Allen's unlimited expense account back half a million dollars. Practice is invariably a lackadaisical affair. Some of Allen's old Rams lie in the grass in brightly colored painters' hats while around and around the track on a bicycle goes Maxie Baughan, an aging red-haired linebacker in an engineer's cap. He jingles the bell on the handlebar and waves to his teammates. Out on the field George Allen is quietly talking to his defense, showing them diagrams after each half-speed play, exciting little enthusiasm, making little noise.

It is hardly inspiring, yet that Sunday the Redskins take victory No. 5 with a 20-0 shutout of St. Louis, and Redskin fans, who for years have accepted mediocrity with the same resigned smiles they wear during rival political administrations, get close to hysteria.[89]

It wasn't just the fans who were excited. Allen predicted things in our first game with St. Louis. He said, "We're gonna shut it down; that crowd's gonna be quiet. We're gonna be winning, and I'm telling you guys, we're gonna be dancing in the locker room after the game."

I said to myself, "*We are not gonna be dancing.*" Sure enough, though, we were. We were giddy.

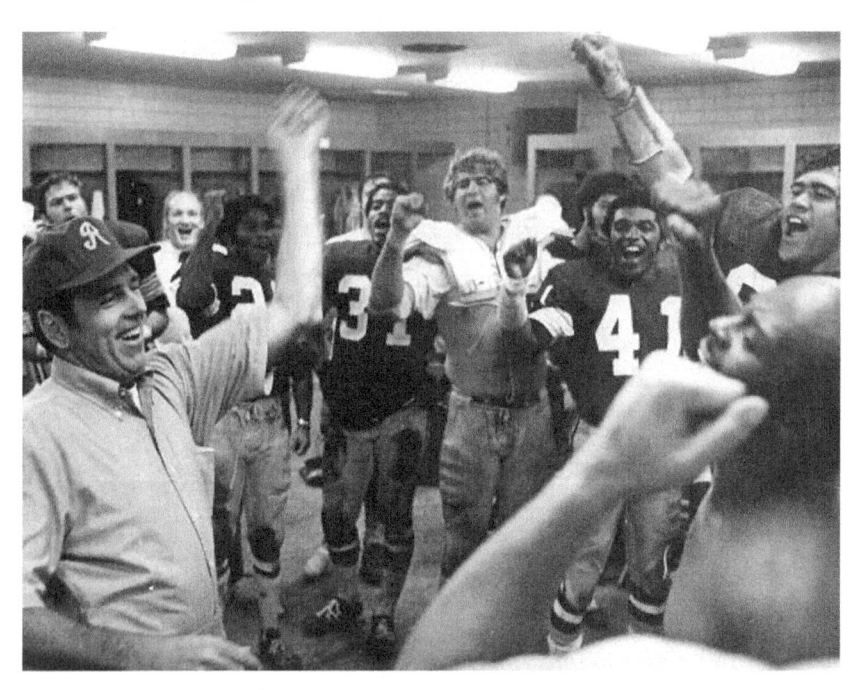

Celebrating with Coach Allen after a big win

---

89 Marshall, Joe. "YOU WON'T HAVE WASHINGTON TO KICK AROUND ANYMORE." *Sports Illustrated Vault.* https://vault.si.com/vault/1973/01/15/you-wont-have-washington-to-kick-around-anymore.

We beat St. Louis and the next team and the next team. We beat Dallas; we're just off and running. It was a team effort. After games, we'd come into the locker room and, yes, dance and sing. It was fun. The team was good: Larry Brown could literally bounce off opponents when he was hit and could continue to drive himself forward and remain balanced, always gaining yards. If you hit him on his left side, he'd bounce off of you, and instead of being pushed right by the momentum of the hit, he would fly out to the left, cutting back against the grain.

Charlie Harraway was a good runner, too. Jerry Smith, at tight end, spent hours perfecting his routes. This discipline led to his being one of the best pass-receiving tight ends in the NFL. Charley Taylor was an incredibly gifted athlete, with speed, strength, and toughness. Along with Roy Jefferson, who was smooth as silk, they were outstanding wide receivers. And the defense was special.

We weren't a ragtag group anymore. We were playing as a team, not just leaning on Sonny Jurgensen. I was elated. Kilmer was great, and everybody needed everybody.

When Nancy and I went to parties at the Kennedy compound, we passed out game tickets, which were the new hot commodities. At games, Nancy parked in the players' parking lot right in front of the stadium. I parked way in the back where the general public parked because I came early. There was little activity going on in the parking lots, and it was easy for me to get out after the game. As I walked toward the stadium, kids started following me and asking me for tickets. I decided to sell them tickets for $5 each with the understanding that their school work had to be stellar. They had to show me their grade cards to get tickets, which they did.

Years later, I was on the DC Metro, and a man approached me and asked if I was Ray Schoenke. He said that he had been one of those kids and that I had inspired him to excel in school. He told me he now had a good career with the Metro system, and he wanted to thank me. I still cherish that moment.

I had lots to feel good about when I was handing tickets out to kids. I was feeling good about my performance on the field and, on my off days, feeling good about recruiting ballplayers to get involved in the McGovern campaign. I was burning the candle at both ends, and the sense of total engagement was satisfying.

Kilmer led the team to a 9-4-1 record and its first postseason appearance in 26 years, as the wild-card team, playing in San Francisco.[90]

As we were preparing for the game, President Nixon accepted Coach Allen's invitation to visit practice at Redskins Park in suburban Virginia. Nixon came, chatted with Allen, and milled around with the players. Everyone was excited to have a picture taken with the president.

Except for me. My anti-Vietnam war views were well known, and I was quite publicly supporting McGovern, so cozying up to Nixon was a non-starter for me. When everyone got together for the picture, I strolled over to another practice field, several hundred yards away.

This act of resistance filled the notebooks of many reporters. It gave me uncomfortable national attention. Some teammates resented my boycotting the photo. My brother Walter called me up and told me I was stupid. Mike McCormack, my line coach, accused me of disrespecting the Commander in Chief.

"I'm an American citizen, and I have that right," I said.

"No, you don't!" he exclaimed.

I immediately questioned his familiarity with the Constitution,[91] but right then, because of that comment, I felt that I could be in trouble. But I felt that as long as I played good football, I wouldn't get cut. We lost, 24-20, to the 49ers. I had a previous run-in with McCormack where Nancy played a role, which probably did not help the situation. In 1972, after a game, I saw her poking McCormack

---

90 Tarhog. "Redskins History 101: Legends of Lore – Billy Kilmer." *WASHINGTON FOOTBALL TEAM, EST. 1932.* 16 May 2005. https://es.redskins.com/topic/99309-redskins-history-101-legends-of-lore-billy-kilmer/.

91 United States Courts. "What Does Free Speech Mean?" https://www.uscourts.gov/about-federal-courts/educational-resources/about-educational-outreach/activity-resources/what-does.

in the stomach. I ducked sheepishly behind the fans. Keep in mind McCormack could have me fired. I came out later, and she said, "You're gonna be mad at me."

"Why?" I asked.

"Well, I saw your coach, and I told him he is not playing my husband enough. I stuck my finger in his big fat belly while I was doing it."

"Holy shit."

"I enjoyed that," she said.

"I'm in trouble now."

When I saw McCormack later, I said, "I apologize for my wife."

But I actually agreed with her opinion that I wasn't being played enough. In retrospect, she realized that her anger, frustration, and heightened sense of loyalty to me could have cost me my job, and she regretted confronting McCormack. I had been replaced by a younger player after I had played a perfect game. While I recognized that my replacement was a very good athlete, I theorized that my not playing had much more to do with my political stance than it did with my performance or his, for that matter. He indicated to me that even he was surprised he was replacing me.

A reputation for being politically active doesn't go away. It sticks with you. A lot of teammates and fans resented my involvement, but that didn't bother me. Hall of Fame quarterback Johnny Unitas saw me at an airport later that year.

"Stay away from me, you dirty fucking commie pinko bastard," Johnny said.

I knew I was on George Allen's shitlist because of my politics, even though his boss, owner Edward Bennett Williams, was known to be a huge Democratic supporter. But when McCormack criticized me for shunning Nixon in a tense conversation that was broken up by one of the managers, I understood that my job might be in jeopardy. They had started replacing me with my backup after the 1971 playoffs when I'd gotten hurt.

Then, McCormack came to me on the Redskins training field right before the 1972 season and said, "Coach wants to talk to you."

I headed over to talk to Allen, who was standing in the end zone. "It's been brought to my attention that you've been disrespectful to our Commander in Chief," he said. "And you've been disloyal to the team." Players were walking by and some stopped to watch the exchange.

I exploded. "If you want to cut me, cut me," I answered, "Don't use loyalty as your reason. That's bullshit." I held up my pinky and said, "I have more loyalty in this little finger than anybody on this entire team." I stormed off the field and into the locker room.

I was honestly mystified—and horrified—at how implicitly criticizing the president could be seen as a betrayal of my team. I viewed politics as a contest of ideas, and I looked at my involvement as the moral duty of any citizen. Allen did not appear to feel this way. He had taken it personally that one of his players came out publicly against his friend.

The sense of unease continued through the 1972 exhibition season. The week before the season opened with our first regular game, when the coaches made their final decision on the team roster and the last cuts, I walked into Allen's office on a Tuesday.

"I'm not going out there until you tell me whether or not you're going to cut me," I said.

He hemmed and hawed and finally blurted out, "No, we're not going to cut you."

He didn't cut me, but I got demoted. I played backup.

We went 11-3[92] in the regular season, even with Sonny tearing his Achilles tendon in the seventh game of the season in New York. Billy took over, and in the playoffs, we beat Green Bay (16-3) and Dallas (26-3) to win the National Football Conference championship. I had great games in the playoffs. Against the Packers, the regular right

---

92 Marshall. "YOU WON'T HAVE WASHINGTON TO KICK AROUND ANYMORE."

guard, John Wilbur, was hurt, so I played right guard. Then, I played left tackle against the Cowboys after Terry Hermeling got hurt.

But I am getting banged up a bit myself. I go to see the doctor, Stan Lavine, during the season, and he looks at my knees and X-rays and says, "You can't play anymore."

"Stan, don't tell me I can't play; tell me *how* I can play."

"You guys are all crazy," he says.

He wasn't wrong. By that time, I was actually known in the locker room as "the Mummy" because of the endless yards of athletic tape I used to hold myself together for practices and games.[93]

CONTROLLING MY DESTINY

Those last three years with the team, I either started or was a backup, and I had some great games. In 1973, we were 10-4 and lost to the Vikings in the playoffs. The Vikings had a defensive tackle who was one of my nemeses: Alan Page. The Vikings' defensive line was known as "the Purple People Eaters" because they were so good at sacking or hurrying a quarterback, and Alan is considered one of the greatest defensive linemen ever to play the game.

Alan was smart (in his post-football legal career, he ended up as a judge), but more importantly, he was quick. His first move was to grab you underneath your armpits and grab ahold of your pads from underneath; he jerked you, trying to control you that way. He was so fast that he could grab you before you could do anything; then he threw you. Well, when he grabbed me, I clamped my arms down over his, and we locked in. He was trying to throw me, but he was throwing himself at the same time. We'd end up locked together. He couldn't get his hands loose, and I wasn't about to let go.

---

[93] Shapiro, Leonard. *Perspective.* "They Were the First Redskins to Play in the Super Bowl. Decades Later, They're Paying the Price." *The Washington Post,* WP Company, 3 Feb 2018. https://www.washingtonpost.com/outlook/they-were-the-first-redskins-to-play-in-the-super-bowl-decades-later-theyre-paying-the-price/2018/02/02/05d967c0-ff88-11e7-9d31-d72cf78dbeee_story.html.

He'd try to get his hands back, and I'd get in his face and say, "Quit grabbing me, man."

The coaches looked at us in the films, tussling like two jiujitsu fighters struggling for a takedown, with neither of us gaining control of the other, and say, "What the hell are you doing, Schoenke? You're dancing out there!" It wasn't an intellectual battle; it was strictly physical.

Defensive ends come at things differently. Ed "Too Tall" Jones played for the Cowboys. When he hit the league, he was dynamite because he was so tall and fast, and he rushed from the outside. He played right defensive end against the left offensive tackle. He came around the corner on a tackle and slapped you on the side of the head to stun you, then turned into you with great strength and speed, knocking you to the ground and heading straight for the quarterback. This was a right-handed quarterback's blind side, so when Too Tall came in and hit the quarterback, it could be devastating. In 1974, I played left tackle, and I faced off with Too Tall. I knew his game. He was going to try to come in, grab me, slap me on the side of the head, pull me out of the way with his right hand, plant his right foot, pivot, run five yards straight at the quarterback, and just kill him. I had studied film on him for hours to figure out how to time my block—how to time things and adjust to his moves. I had to hit him just when he planted his right foot to pivot. That's when he was potentially off-balance and vulnerable. He was using his physical strength to defeat me, not his head. I was using my head—technique and timing. If I could hit him right then, as he planted his right foot, he'd go over like a big tree. I tried it, and it worked. He couldn't figure out what the hell happened. Billy Kilmer saw Too Tall lying on the ground after he threw the pass.

"Can I give you a hand?" Kilmer asked with a smirk on his face.

Too Tall was furious. "Go fuck yourself." (Too Tall will say he doesn't swear. That's what I *thought* I heard.)

That season, 1974, I started 13 games. We played the Dolphins, the repeat Super Bowl champions from the year before, and when Sonny drove us to the winning touchdown late in the game, we won, 20-17. That was awesome, a chance for both of us to play a game as big as the Super Bowl. For me, it was a chance to go up against Bill Stanfill, one of the greatest Dolphins ever, and to show I could block against the best. He was similar in quickness to Bob Lilly in terms of his quickness off the line of scrimmage, but he was a defensive end, and I was offensive tackle. Like Lilly, he crowded the line of scrimmage to get close to me. So I risked a penalty by moving so far back from the line of scrimmage that in films my coaches said I looked like I was a slot back. I defended myself by letting them know that he was so fast off the line, I needed the extra space to counter him. They told me that I was lucky I didn't get a penalty. Because I was so far away, I had plenty of time to anticipate what he was going to do, and I was successful at stopping him. For Sonny, it was his swan song—his last season before he retired. Sonny was incredibly talented; he needed only three seconds to get rid of the ball—to put it where he wanted. He very seldom needed more.

Later, we're playing the Eagles. All-Pro offensive tackle Jim Tyrer, my backup at the time, cornered the line coach, Bill Austin, and urged him to put him in the game. Jim, who was an All-Pro, had been traded from the Chiefs in late August of 1974 for three draft picks and came to the Redskins for his 14th and final season. Remember, at this point, I was almost in my last season, too. Everyone knew George Allen liked his veterans.

Tyrer kept saying to the coach, "Schoenke shouldn't be playing. You traded for me. I'm the guy." They took me out of the game in the second half and put Tyrer in. The defensive end got around Tyrer, and the first thing you knew, I was back in. Word had come from the quarterback. Billy Kilmer wanted me back in the game.

We finished 10-4 that season. We lost, 19-10, to the Rams in the playoffs. I hurt my knee in that game, playing against Fred Dryer, but I played the whole game.

"You didn't have a knee, did you?" Kilmer asked me later.

My last year at the Redskins, 1975, I started 10 of our 14 games, which was tough given my role. We finished 8-6 but did not make the playoffs. I was the first backup—the first person to replace any guard or tackle on the line when someone got hurt, my signature role, which I had played for four seasons. Each position required different positioning of my feet and blocks with different styles, one requiring me to counter a rush from the inside straight over me to one where my opponent predominately rushed me from the outside to my outside shoulder. But I was used to it, and the team valued my ability to play multiple positions as one of my greatest assets.

In the game against Cincinnati, I'm playing left guard, and the coach says, "You gotta play right tackle."

"What's wrong?" I ask.

"George Starke is hurt."

I go down there, and I say, "George, what's the matter?" He's barely able to say anything, moaning with his mouth wide open. He has a bone sticking straight up out of his thumb like another thumb. I say, "George, *just tape it up*! Didn't you take any drugs?"

He shook his head. "I don't take drugs."

I was pissed. It was the third quarter; we were behind; it was hot, and the Bengals were in control of the game at the time, and we were fighting to get back into it. If he had taken some drugs, it would have helped to deaden the pain. He wouldn't even know he *had* a thumb. So I had to play his position. When you do that, the guys that you're up against know you're adjusting, and they try to mess with you. They try to confuse you by running stunts with the defensive end knifing to the inside and the defensive tackle coming around him and driving for the quarterback.

These guys start taunting me, making fun of me on the field during play. They yell things like "Hey, Schoenke, you're a fuckin' Commie." But I manage to hold 'em off. That gave me a lot of points.

One of the Bengals' defensive tackles, Mike Reed, in addition to being an All-Pro player, was also a classical pianist in the off-season, and later became a country singer. Too bad it was George whose hand looked like he was holding a chicken bone. If Reid's hands looked like mine or George's, he would never have been able to play the piano. His fingers and thumbs must not have been dislocated as often as mine. Or maybe that's why he started singing. George (in spite of this injury) went on to become the head "Hog" in the Gibbs dynasty and had an outstanding career with the Washington Redskins. We continued to have a relationship after our football careers ended. I recently spoke with George and joked with him about his thumb. He told me that 10 years later, he was in a game against the Philadelphia Eagles cutting off Pro-Football Hall of Famer defensive end Claude Humphrey:

The surface of the turf we were playing on was not good and was rough, and as he was cutting up the middle, my hand got caught on the turf, and all of the bones in that same hand broke. I didn't even consider leaving the game. They looked at it on the sideline and informed me that the hand was severely broken, and I assured them I was well aware of that and went back out on the field, attempting to conceal the injury from Claude Humphrey, who was right in front of me. I'm sure he knew that my stance was off because my "down" hand was not really touching the field, but had he known the hand was broken, he would surely have grabbed that hand as soon as the play was called. I now know Ray was right. 10 years later, I would have stuck the skin back around that bone on my thumb, taped it up, and returned to the field. What I realize now is that that over the years we play, we gradually transition from normal humans into warriors who literally have to be carried off the field.[94]

---

94 Note: Quote from a phone conversation I had with George in 2022.

My own greatest moment came against the top defensive lineman in the league, Jerry Sherk, who was with the Cleveland Browns. He was a superior physical being—relying on his quickness and strength. But more importantly, he was *smart*. Trying to outthink him was one of the most fun experiences I had in football. You use your brains and combine this with your physical ability. Most of the guys I played against were just big brutes. I want to say I held Sherk out every time, but I didn't. It was still the pinnacle of my career. In him, I had met my match.

After retiring from football, Sherk worked as a sports photographer and then returned to college and got his master's degree in counseling psychology. Like me, he was concerned about what happens to an athlete after he is "done being a hero."[95] Unlike many football players, I was aware of this reality and started preparing for my post-football life while I was still playing. The biggest problem is the financial disruption, which I had covered. According to Sherk, players enter "a confusing season of life" and "are left depressed, injured, unemployed, and bewildered when the cheering stops and the stadium stands empty."[96] He became an expert on mentoring programs and has had a successful career developing mentoring programs and promoting mentoring at many levels.

The playoff game against Dallas was an especially thrilling night. It was New Year's Eve, and we were playing at RFK Stadium. The town's football fans no longer tolerated defeat, and they bellowed deafeningly. With Billy Kilmer leading us, we buried Dallas 26-3.

It was our first division title since 1945 and our first playoff win since 1943. It was Allen's first-ever playoff win. That evening, Nancy and I went to Christmas service at our church, and when we walked in, everybody stood up and applauded. The whole town was euphoric.

---

95 Milt Right and Associates Inc. n.d. https://www.miltwright.com/jerry-shark-bio.
96 Ibid.

The Washington Redskins were headed to the Super Bowl for the first time—Super Bowl VII, the epic matchup between the teams of George Allen and Don Shula. The Miami Dolphins were (and remain) the only team in National Football League history to finish the regular season and the postseason undefeated. Yet we were making our first-ever Super Bowl appearance and were slightly favored to win. It was among the most important of games for both franchises, and for many of us, it represented the ultimate achievement of our playing careers.

Leonard Shapiro of *The Washington Post* described the game:

That game was the hottest in Super Bowl history (it was 84 degrees in Los Angeles that afternoon). It is also the lowest-scoring. Washington held Miami to two touchdowns, shutting out the Dolphins in the second half. But Washington's offense never could score, and the Redskins' only touchdown came on a fluky fumble recovery after a blocked field goal in the fourth quarter that is still recalled as one of the more bizarre plays in Super Bowl annals. Miami won 14-7—and finished the season 17-0.[97]

Making it to the Super Bowl was huge, but to me, the spirit of the team was something to behold. Because I played well at two different positions in the two playoff games, the most important games in the history of the franchise, even though my knees were shot, I felt elated. I knew that no one else on the team could have done that.

Later, after the playoff games, McCormack told me, "I knew you could do it."

I wanted to say, "Then why wasn't I starting the entire season?"

Another example of the team spirit was the attitude of the team toward Jerry Smith. Many of the players knew he was gay and totally accepted him, which was a significant thing in 1972 among athletes.

---

97 Shapiro, Leonard. "They were the first Redskins to play in the Super Bowl. Decades later, they're paying the price." *The Washington Post*, 02 Feb 2018.

He was tough as you can be. And incredibly talented. Once he tore his stomach muscle, and his scrotum was filled with blood, but he refused to come out of the game. The new team doctor at the time was afraid to tell the coach he could not play, and Jerry wanted to play, so he did. He was ultimately hospitalized for the injury.

Sometime after Jerry retired in 1978, I heard that he had contracted HIV and that he was in the hospital dying.[98] I went to see him, and on my way into the hospital, I struggled with whether I would hug him. At the time, HIV was still somewhat of a mystery. It wasn't clearly known where it came from or how it was spread. HIV wards were viewed like leper colonies, and the disease was heavily stigmatized. I walked into his room, and he was lying reclined, somewhat upright, in his hospital bed. He was pale, and his face looked tight and strained. He smiled when he greeted me, but his eyes betrayed the depth of his sadness. He was *so* emaciated, a shadow of the Jerry Smith I knew. I instinctively and without hesitation leaned toward him to hug him, and he struggled to lean forward and hug me back. In my arms, he felt weak and lifeless. It was like holding an empty shell. We were both *so* sad. It was heart-rending. That was the last time I saw him. My life went on, and he was gone, just like that.

I continued to grow in the sport. Years later, *Sports Illustrated* writer Joe Marshall hit the nail on the head in terms of the way my relationship with George Allen was evolving. Moments after the Dallas win, Marshall encountered an old-timer in the Redskins locker room and asked him about Allen's genius:

> *"Take Ray Schoenke," says the veteran. "He sat on the bench all year, and he had to know the plays for every line position. Last week [in the playoffs], he filled in at guard and did a great job. Now today he has to go in at tackle and do another great job.*

---

[98] NFL network. "'A Football Life': How Jerry Smith faced his AIDS diagnosis." https://www.nfl.com/videos/a-football-life-how-jerry-smith-faced-his-aids-diagnosis-279269.

You think George Allen will ever forget that? Ray Schoenke will be on pension with the Redskins for the rest of his life."[99]

The Redskins didn't give me a pension for the rest of my life (the NFL did), but I knew that George Allen had come to appreciate me. As I was getting ready for training camp in 1973, I had a new goal. Although I knew I had proven myself to Allen, I sensed that there was lingering ambiguity. I decided to make a chess move.

"I'm never gonna play for you again unless I get a guaranteed contract." And I held out.

Two days before the start of camp, Allen's secretary calls. "Do you want to hear about your contract?"

"Yes."

And she read, "I, George Allen, General Manager and Head Coach of the Washington Redskins, guarantee to you, Ray Schoenke, your contract for the upcoming season."

"Tell him I'm on my way," I said. He did the same for the next three seasons. A no-cut contract. In a funny way, standing up to him solidified my position with him. I wanted to remain a valuable member of the team's offensive line, moving back and forth from guard to tackle as needed. And he realized that he could count on me and not just to be loyal to the team. I would play any position on the line anytime. It had taken three years for him to figure me out. But then he stepped up for me, and I stepped up for him.

Part of Allen's hesitation had been my dedication to my burgeoning business. But he realized that I could run a business, *and* I could be there for the team. I might come in late, but I stayed late. And I studied every position.

Coach Allen was a different animal. He let me leave early or come in late because he knew I would be ready. I got to know what turned him

---

[99] Marshall. "YOU WON'T HAVE WASHINGTON TO KICK AROUND ANYMORE."

on and off. I had a lot of respect for him as a coach, and he respected my ability, my intellect. I played in key games for him, in different positions, and we won. He had questioned me, questioned my loyalty. But when I said, "I'm never gonna play for you again unless I get a guaranteed contract," and he gave it to me, I think he realized that he didn't have to worry about me. He knew I was dedicated and committed. He could count on me. I got to know his family, and I really liked them. It helped that his wife loved Hawai'i. He and his wife even attended a dinner party at my home along with other Washington dignitaries, including Roger and E.J. Mudd, Ethel Kennedy, and several of my teammates.

Most coaches hate anything that takes your focus away from football. They want players to be totally focused on the game plan and the execution of the plays that are in that game plan—literally, to have tunnel vision. Outside interests are heavily discouraged, and political interests that are at odds with their own are not welcomed and, in some cases, not tolerated. In the end, George appreciated my multiple dimensions. He saw that I was out of the mold but that it didn't compromise me as a player.

During my last year, he called me over after practice as I was walking into the fieldhouse and told me he was actually going out to dinner with George McGovern. And he told me he was going to give McGovern season tickets in a season when you could not get season tickets. I went from being just a player to a player trying to figure out how I could help him motivate the team. Each opposing team had a different personality, and as he'd try to put together a game plan, I tried to offer insight on those teams. Once he trusted me, I had complete trust in him. We developed a bond. In this relationship, I was really learning about leadership. I'd often stay after practice and just talk to him—we talked psychology and the philosophy of the game. I think he knew I was always thinking about the team first.

I made $42,000 each year over the next three seasons—'73, '74, and '75. In 2022, at a modest interest rate, that's $270,000 per year. For those times, this was a lot of money. Players then didn't *have* to work, or at least not seriously, but I had had such a precarious early career that I didn't trust the system. And I was very focused on making a lot of money in life, period. During that same period, my annual income for my insurance business on a part-time basis was about $80,000, which, converted into today's currency, would make my total annual income just over a half million dollars, so I didn't need my football checks. I deferred all of it until I retired. I was building toward that time when I could walk away from the game. That final three years of salary from the Redskins came to $126,000, so I banked the equivalent of $810,175 in today's currency.[100]

I retired after the 1975 season. I had been in the NFL for 12 years. It was time to turn my attention to growing my corporate insurance business, politics, civic affairs, and my family. In the end, I walked away from the game on my own terms, which my teammates respected and which, I think, George Allen respected. He knew I wanted to be the one to call the end of my career.

Our offensive coach, Ted Marchibroda, went to the Baltimore Colts and wanted me to be his line coach, so I briefly entertained the notion of staying in the game as a coach. But I finally said, "Thank you, but no thanks." I wanted to control my destiny, and I'd figured out that the only person who controls his destiny in football or any other industry is the owner.

---

100 Value of 1969 US Dollars today. *Inflation Tool.* "Inflation Calculator – US Dollar."

CHAPTER SIX

Lessons from the Game (1953–1975)

My parents were proud of me but did not see the game quite as I did. My father was the reason I became an athlete, but he wasn't passionate about the pro game. We never had an in-depth discussion about football. My parents lived in Texas and then Florida during my pro football career, but I didn't see them a lot when we lived in Washington. We weren't close. I think there might have been some tension because Nancy was Southern, and my mother was Hawaiian, and they might have had insecurities about that. They did enjoy seeing the children and coming up for games. I could see that my mother enjoyed the status of having a son in the NFL. She also appreciated my business success. I reflect from time to time, like all adult children, about the role my parents played in the development of my character.

My father was a man of few words. He had provided steadiness when my mother was off the wall, fighting the demons of her past. Of course, I got my athleticism from him. I had exposure as a young boy to sports in Weatherford, seeing that the kids who worked out real hard became district champions. I was naturally big and strong and fast, but I also worked out longer and harder than most of my teammates.

I got my drive from my mother. I know that my ability to take Vince Lombardi head-on came from Olivia Haleaka Schoenke. I had some of my father's laid-back affability, but I studied hard; I made sure I knew everything, and if someone like Lombardi questioned me, I could throw it right back in his face.

My professors at SMU also shaped me and encouraged my intellect. They believed I could get a Ph.D., and though I didn't, I benefited from their confidence in my ability to think things through, to analyze. But, of course, when you are a football player, it is your coaches who really shape you, and every one of my coaches was different.

When you get to the pros, your first challenge is that you have to relearn things. I was lucky that with the Cowboys, veterans showed me the techniques I needed to play the game as a rookie. With the Packers and the Browns, veterans showed me the things that were unique to their team and the style of play. The next challenge is to be a player who can execute—not in practice but in a game, and under game conditions, where there's a lot of pressure. But that's just the beginning of making it in the pros.

You must deal with your coach, the system, all the other players, locker-room machinations, competition, roommates. You have to avoid the pitfalls that you will encounter. I learned pass blocking and run blocking, but I had to be able to execute those skills, time in and time out, and sometimes you have only seconds to adjust after an audible. You can't make a mistake, and if you do, you have to keep functioning. I had to develop a totally focused state of mind. Everything has to line up. Sometimes coaches don't like the way a player looks. You're too fat, too skinny, you don't carry yourself well, you are too good-looking, which might suggest you are a pretty boy who doesn't want his face smashed up. Sometimes players are outstanding athletes, and they never get a shot. Sometimes players get shots, and they lack talent. And sometimes players get better over time.

Your success doesn't just depend on you. It depends on the attitude of your direct coach and the head coach who creates the system that surrounds you. You might get a coach who knows how to motivate you through fear or flattery. You might get a coach who's caring and genuinely tries to help you. It's really the luck of the draw. The personality of a coach can even change over time. They are dealing with a whole other set of challenges. The tremendous pressure on a coach and the fear of losing his job can transform his personality over time. Another interesting aspect of being a pro football player is the relationships you form with other players and the effects those relationships have on your perspective of the game and how you handle the challenges.

At first in the NFL, I was just trying to be a good football player, be a good team member. I thought that would earn the respect of my coaches. I thought athletic skills should be enough. I was involved in other things. I got involved in politics because that was my love and interest, but I ran up against a wall. Outside interests were sometimes perceived to be in conflict with caring about football. All I wanted from my coaches was to be graded as a football player. But coaches are human beings. They have perceptions and their own unique instincts. They have personalities. I came to realize that coaches might make decisions based not on your football abilities but on what *they* think is important. You had to fit a mold. Unfortunately, I never fit the mold that most coaches wanted. I was always on someone's shitlist.

After our last season together, Allen gave me a "game ball." After a game, the coaches and the captain picked a player or players who had had a great game and tossed a football to the player with the standard yell. For me, it was, "Hoo-ray, Hoo-ray, Hoo-ray at last; Hoo-ray for Ray, he's a horse's ass." On January 21, 1976, I was given the game ball from Coach Allen, with this inscription:

To Ray Schoenke. We had 5 great years together. You are a winner and always will be. Stay in shape. Your friend, George H. Allen

REFLECTIONS ON COACHES AND HOW THEY CREATE WINNING TEAMS

I have had the privilege of playing for some of the greatest coaches in NFL history. Three of them were Hall of Fame coaches—Vince Lombardi, Tom Landry, and George Allen. Some had winning teams while I was on the team, and some developed a winning team over time. Based on my experience, several factors contribute to how coaches lead a team to victory. First, the personality of the coach and his coaching style affects whether or not a player is inspired and wants to please the coach. There are differences between how criticism and praise from a coach affect a player and ultimately how motivated that player is and how he feels about the coach and his motivational techniques (or lack of them.) The two factors most critical to developing a winning team, in my opinion, are the system the coach uses and the ability of that coach to select a winning roster of extremely talented players who believe in or are willing to adhere to the system or bend to the will of the coach and his leadership, whether he is a tyrant, an intellectual genius, yells at you, is calm and composed, or ignores you completely.

Having a winning team is inspirational regardless of what a coach puts you through to get there or whether the coach himself is inspirational. When you play well and win, you gain recognition from the coach, the team, the fans, and the city you play in. What follows is an overview of the coaches I have played for and the effects these specific factors contributed to producing a winning team or failing to do so.

BEGINNINGS: THE JUNIOR HIGH SCHOOL YEARS

Garrett Fagan, associate professor of Classics and Ancient Mediterranean Studies and History at Penn State,[101] refers to the public's obsession with contact sports as "a consistent appetite for violence as spectacle," and current football players are often compared in articles

---

[101] Pennsylvania State University. "Probing Question: Is football similar to Roman gladiator games?" PHYS ORG., Sept 2009. https://phys.org/news/2009-09-probing-football-similar-roman-gladiator.html.

to ancient gladiators. I often refer to my experiences on the field as participating in what I call "controlled violence." When you are 12 years old, put on a helmet and pads for the first time, and have to hit people, it is frightening and unnatural. It is incredibly intimidating. You are full of fear that you are going to get hurt. You have to relish hitting people and trust that the gear you have on is going to blunt the force of hitting someone. It still hurts. You have to reconcile yourself with that.

COACH WHITE, WEATHERFORD JUNIOR HIGH, WEATHERFORD, TEXAS—AGE 13

Coach White radiated confidence and was both nice and tough. Even looking at him was inspirational. His nose had been smashed and flattened against his face in competition, which affected how he sounded when he talked. He always sounded as if he had a cold. He walked with a jaunt and radiated a kind of physical confidence that suggested no one could mess with him. He was a champion golden glove boxer and used a boxing analogy to coach—being tough and taking hits. Coach White talked about being in the ring and getting the crap beaten out of him. We felt if he could handle that with no protective gear, we should be able to do it with all this gear on. We also learned that if your opponent doesn't get up, you feel good.

He was a very creative offensive coach. He wasn't afraid to use the pass as a weapon, which you typically don't see at the junior high school level. The game was new to us in an organized way. All we had done is play pickup games. However, I had learned to tackle to a certain degree defending myself against bullies on the playground. It was an easier transition for me than for some of the kids because I had already experienced the pain involved in tackling someone without gear, and I was bigger and had better athletic skills than most of the other players. I probably had less fear than most of the other guys. Coach White gave us an idea of how coaching works and what we had to accomplish to play on a high school team. If I kept making a mistake, he stopped, got my attention by getting in my face, told me I could do better, and showed me again.

Coach White also spent individual time with me to improve my skills. Not just any coach will do that. I did what I was told, and he praised me for following directions. Later in my career under Lombardi, I began to fully understand how powerful praise is as a motivator. It literally becomes what you live for in an atmosphere where you risk injury or fear losing your job, play injured, and face highly skilled opponents who can take you out of the game in a single play just to hear a coach like Lombardi yell, "GODDAMMIT, SCHOENKE! THATTA WAY TO BLOCK, SCHOENKE! THAT'S WHAT I CALL A GOOD BLOCK!"

White's system involved a dominant offense combined with good defense. He had a running game that could go outside and inside. He was good at grooming and locating talent at the junior high school level, so he had a great roster of players, and he had a good defensive line. He looked to his quarterbacks to lead the team and implement his system. He had a winning team.

COACH ALLEN, WEATHERFORD JUNIOR HIGH SCHOOL, WEATHERFORD, TEXAS—AGE 14

Coach Allen was a very quiet, even-keeled coach, who was smart and was willing to take the time to ensure his players knew the basics. He was a technical coach who emphasized the importance of team play. At our tender age, he was protecting the fragile egos of sensitive young athletes who might give up football if he was too harsh. He was fair, which I define as a balanced mix of criticism and praise, and not using praise to make a player feel that he was better than someone else. He certainly kept my ego in check. He knew how to praise a talented player without turning him into a hot dog. He corrected players in front of the team in a quiet way when they made mistakes. He taught us to play for our teammates, not for ourselves. He worked with players individually and as a team. He was molding young players with his system, which was a thorough offensive and defensive system that he knew how to implement in young players, and his roster was loaded with talented eighth graders fed in from grade schools all over the city. He had the two components necessary to have a winning team—a good system and talented players—and he had a winning team.

THE HIGH SCHOOL YEARS

At the high school level, you are playing with teammates and against opponents who are often more mature and more athletic than you are as a freshman and/or sophomore. Because of your inexperience, you are easily taken advantage of physically and mentally. Once you adapt to the system your coach is using and the basics of tackling and blocking at a higher level than you encountered in junior high school, you gain confidence and garner praise. With that comes the potential for recognition.

COACH MONAHAN, PUNAHOU HIGH SCHOOL—AGE 15 AND 16

Coach Monahan was a no-bullshit kind of guy—direct, tough, and fair. He was very direct and made it clear what he expected. He came out of the Ivy League and was very disciplined. He had served as an officer in Korea as a Marine, so he was also a disciplinarian. He presented as a man who was in great shape, which garnered respect from us as players. He praised intellect. Part of football is executing as many as 40 to 60 plays in a single game, so being able to memorize plays and effectively study other players is a big part of the game. If you have studied a player and know how to counter his defenses, you can quickly and efficiently anticipate what he is going to do. Monahan was working with more experienced, older kids, who were more mature and better athletes, so he could afford to be very demanding.

At the end of practice, if he was very upset with us, he made us run the "bowl" up and down that steep slope. Depending on how pissed off he was, he might make you do it two or three times. Transgressors tried to outrun us, and if we caught them, a lot of the guys kicked them. Coach had informers, so he was able to enforce curfew. He punished the whole team if a guy was late to practice or failed to meet curfew. His offensive and defensive systems were set, and you were expected to be able to run them efficiently and perfectly. He played a running game with simple passes. He didn't believe in a lot of different types of fake plays. He believed in going straight at the defense with a running game and limited passing. His players were picked for him by the athletic director, who looked for players in the city and suburbs of Honolulu and also drew players from organized sports teams on the outer islands and offered them scholarships to Punahou.

He had a winning team because he had the two central components necessary to win—a strong, executable system and a powerful roster.

COACH COFFEE, WEATHERFORD HIGH SCHOOL, WEATHERFORD, TEXAS—AGE 17

Coach Coffee was a quarterback in college. He was upbeat and positive. He was very handsome and never looked sloppy. I was impressed by the fact that he always looked good and never seemed to sweat. His looks generated positive attitudes toward him. When he spoke, he spoke clearly and precisely. He was thoughtful. When he explained things, he was polite and treated everyone with respect. He didn't threaten or degrade us when he was upset. He was smart and disciplined, and he believed in throwing the ball. He had a disciplined offensive system, and he was a very creative offensive coach.

In high school football, there are not many teams that have a wide-open offense. They tend to be more fundamental. He went over and over the timing of plays and taught us how to deal with the different defenses we would encounter. He needed key players, particularly a quarterback who could throw the ball accurately. He also needed a strong running game to complement the passing. He found the talented players from local junior high schools that he needed to execute his system. He took all this talent and organized it and put it together in a systematic way so players knew how, when, and where to execute under game conditions and under enormous pressure to win. Familiarity with the system led to success. We had one of the best high school teams in Texas that year.

THE COLLEGE YEARS

College football was straight-ahead stuff. You learned that you had to block or knock the guys in front of you out of the way so somebody could run past you. The few times the ball was thrown, you had to stay in front of the guy, and it was relatively simple.

COACH MEEK, SMU—SOPHOMORE AND JUNIOR YEAR

Coach Meek was a gentleman, but he was not an inspiring coach. He wasn't a warm, personable guy. He looked and acted like you would think George Washington would have. He didn't get his hands dirty. He let his assistants do that. He built a reputation out of the University of Houston based on a bunch of renegades, players who weren't full-time students and were "hired guns" brought in to play football. He built the team around Don Meredith because Don was very flexible, and he had also a good roster. After Don and most of his teammates graduated, and his backup quarterback flunked out, Meek went through one sophomore quarterback and four freshman quarterbacks, all of whom were All-State, and all of whom failed miserably because they had no leadership skills or the skills necessary to be an effective quarterback.

An example of this was the last of this group. We were playing Rice. He looked at me in the huddle, and he said, "What play do you guys wanna run?"

"You're the quarterback. It's your job to call the play," I replied.

He called the play, but it didn't give us any confidence, that's for sure. Meek's system was very dependent on an extremely effective passing quarterback and a very tough defense. He relied on his assistant coaches to implement his system, both offensively and defensively. His roster was simply too unstable for the team to have continuity or to be a winning team against the outstanding opponents we were playing against. We lost all our games that year.

HAYDEN FRYE, SMU—SENIOR YEAR

Coach Frye was an extremely confident man. He was hard-nosed and very demanding—an "in your face" kinda guy. He came off as very ambitious and full of himself. He didn't hesitate to sacrifice a player to achieve his goals. He tried to be legitimate, but he wasn't afraid to break some rules. He didn't like having one member of the team getting a lot of attention. He was willing to sacrifice a single player to unify the team by turning them against any single player who was the focus of media attention. He fed off the team's resentment toward that player. It was a kind of an 'end justifies the means' approach. He was able to inspire the team by ridiculing me, for example. The team enjoyed this. He took this approach to motivating his team, which was not good for me.

His system was a running system built around Arkansas football, which at the time was a very fast game off the run, and all passes were fake off the run. However, his roster was weak. He lacked a reputation as a head coach that possibly would have attracted talent, so he had to use the team he had on hand. He wore players out, and his system was very demanding on the team in a hot environment and led to a risk of heatstroke or even death. His system was very new, and he didn't have the personnel to complement it. However, over time, he built a winning team, used this system, and took it to the Cotton Bowl.

THE NFL: DALLAS COWBOYS, GREEN BAY PACKERS, CLEVELAND BROWNS, WASHINGTON REDSKINS

Coaches in the NFL are their own breed. There are a lot of assholes and a lot of failures. But the good coaches allow you to learn about leadership—if you're interested enough to learn. A coach is dealing with a sport that's violent; he has to be able to motivate players to do things that are violent that can hurt them, that can scare them. He has to motivate men to become part of a team and to do things that are potentially dangerous. He is putting a man in a position to see an opponent who is ready to knock the shit outta him who must move quickly enough to counter an attack and knock the shit outta that guy first.

A coach also has to deal with players who make mistakes and pressure them not to make mistakes when it's inevitable that they will. And they will get hurt. And then they will get rehabilitated if they are lucky, and the coach needs to convince them to do it all over again, at 100 percent, even though they may not really be able to and may still be healing from an injury. Injuries include things like torn cartilage, torn ligaments in knees, ankles, fingers and shoulders, dislocated shoulders, elbows, hips, ankles, and fingers, rib injuries (separated rib cages, broken ribs), broken bones (noses, ribs, legs, ankles, fingers), concussions, brain damage, eye injuries and temporary double vision, lost or loose teeth, heatstroke, loss of consciousness, spine injuries, heart attacks, permanent or temporary nerve damage, severed fingers. You often have to play with any one or more of these injuries, and risk reinjury, exacerbating a current injury, or even the loss of your career.

Without coaches, men will not walk onto the field. Good and bad coaches put a lot of pressure on players and demand perfection, and if players don't give it, they get chastised and can lose their jobs. Consequently, a lot of players play hurt, and some succeed, while others are not so fortunate and, in the process, destroy their careers, their bodies, or both.

TOM LANDRY: DALLAS COWBOYS

Tom Landry was cold and impersonal. He didn't inspire players by connecting with them, and he didn't invest in building a relationship with team members—or at least not with rookies like me. In essence, his style was a fear-driven approach to coaching even though he didn't yell or scream at players.

He had a system he believed in and wouldn't deviate from. His defensive system was known as the "Flex Defense." After carefully studying films on the opposing team, Landry designed a defense where the defensive tackles and defensive ends were staggered strategically along the line of scrimmage, either on the line or a yard behind the line positioned directly in front of the opposing offensive linemen or to their inside or outside shoulder. This was in response to a call from the defensive captain based on the formation of the offensive linemen and backfield after they left the huddle. This defense could make it more difficult for the offensive linemen to block the linebackers, who were behind the defensive linemen or strategically placed in gaps.

One of his most effective offensive systems of several that he used was shifting his offense prior to the snap of the ball by having the linemen at the line of scrimmage with their hands on their knees. At a signal from the quarterback, the linemen would all stand up and then go down into a three-point stance. During the brief time the linemen were standing, the backfield and/or receivers would change their positions to create confusion, which could cause the other team to have to make rapid adjustments as the ball was being snapped. You adhered to this system. There was no gray area.

Players were expendable and easily replaced. Gil Brandt, the personnel director, claimed to have 20,000 names on his computer that he could draw from. It took five years for Landry to build a winning team for several reasons. One example of this is my line coach on the field, who was a head coach at the college level and did not understand line play in the NFL. He was in charge of making sure players made the transition between college play and the pros. However, he couldn't tell me how to make this transition or execute the system in my position because he had no idea how to do it himself.

Landry's lack of oversight of his line coaches set up players like me in a situation where the line coach could drive a wedge between a player and Landry. In the pros, the game is 60-70 percent pass blocking. Most college offenses were built on the run and not the pass at that time. When you came into the pros, the rules were more lenient for defensive linemen. If you didn't understand pass blocking techniques, it was very difficult to make the transition because the defensive player could grab you or punch you in the head and then throw you, which was legal in the pros at the time. If you didn't know how to counter that, you got annihilated. My line coach assumed if I was an outstanding player at the college level, I would understand how to do this, but I had to figure it out on my own. It was easier for players who had come from a passing game in college to make this transition. That was not the case with me.

I was in the early stages of Landry's system and played as a starter, but I had to play in games where I didn't have the skills that were necessary to be successful, and the veterans on the team weren't willing to share techniques with me because I was new and a competitive threat. It was like being thrown into a pool without knowing how to swim. Landry was lucky to have been given the time to overcome these issues and build his roster.

He also didn't address the racial issues on the team at the time, which were profound. All he cared about was recruiting and hiring great Black athletes from Southern schools that he could hire for low wages and easily replace along with exceptional southern White athletes in a segregated state, which he could also easily replace. This set up a potentially highly combustible situation and perpetrated the racial tension existing in society at the time. I assume that he thought the team would be unified by winning, which seemed to work for him most of the time.

When he had a winning team, and there was pressure on the Cowboys from the Redskins in a game, we knew we were breaking them, that we were on the way to victory, and that the Cowboys were losing cohesion when his White linebackers started yelling racial epithets at their own defensive Black linemen. It is very difficult for a system to work in that kind of atmosphere. A system only works when players are unified. Players who are unified pull each other together when a player makes a mistake. Players who are not unified usually turn on each other. There were cracks in Landry's system, and former Cowboys, both Black and White, knew how to widen that crack. But the bottom line was he still built winning teams.

BLANTON COLLIER: CLEVELAND BROWNS

Collier was a cordial but somewhat distant coach who really expected the players to understand what he wanted when he told them what to do. At the Browns, Collier seemed above the fray taking place on the field because his players knew the plays. It was an unusual team because everybody, particularly the starters, knew what to do and had been doing it for many years. They knew the plays, the defenses. He assumed you had the intellectual and athletic capacity to execute a play without running it on the practice field. He didn't need to motivate the team. When you came in there, you had to fit into an established system. He encouraged mental preparation as much as physical preparation and encouraged players to practice mentally as much as they did physically. He was looking for a roster that was pretty much a "finished product." Motivation was built in because his roster was made up of mostly veteran players who were familiar with the NFL and who had won with his system under Paul Brown. There was very little coaching necessary. Belief in the system was a motivator. They knew the system worked. They had great talent, and the only team that was in their way was the Green Bay Packers. They hated the Packers. Period. He consistently had winning teams.

OTTO GRAHAM: THE WASHINGTON REDSKINS

My first coach at the Redskins, Otto Graham, was a real gentleman. He was thoughtful, never mean, and never used fear to motivate players. He didn't chew people out. He showed his disapproval by being angry but never abusive. He ultimately struck me as naïve, but he shouldn't have been. He had been very successful as a quarterback in the NFL for the Cleveland Browns. He or his assistants informed you if you did something wrong. He encouraged a strong intellect and character that led to a player studying and executing pre-drawn-up plays well. In many ways, he represented the kind of human being I wanted to be.

But Otto was *too* nice. Putting a team together and playing in the NFL, at least in our generation, was difficult. Every game was a struggle. Otto won 50 percent of the games, but to make the playoffs, you had to win 80 percent. Unfortunately, his system was not a winning system. He had a passing attack. His mindset complimented our star quarterback, Sonny Jurgenson, and he had a good offensive roster. But he lacked a strong defensive team, so his team could score but couldn't defend itself. He was possibly not involved enough in the selection process to build an effective defensive roster. He did not have a winning team.

VINCE LOMBARDI: GREEN BAY PACKERS, THE WASHINGTON REDSKINS

Lombardi was a great coach, but he was incredibly mercurial. He was a genius in that he motivated through fear and knew how to dole out *and* withhold praise. He had a good system that was easy to understand and execute. He did not inspire you, but rather drove you toward excellence through fear and a need for his praise because his criticism was unbelievably intense, and his praise was equally intense. You eventually became inspired simply due to being on a winning team. Inspiration was a *result*, not a cause, of this type of motivation. He had good-to-excellent players. He felt if he had good players, his leadership would be enough to drive them to victory, which it did at the expense of players who could not handle his kind of pressure or were unable to play injured.

Coaches who raise their voices at players can be very demeaning. He destroyed the careers of many players who simply couldn't hold up to his in-your-face style of coaching or who succumbed to injuries or played with injuries that took them out of the game or ruined their careers along with their bodies. Lombardi sought out players who could handle violent criticism and could play injured. His system worked, and he had winning teams at the expense of the careers of many players. However, he did have redeeming qualities. Behind all the bluster, the volcanic anger, there was affection and a huge payoff—being on a winning team.

GEORGE ALLEN: THE WASHINGTON REDSKINS

George Allen had two personalities—one he had for the team, and one for behind closed doors. In front of the team, he was very clear that there was only one standard, and that was winning, and we had to win. He was upbeat and positive. He was always clapping his hands and cheering the players. Behind closed doors, he was more open to discussing the problems and issues related to players. He said to us when we started that we were going to be well-prepared, play with enthusiasm, have a team made up of great older veteran players along with young players, and declared that with his system, we would win. His roster was mostly older veteran players who came from winning teams who understood what it took to win, and he relied on their leadership to inspire the rest of the team because of their experience and ability to avoid mistakes. He used long, exhausting practices, and often, players complained behind his back. Repetition was his style.

His system was based on a belief that you could win through defense, and it was drilled into his players. It was very intense. He believed that defense was the most important thing, then special teams, then offense. He was primarily a defensive coach. He simply didn't want a lot of offense.

He said, "All I need is three scores, then we'll hold them to two." In either case, the defense was gonna win the game for us. Sonny Jurgenson was a problem for him. Sonny would say, "Screw that. I wanna win by 50." Allen felt that trying to score too many points by the pass on offense was too dangerous. He didn't want to risk interceptions or fumbles. Winning became the inspiration that shut down any complaints and criticism about the long practices. He had a defensive system that worked and veteran players who knew how to execute it. He had a winning team. When we won, it generated glorious mayhem.

JUNE JONES, UNIVERSITY OF HAWAI'I, SMU

I was never coached by June Jones, but I had the privilege of watching him coach at SMU for a week. June Jones is very calm and easygoing. He never raises his voice. He treats players with respect and shows that he has high expectations of them. He inspired his players at SMU using a proven system that he brought from the pros. He automatically garnered respect because of his reputation. This made it easy for him to recruit athletes who complimented the unique offensive system he had helped develop called the "run and shoot."[102] This ensured a roster of great players who would adhere to his system unflinchingly. He thus had a winning team.

OBSERVATIONS AS A PLAYER

To me, the ideal, most inspirational coach would be a fundamentally nice person—not demeaning or loud, who is respectful of the players and doesn't motivate through fear and threats of losing one's job. It would be a coach who has a proven system that is understandable and executable offensively, defensively, and with special teams. He has the personnel in all the positions on the team who can study and effectively execute the plays that are given to them, can adhere to the system,

---

[102] Coach Martin. "Run and Shoot Offense Football Coaching Guide." *Football Offense*. https://footballadvantage.com/run-and-shoot-offense/.

and can handle adversity. He is a coach who has leadership skills or who can pick players who will convince other players to execute his system and take them through the uncontrollable and difficult challenges they will face until they win—unpredictable or harsh weather, injuries, faulty equipment, field surfaces, personnel changes, illness, lack of sleep, substance and alcohol abuse, among others.

Unfortunately, there is no such coach, but in my experience, some coaches have the critical components that lead to a winning team even when they don't have an ideal personality and are not inspiring. The most critical component is a proven system. If a coach has that, even without an abundance of players who are experienced All-Pros, he can build a winning team if the team will adhere to the system and accept his direction and leadership or bend to his will.

Inspiration is not the same as motivation. They are not synonymous.[103] Inspiration motivates. Praise motivates. Fear motivates. Individual attention and support motivate. One *leads* to the other. Motivators can either enhance performance through inspiration, praise, and individual attention or can destroy an athletic career through evoking fear. Because of my volatile childhood experiences, I thrived in an atmosphere of fear and uncertainty. I had established an internal belief system that suggested that, at any moment, what appeared to be stable could, without warning, deteriorate into chaos and lead to failure. Life had supported this belief. It was easy once something went wrong to say, "See, I knew it was all going to fall apart! It was only a matter of time." It was this belief that drove me, and instability, losses, and failures supported this belief system and solidified it over my lifetime. Of all my coaches, Vince Lombardi fit into this belief system the best, which was why I performed so well for him in spite of feeling every game as if my life, physical well-being, and job were in jeopardy.

---

103 Surbi, S. "Difference Between Motivation and Inspiration." KEY DIFFERENCES. June 2018. https://keydifferences.com/difference-between-motivation-and-inspiration.html#ComparisonChart.

What I really wanted and needed was to motivate *myself*. George Allen accused me of being disloyal to the team and threatened my job security. But he was the only coach who took the time to understand me. He gave me a guaranteed contract and trusted I was a team player who wanted the team to win and knew I would be ready every Sunday to play whatever position he wanted me to play. Of all my coaches, I feel I played the best for George Allen because over time, our mutual trust was highly motivational, and we developed a relationship that served both me and the team. By ensuring my contract, I became motivated to play a leadership role on the team. This inspired me to become the natural leader that I am, to speak out and stand up as a player and tell the other players what I felt we needed to do, which I did for the next three years until the end of my career.

Landry is probably the most interesting of all the coaches I played under because he was dispassionate, impersonal, and distant, treated players as if they were completely expendable and replaceable (because they were), ignored incredible levels of racial tension on his team, and still developed a winning team because the fear of losing their job made his players adhere to the system until winning became a reason to adhere to that system.

Some players adhere to a system to keep their job. Some players adhere to a system because the system is proven. Some adhere to a system because they want to support the coach or are bending to the will of the coach, and some adhere to a system because they are inspired by the coach. Unfortunately, being inspired by your coach is not the basis for a winning team. The decisive factors are having a proven system and a carefully selected roster of talented players who will adhere religiously to that system for whatever reason they are motivated to do so and will follow the leadership of the coach who developed that system.

As we make that total commitment, we are prepared to sacrifice our bodies, possibly die, and face serious injuries that could ruin our quality of life. We leave our stench, sweat, snot, vomit, blood, skin, fingernails, and teeth on the field, and later, in the locker room, we assess what that field took from us. The stories in that DNA tell the history of every team, both the winners and losers, and mark the differences between the players who are willing to adhere to a proven system, follow the leadership of a coach, and sacrifice everything on that field to win, and those who aren't.

CHAPTER SEVEN

The Silence After the Cheers— Schoenke & Associates (1974–1980)

In the late 1970s, I called up Leonard Rodman and invited him to lunch at Alfio's La Trattoria, next to his flagship drugstore on Wisconsin Avenue in Washington DC. *The Washington Post* described Rodman as "an ebullient, cigar-chomping showman who liked to arm-wrestle with staff and chat up customers."[104] He had challenged me to a duel several times.

At the time, I had left the Redskins and was trying to build my business into a major enterprise. My goal was to make $1 million a year, and I was determined. I wanted Rodman as a client.

I had first met Rodman at a function for the county paper after I had secured the publisher as a client. Rodman said then, "Hey, I'd like to arm wrestle you."

I answered, somewhat bemused, "Well, maybe we'll do that sometime."

Somebody else leaned over to me and said in a quiet voice, "The guy's for real. He's a monster; you don't want to arm wrestle him because he has broken people's arms."

Leonard Rodman was born in Baltimore, where he attended pharmacy school and began his career as a pharmacist. He was a star boxer on the University of Maryland's boxing team and eventually won two professional bouts, both by knockout. After serving in the Merchant

---

104 Levy, Claudia. "Leonard Rodman Dies." *The Washington Post*, 15 April 2003. https://www.washingtonpost.com/archive/local/2003/04/15/leonard-rodman-dies/17d78f9f-5cc6-4489-81cf-7f8843969f7f/.

Marines in World War II, he started working for an uncle in NW Washington, DC, a business he eventually bought from his uncle.

The Rodman business empire featured gourmet and specialty foods, discounted items, and even home appliances. The business attracted an international clientele and even included dignitaries like President George H. W. and Barbara Bush.[105]

I saw Rodman a couple of times after that first meeting, and each time he said, "Come on down, we'll talk. But hey, you gotta get ready to arm wrestle, baby!"

Finally, I called him up and said, "I'd like to do business with you," and we set up lunch at the Italian restaurant. We talked about a lot of things, and sure enough, he challenged me to a duel. "Well, here's the deal," I said. "If I win, I want your account. No ifs, ands, or buts!" I added, only half in jest, "And if I lose… I still get the account."

The plates are now emptied of pasta, and he clears them—it's probably 3 o'clock, and the lunch crowd has disappeared. I apply the lessons someone had given me on how to arm wrestle. You put enough energy in to reach a stalemate, keeping your forearms straight up and your hands entwined. You count to five. Then you explode. You put everything you've got into it and just muscle your opponent down. That's exactly what I do. I can tell Rodman is slowly folding, and then he just lets go. I say, "I won! You're my newest client!"

He says, "OK."

When I got home, Nancy said, "What's wrong with your face?" I went and looked in the mirror. I had busted all the blood vessels underneath my eyes. That's the amount of pressure I put on myself.

"But honey, I got the account!" I said, elated.

She said, "Was it worth it?"

It was.

---

[105] Ibid.

FOLLOWING THE MONEY

Owning an insurance business hadn't been part of my plan.[106] At SMU, I had dreamed of law school and maybe even a life in politics. But I dropped out of law school to curry favor with the Cowboys and focus on my football career. The off-season posed a dilemma. I didn't want to just vacation like a lot of my teammates. After I had proven to myself that I could sell insurance to college seniors at SMU, I started branching out, selling to professionals and business owners. At first, I wasn't enthralled with the business because you're selling packages for death benefits, but I looked at the insurance companies I worked for and realized that if I stayed focused and selective, I could make a lot of money at it.

Once Nancy and I moved to the Washington area in 1969, I started building a bona fide profession. My experiences with the Cowboys, the Packers, and the Browns had taught me not to count on the NFL for long-term financial security.

After working for Raymond DuFour in Georgetown, I saw new possibilities for business and corporate-owned insurance programs. It would require more products than just life insurance, but I saw that an insurance company that dealt with large to moderate companies might be my salvation. After the Special Olympics, I was making about $25,000 a year playing football ($191,564 in 2022), and I wanted to double that in my off-season career.[107]

After leaving DuFour Insurance, I was eager to take advantage of the opportunity to earn more, so I started my own agency, Ray Schoenke & Associates, and affiliated myself with different insurance agencies in Virginia and Maryland. I was now clearly beginning to formulate my exit strategy from professional football by building ties in the business community. I leveraged Ray Schoenke's Montgomery County Redskins Luncheons into a lot of corporate-level prospects.

---

106 Section reviewed by Ray and Schoenke & Associates lawyer.

107 "Value of 1969 US Dollars Today." *Value of 1969 US Dollars Today - Inflation Calculator*, www.inflationtool.com/us-dollar/1969-to-present-value?amount=25000.

Going from the locker room to the boardroom

By the time I left the Redskins, though, I had set my sights on working with large companies rather than individuals, and I was building a national insurance brokerage agency. The first significant account that came from these efforts was with the Montgomery County newspaper, the *Sentinel*, and its affiliate Comprint Printing Company, which earned me a commission of $50,000. This account was my jumping-off point. Ray Schoenke & Associates began dealing exclusively with large private corporations.

Landing the Rodman account did not mean a lot to my business financially, but it was a feather in my cap since Rodman's Discount Food and Drugs was a Washington, DC institution, and Leonard Rodman was a respected businessman. It earned us recognition as a "go-to" firm for business insurance. There was another perk: Rodman introduced me to his lawyer, Sid Silver, who became my counsel and in turn introduced me to a myriad of attorneys in the DC area.

One of those attorneys, a tax lawyer, approached me and suggested I connect with a man named Joel Koenig who, he said, "knows more about life insurance than anyone alive." Koenig, he added, had been selling insurance to large, privately held companies. Koenig was scheduled to make a presentation to a group of lawyers and accountants. I decided to attend.

Joel Koenig had the appearance of a mad professor. He was medium height, slightly overweight, tightly wound, with a little black mustache, and as he spoke, he paced back and forth trying to make his points. I didn't have the foggiest idea what he was talking about, but I noticed that all the lawyers and accountants were enraptured. The lawyer who had told me about him said that Joel, who had a background in an actuarial firm, stood out for his knowledge of using insurance products to solve large corporate executive firm compensation issues. "Joel's a brilliant guy, but he's not a marketer. You're a natural marketer, but you don't have his technical skills."

I talked to Joel afterward and soon proposed a partnership. Joel was brilliant. My new role was to be the organizer and the "rainmaker." I opened doors for meetings. As Schoenke & Koenig, our new company, we focused our efforts on large private corporations and mid-sized, publicly traded companies. My role was to run the operation and be the lead marketer. Joel was our technical, actuarial arm. Within a few years, we were very successful. We qualified for the Five-Million-Dollar Roundtable, a global association of the most successful independent insurance and financial professionals in the country.[108] Joel was a member and encouraged me to join and attend meetings.

Joel had taken me into a world where the best marketing minds in national life insurance got together. At one roundtable meeting, the featured speaker was Peter Mullin, out of California. His presentation centered on how publicly traded companies could acquire specifically designed insurance products that were in compliance with all applicable tax, securities, and state insurance laws, and could meet the financial criteria and accounting standards required when financing large executive compensation programs. Peter was very clear, concise, and logical. I realized that we needed him to do our presentations. So I initiated a conversation with Peter to establish a joint venture. I got pushback from Joel but stayed firm and convinced Joel that Peter should be a partner in our business venture.

I listened to Joel; I listened to Peter, but still could not grasp all the nuances associated with this concept. I asked myself, "*What should a savvy businessman do in this situation? Surround yourself with the right people to complement Joel and Peter.*" I hired Kevin Ballou as our in-house legal counsel. Kevin played a key leadership role with our management team and dealt with all the legal responsibilities that were directly involved in all of our proposals, marketing discussions with the lawyers of potential clients, and with the outside counsel we hired who had unique specialties. I also hired several technical people who had legal, actuarial, finance, and accounting backgrounds to prepare for a presentation to a large defense contractor in the area, Fairchild Industries. I knew if we went in with just Joel and me, Joel would present a dozen of different scenarios, possibly confusing the Fairchild executives. All that was needed was two or three scenarios at the most. While Joel was very knowledgeable, he tended to provide too much information. As I liked to say, "If I asked Joel what time

---

108 Wealth Management.com. "Joel Koenig." Informa USA, 3 May 2021; https://www.wealthmanagement.com/author/Joel-Koenig.

it was, I would first be told how to build the best watch in order to get the most precise time." Peter was Joel's antithesis. Peter gave his presentations in less than an hour, answered all questions—whether about finance, taxes, legal, accounting or insurance—and had the corporation's executives captivated by the end.

The presentation to Fairchild went just as I had envisioned. It went off like clockwork (pun intended) and marked the largest transaction closed to date by our firm. The commission to the firm was in the neighborhood of a quarter million dollars.

STRIVING FOR GREATNESS

With our successful entry into the corporate-owned life insurance market, COLI, every time our firm reached a new plateau, I set my sights on the next peak. We joined a national consortium of companies similar to ours, the Management Compensation Group (MCG), at the insistence of Peter. This alliance placed us in an entirely new arena. Our target market was large publicly traded companies with hundreds or even thousands of employees.

The MCG consortium was structured with 13 independent national offices, so if a member firm entered another firm's geographical territory, a call was to be placed to the "home" firm. The call would seek approval for entering their territory or even offer the "home" firm the opportunity to participate in the case. Schoenke & Koenig became the Mid-Atlantic regional office of MCG, covering Maryland, DC, Virginia, West Virginia, North Carolina, and South Carolina.

From my athletic career, I knew leadership, motivation, organizational structure, and how to coordinate a team effort to win where it counted. But I quickly realized I was a novice within the MCG structure and needed to shorten the learning curve fast—or sink. I needed expertise in the business, tax, finance, legal, and accounting areas, and then my job would be to manage the whole project. It took a few years, but with Joel's help, we were able to hire technical people with expertise in all the relevant disciplines. I was now in a position to begin protecting my territory from MCG interlopers.

One piece of the puzzle was missing. Peter had been our lead guy on all major cases to date, but he kept too much technical information and analytical data to himself, and he was taking half of all the commissions. With my team in place, I wanted to reverse-engineer the process and rely less on Peter, the MCG consortium, and other outside partners. I had been building an entire program in-house with the support staff required to handle the administration of all our large corporate accounts.

I approached Bruce Tyson—a well-known financial guru and Peter's right arm in designing proposals—to break down each element of the proposal so my team and I could handle all aspects from beginning to end. I appealed to Bruce to help us figure out how to do some of this ourselves.

Bruce said, "Put us up at the Hay-Adams Hotel in DC and get us tickets to the Bruce Springsteen concert, and I'll show you how it works." I booked the hotel. Springsteen was playing at the Coliseum, where the NBA Bullets played their games. Because I knew the GM of the Bullets, I got the tickets, and Bruce made good on his promise. He and Shelley came to DC; he gave my company a seminar, and they went to the concert. Once my team assured me that they fully understood all the elements, I pulled a 'Ray Schoenke' and renegotiated Peter Mullins's contract. From that point forward, I was in full control of our destiny as an executive benefits and consulting firm. Eventually, I bought out Joel, and the company became Schoenke & Associates once again.

Over 25 years, I built Schoenke & Associates into a 50-plus employee firm based in Bethesda, Maryland, with satellite offices in St Louis, Missouri, and Honolulu, Hawaiʻi. Our market was large corporations in the Mid-Atlantic region, the Midwest, and Hawaiʻi. Our success was of course based partly on my drive to become something. But it was also attributable to the expertise of our employees, who spent countless hours researching, evaluating, and then assigning the best insurance company and the best individual insurance policies to fit each client and allowing them to achieve optimum results. This kid-glove customer service became our calling card. We became a premier brokerage firm specializing in the design and administration of insurance-funded executive and employee benefit programs. I established longstanding relationships with international, national, and local corporations, including Marriott International; Fannie, Freddie, and Sallie Mae; Bank of Hawai'i; MBNA; Black & Decker; Norfolk Southern Railway; and McCormick & Company. We also had Baltimore Gas & Electric, Potomac Electric, and Hawaiian Electric. And I had become a fixture in the business community in Honolulu as well.

We specialized in executive benefit and compensation consulting for large publicly traded corporations. We used specially designed, cutting-edge financial products from the life insurance industry that would assist corporations with paying full retirement benefits to highly compensated key executives and employees without hurting their company financially. We complied with existing tax, accounting, and securities laws, and worked with insurance and annuity carriers to design products specifically for us.

The programs we implemented were governed by a myriad of state and federal laws. Vigilantly following proposed regulatory changes was a never-ending job. So politics and lobbying became a must, which I happily became involved in. In fact, I relished it, as politics always fascinated me. Much of our work was governed by the House and Senate Finance Committees of Congress. I hired the lobbying firm of Patton Boggs and became friends with lawyer Tommy Boggs, the son of the legendary congressman from Louisiana, Hale Boggs, and his co-equal Lindy Boggs, who succeeded her husband after he died in an airplane crash. Tommy and I had gotten to know each other through Democratic circles and through hunting on the Eastern Shore of Maryland. He had run for the congressional seat representing Montgomery County, where I lived, and he was very active in Democratic politics on a national and state level in Maryland. We saw each other often at events and engaged in the cursory greetings, "Hello" and "How are you?" However, we never had any in-depth political conversations until later when I retained his firm.

EXPANSION

I wanted to open a Midwest office, so I hired my brother Walter, who'd worked his way from being an athletic coach to selling bowling alleys to selling AstroTurf. I said to him, "Try to make contact with banks that have 10 billion in assets or more. All you have to do is open it up, and I'll send technical people who will do all the numbers, and you close it out, and I'll give you half the case." He was an excellent salesman and incredibly well-organized.

I, of course, relied on other people for organization and moved very quickly. I got to St. Louis one time, where Walter had a meeting set up, and as soon as it was over, I said, "Let's go to the next meeting." He had everything scheduled tightly, and I destroyed his plan by demanding that we set up another meeting immediately. He got so mad he accidentally locked his keys in the car. He was a nervous wreck. I realized we couldn't work together. So, I let him work with one of my associates, John Blottenberger, and the two of them did marvelously well together.

Many people never understood how I became so successful. When I was with Joel, they assumed he ran everything because he was so brilliant and knowledgeable, and I was viewed as a jock who was only good for marketing and being driven around in a limo with all these lawyers and accountants. In reality, Joel was the technical wizard, who understood how the life insurance product conformed with the relevant accounting, tax, and federal regulations; however, his strength was not communicating these vast, complex amounts of information in a proposal in a simple way that made sense in a presentation, nor was he good at managing people.

On the other hand, I was the marketer and ran the company. I created the framework for simplifying the information, marketing it, and closing the accounts. My framework was eventually implemented by account executives we hired, who became responsible for each aspect of their assigned accounts after Joel explained everything to them. He was always available as a resource, as was I. They also managed their own teams and addressed the tax, legal, accounting, financial, and cost ramifications, as well as the compliance reports. They also managed the staff who addressed the technical issues and made the product when presented to a potential client easy to read and understand. This structure made it possible for me to expand the company substantially because I was able to oversee the cases and focus on marketing, which I was constantly doing. I was responsible for getting all of the new prospects and closing the cases. I was driven to succeed. I was always self-motivated, and I had focus. My drive had served me well during my entire athletic career, and I had simply redirected it into the business world.

I never stopped climbing the next peak. I had reached my personal earnings goal of $1 million annually. Schoenke & Associates had become a premier brokerage firm; I became independent. But I wanted something else: I wanted other CEOs to see me as an equal. I emulated them, trading in the business van, owning a closet full of tailor-made suits.

There were a couple of dimensions to the image I tried to create as a businessman. Some of it was strategic. "They see you before they hear you," was my motto. When you walk through that door, you're going to make an impression. I wanted to have on an Italian suit, Italian tie, white shirt, shoes polished. I wanted to look like a million dollars and to look like I knew what I was talking about. I recognized that, in the back of their minds, they were looking at a football player first, then maybe a Hawaiian guy second, then a business guy. I always reminded myself that in the business world, people were looking for answers to major problems. I couldn't come off as this jock who didn't know anything who had all these people around him who did all the work.

They had to understand that I ran the show; it was my baby. That's where the clothes and the limousine and the chauffeur came in. I had to convince them that I was there to do business, and I knew what I was talking about. For the first meetings, where I talked to the CEO or president, I went by myself. When I showed up in a limo, and Nate, my driver, jumped out and opened the door for me, I was acting like their CEO. Some CEOs might have wondered "Who the fuck does this guy think he is?" but I wanted to establish that I was on their level. And the limo and driver saved me time and stress. I didn't have to worry about driving, traffic, or how to get there, or the many speeding tickets I accrued when I drove myself.

I walked in like I owned the world. I'd explain what we wanted to accomplish; then, the CEO usually handed me off to his treasurer or Chief Financial Officer, who set up our next meeting. At the meeting, I walked in with the account executive who became responsible for the case, a lawyer, and an accountant, so as to be ready to cover any finance, legal, tax, and accounting issues or concerns.

George Solomon teased me about the limo when he had me on as a guest when he hosted the *Washington Post Live* TV show in the 1980s. He made fun of me by talking about how I showed up at the studio in a limousine driven by my driver, Nate, who even wore a cap, and he commented about how unusual it for a professional football player to have a more lucrative career *after* he leaves the NFL.

I may have emulated other CEOs, but my coaches were my true role models. I had learned from high-powered men like Tom Landry, Vince Lombardi, and George Allen. I understood them. I knew how to set goals, establish a game plan, call a meeting, follow an agenda, and motivate my team to execute and win.

BULLIES IN THE BOARD ROOM

I was determined to be successful, but it was cutthroat. And if you were a competitor who got in my way, or if you acted unethically, I was ready to tussle with you the way I had with Alan Page or Buck Buchanan. I was ready to confront you. Football, again, was my guide.

This happened at one point in the Management Compensation Group. Three or four guys in the organization (out of LA, Portland, and Philadelphia) were so dominating that they could run roughshod over regional offices. These predators were brilliant, dynamic, and hugely successful, but they'd just as soon use you and throw you away. Other colleagues in the group weren't tough—they said, "We don't know what to do" or "They won't listen to me" or "I can't get kicked out of the organization." So the predatory members showed up and just stole business away. One of them tried it with me. His group was talking to Martin Marietta, which was in my area.

"Hey, I thought there was an agreement here," I said.

"Well, there is, but who's gonna call the police?" he replied.

I was offended by the lack of ethics. I found out that a very successful group out of Portland was behind the poaching. I called them and asked, "How come you guys didn't call me?"

"We forgot," they said, as if it was a joke, not that big of a deal. They tried to blow me off.

"Really?" I answered. "You forgot, huh? Let me tell you what's gonna happen. Next time you come into town, and I don't know about it, your men will never make it back to the airport."

"Are you nuts?"

"Am I nuts? This is my *life*! I have put everything I have into this thing! We have a signed agreement here with all the offices in the group to notify them if you're coming into their territory to market. If you don't wanna agree to it, fine, but if I catch you, you're in trouble."

The guy I was talking to said, "What are you going to do about it?"

"I'll break his back."

"OK, then we'll shoot you."

"Just make sure you kill me."

One of the Portland guys did it one more time, and I went after him. He was a small-statured guy, a marketing guy, so it wasn't really fair. And he was just following orders. When I confronted him, I asked a simple question: "Do you like walking?"

He went back to his group and said, "Schoenke scared the shit outta me!"

I told the others, "Follow the agreement. Don't mess with me again."

That wasn't my usual style, but I could get nasty when pushed. I was used to bullies—I knew them in the seventh grade in Weatherford, Texas, in high school at Punahou, in college at SMU, and in the NFL. My coaches might have taught me how to deal with successful CEOs in big corporations, but the offensive line taught me how to deal with guys who were trying to screw me.

Occasionally, I showed flashes of the rough lineman (or maybe behavior modeled by my coaches) in our company meetings. They were always on Mondays. Once, one of my project managers called in and said he thought he had a temperature. I said, "Get your goddamn ass in here! I expect you to be here within an hour!" BAM. I hung up the phone. He comes in with a towel around his neck, he's so feverish, and he's pissed.

I said, "Get sick on your own time!" Sometimes I sounded like Lombardi. I wasn't gonna hear "No." This guy was one of my favorites. Imagine what I was like with the other marketers. As far as I was concerned, a fever was nothing but a pussy injury.

I'd like to think that most of the time I was more George Allen than Vince Lombardi. (I wish I could say I was Otto Graham, but I was not that kind of gentleman.) My experience with football coaches gave me the skills to organize and run things. I knew how to walk in and meet a CEO and present a case. I put together a team, and I became successful.

EXPANDING MY VISION INTO A NEW ARENA: THE POWER OF DONATIONS

If my experiences with coaches gave me the skills and the confidence to enter the business world, my early behind-the-scenes experiences in election campaigns helped me develop confidence in the political arena. Once I left football, I saw myself more and more as a leader, and once I became a successful businessman, I started to bring together the various threads of my life.

I had long had an interest in politics. At SMU, I ran for president of my senior class, though because I was happy to call myself a leftist, I lost that race. I was often a leader on the football field and gained a certain amount of respect from my teammates, although I wasn't necessarily the captain of the team. When John F. Kennedy was killed, it affected me deeply and caused a split between me and my conservative teammates. Nancy and I started having conversations about how we might best support civil rights causes. It was very clear to me that some people had privilege, and others didn't, that racism existed, and it hurt people—me included.

I wanted to put my energy into making sure that everyone was treated with dignity. I was aware of how desperate the Vietnamese were to have their freedom. And we started joining anti-war marches. I was in a unique window, where I never qualified for the draft. First I was in grad school; then I got married, and then I had a child, all of which gave me a deferment. However, in spite of my negative feelings about the war, I felt guilty for not serving. When I was still in Dallas, I went down to the National Guard Headquarters to sign up. I knew the commander.

He sat down with me and said, "Your signature won't be dry, and your ass will be in a rice paddy field in Vietnam. You just had a baby, and you don't need to do this." The ink never got put on the paper.

When I joined the Redskins, I went up to Congress and introduced myself to the delegation from Texas and Hawai'i. I was warmly received because I was a football player, and having SMU as my alma mater helped open doors with the Texas delegation. Having Punahou as my alma mater, and, more importantly, being Hawaiian, made me welcome at the Hawai'i delegation. I was interested in island politics, and I wanted them to know that. I was trying to build a base, and I was also looking for ways to plead certain causes. Eventually, I became very involved in efforts to advance legislation like the Akaka Bill, which would give specific rights to native Hawaiians.

I even entertained the idea of working on the Hill and still doing my business. But Senator Ralph Yarborough, a very liberal Texas senator said, "Everybody up here is chasing money. Stay in your insurance business. Make a lot of money, and then come up here."

After Ethel Kennedy had helped me promote the regional Special Olympics, and she began to invite Nancy and me to events out at Hickory Hill, I started meeting a lot of Democrats, celebrities, and political activists. The war was raging—and enraging leftists like myself. I came out of SMU with a basic understanding of the history of the struggles in Indochina—of people trying to gain a modicum of decency in their lives and being able to provide for their families. Those struggles were going on throughout the world, including in the US.

When the Vietnam War began to escalate, we stepped in because of Communism, and when Nixon started pushing the war, I knew I had to do something. I identified with the Vietnamese—maybe because I was part Hawaiian. As a brown person, I'd had brushes with intolerance; I had witnessed racism, whether directed at me or others, and I felt great empathy for the Vietnamese because they were dehumanized due to their ethnicity. I was definitely not a knee-jerk anti-communist.

I thought I should endorse a candidate and get involved in the 1972 presidential campaign. Between the people I was meeting on the Hill and those I was meeting out at Ethel Kennedy's home in McLean, I felt at ease, even if they might have viewed me as a political novice. But I enjoyed the discussions and started gaining confidence. I started asking people what they thought of Senator George McGovern of South Dakota, who was the loudest voice among politicians objecting to the war and was staking out the moral high ground when it came to Vietnam.

Of course, my support of McGovern and my refusal to take a picture with Nixon and the Redskins in the fall of 1971 drew criticism from George Allen and drew fire from some of my teammates. And it drew public attention to my political activities. A lot of people, in the business world as well as in professional sports, disagreed with what I was doing. But I was willing to take that chance and possibly lose business and my job with the Redskins. I liked being out there, fearless in many ways. It was a calling. I knew that, somewhere down the line, I would run for office.

When I retired from the NFL, my political involvements prompted speculation that I would run for Maryland's Montgomery County's open seat in the House of Representatives. But I didn't. I wanted to be more than a football player-politician. I wanted to participate in my children's lives. I wanted to have family outings, coach my kids' teams, watch their swim meets, attend all of their school performances (and I mean *all*), and take them to Hawai'i, all of which I did. I wanted to be a dad. Whether it was a swim meet, a performance, or an event of some kind they were participating in, I made it a point to be in the audience. My rule was if they were in front of a crowd, I was going to be in that crowd—no matter what. My kids' lives were not going to be one of those movies where children look out into an audience and their dad isn't there. They always looked for me, and they could always find me. By this time Eric was 11; Page was nine, and Holly was four.

Also, to be honest, I did not want to start at the bottom, working my way up from state government in Annapolis to a US representative or senator, going to committees, and sitting there for 10 years, and only then run for the office I was truly initially interested in.

There was another reason I passed up the 1976 race. I wanted to be financially independent. I wanted to stick with my growing insurance business. I hadn't forgotten what Senator Yarborough had told me about building an economic base. And I'd seen that people with money could skip a lot of seats. I could learn a lot and earn loyalty by contributing financially to political campaigns. If I wanted to run, I had to pick a time when I thought I could do it—when the governor was in trouble, when I had $4 or 5 million to spend. I figured I was going to have to come out of left field, with a different story. It wouldn't hurt to be able to say I had built my own business over many years and figured out how major US corporations tick.

So I stayed involved in issues, working on campaigns, including those of Michael Dukakis, Bill Clinton, and Bill Bradley. And I began to make sizable donations. Becoming a political donor put me in good stead with politicians and with the party. I met influential people like Ron Brown, a lawyer with Patton Boggs and a veteran of the presidential campaigns of Teddy Kennedy and Jesse Jackson. He was elected chairman of the Democratic National Committee in 1989, and he put me on key committees and made sure to introduce me to figures like Jesse Jackson and Bill Clinton, for whom Brown later served as Commerce Secretary.

At the time, I saw something great in Jimmy Carter, the same warrior mentality I had seen in McGovern. A man who presented as a Southern gentleman, which belied his background as a graduate of the Naval Academy. Jimmy Carter had quite a few more dimensions beyond being a "peanut farmer" although he was very proud of his humble background. In addition to representing himself as a man of the people, which he easily could do, I saw a man who was decent, a man who cared deeply about his family and his country. His military background gave him a crucial warrior mentality that could be brought to bear in the highest office in the land, and he had been a governor, so he also knew his way around the political arena. He wasn't afraid to make a stand, which was reflected on his second day in the White House when he pardoned draft evaders, an action that I greatly appreciated.

FAT GIRL SINGS

Jimmy Carter
7/77

Chatting with President Carter at a White House lawn event

It was during the Carter campaign that I found a new role as a political fundraiser. I organized Artists and Athletes for Carter. Partly as a result, during Carter's term, I even had an office in the East Wing of the White House. Gretchen Poston was the social secretary, and she was using me to get to athletes for Carter. They had used some of these celebrities when he ran the first time, but after he won, they hadn't called anybody to the White House. They didn't even invite the Pittsburgh Steelers after they won the Super Bowl, which was becoming a tradition. Celebrities could get bitter about not getting a call. My job was putting out fires. I was also calling celebrities trying to make nice to them and inviting them to the White House—especially opera stars and country singers.

I'll never forget the time Willie Nelson played on the White House Lawn. The band was setting up outside, and the guys were saying, "Hey Schoenke, you got any weed, man? Can you get some weed for us?"

"This is the White House! I am sure I cannot get you any marijuana," I said.

Later, the guys called me over. "We got some!" they said. "You want some weed, man?"

Carter's term in office was filled with images of long lines at gas pumps. His loss to Ronald Reagan in 1980 was disheartening to me. One of the endorsers in Carter's campaign for his second term was Lyle Alzado, one of the fiercest defensive linemen in the NFL. He was known to take anabolic steroids specifically to help make him crazy fierce. Whereas many of us took amphetamines to ward off exhaustion and deaden pain, Alzado would get so high from his drug cocktail that white, foamy saliva would run out of the corners of his mouth as he stared across at me on the line of scrimmage.

In 1974, when the Redskins played against the Denver Broncos, I had the dubious privilege of having to block Alzado. He comes at me, attacking me by trying to intimidate me by punching me in the face and swearing at me while trying to grab me or throw me. Needless to say, before it is over, we are in a slugfest. It's a Monday night game, and he tells Howard Cosell, Frank Gifford, and Don Meredith how many sacks he's going to get against me. It becomes obvious toward the end of the game that he isn't going to get any. We are winning, and after a play, as we look at each other, he slugs me right in the face, at which point I retaliate. Then, he starts yelling at everybody on his team to "get Schoenke."

My teammates, being the great comrades that they were, said, "He's over there; go get 'em!" As the game was winding down, they sent in a new quarterback, Joe Theismann. This was in his first year on the team. He came in at the end of the game to get some experience, where at a time like that you usually run the clock out. Typically, you have running plays, where the clock continues to run as opposed to a passing play, where the clock stops after the passing play is over or is incomplete.

So Joe starts calling passing plays, and I tell him, "If you call one more pass, I'm going to give you a 'look out block,' which means I'm not going to block my guy."

His answer was, "You wouldn't."

I said, "You call one more pass, you're going to get that. I've got a madman over here I'm trying to contain, and I'm gonna let him rip your head off." Joe ran out the clock. This madman was desperate to meet and travel with President Carter. My job was to follow the campaign guidelines, which was not to put Alzado with the president. It took everything I had to get him to attend other events before he had a chance to meet Carter. Eventually, I insisted that he would be allowed to meet Carter, and when I saw him again, he didn't hit me in the face.

Ethel Kennedy had a lot to do with the confidence I brought to my political involvement. While she probably invited me to her parties because I was a football player who could carry on an intellectual discussion, or at the very least delight the older ladies at a table in a corner, I'm not sure Ethel realized I also had a business. One night, Gloria Steinem was seated at the same table I was. She later asked Ethel, "Who is that good-looking insurance man that I was sitting with?" as if she had uncovered an interloper.

"There's no insurance man at my party," Ethel replied.

Steinem said, "Yes, there is!" Nancy and I got a good laugh out of that.

Nancy and I had become very good friends with two other regulars at Ethel's parties—CBS correspondent Roger Mudd and E.J., his wife. He was being groomed to succeed Walter Cronkite as the anchor on the *CBS Evening News*. When Dan Rather got the gig instead, Roger was devastated. He had spent every weekend substituting for Walter Cronkite and assumed he would replace Walter when he retired. However, Dan Rather was making a name for himself reporting from Vietnam, and when the time came for Cronkite to retire, Rather got the job. Roger moved on to NBC and then PBS. E.J. Mudd, Roger's wife, hosted parties for Washington elites in their home, and Nancy and I were often guests. Nancy and E.J. greatly enjoyed each other's company.

But after 10 years of being regular guests at Hickory Hill, all four of us were wanting to be a little less tethered. We never had the nerve to refuse an invitation even politely, sensing that that might burn a bridge. We ran scenarios about who would do it first. As it happened, both Roger and I acted at about the same time. And it was over politics.

When Teddy Kennedy decided to run for the 1980 Democratic nomination for president, Ethel said to me, "You need to get a bunch of football players and get up to Boston when Teddy announces his candidacy."

I punted on that request and left for Hawai'i. While I was gone, a few days before Ted announced his campaign to defeat Carter, Roger interviewed then-Senator Ted Kennedy, who at the time was leading the race in the polls.

> *"Why do you want to be president?" Roger began. Teddy Kennedy hesitated, apparently caught off guard. "Well, I'm—were I to—to make the, the announcement and to run, the reasons that I would run is because I have a great belief in this country," he stammered. He twitched and squirmed for an hour, stumbling through Roger's questions. The reviews indicated that he conveyed nothing so much as self-doubt and flawed preparation.[109]*

I got back from Hawai'i, and Roger couldn't wait to show me the tape. I saw it and said, "The sonuva gun doesn't know what he wants!"

We both knew that the interview was going to make Roger persona non grata at Ethel's.

"I need a buddy with me!" Roger said.

---

[109] McFadden, Robert D. "Roger Mudd, Anchorman Who Stumped a Kennedy, Is Dead at 93." *The New York Times*, 9 Mar. 2021. https://www.nytimes.com/2021/03/09/business/media/roger-mudd-dead.html.

I *was* his buddy. I told Roger I wasn't gonna support Teddy Kennedy. I told Ethel I wasn't going to go to Boston with a batch of football players. I endorsed Carter.

So we were done with Ethel. However, the dinners had given Nancy and me access to a constant flow of Washington elites who made our lives interesting and fun. I had enjoyed meeting the politicians and celebrities who were there and became more confident over the years because I could move in that world.

CHAPTER EIGHT

My Family and Hawai'i—Returning to My Ancestors (1965-2000)

DIFFERENT PERSPECTIVES OF THE SAME EXPERIENCE

I made countless trips back to Hawai'i, starting in 1965, both personal and business-related. Nancy and I had married in April 1964 and had taken a quick trip to New Orleans for our honeymoon. During the next football season, I saved up because I wanted to take Nancy to Hawai'i, and I wanted to take her in style. We boarded the luxury ocean liner *Lurline* out of San Francisco. We had found out she was pregnant right before we left, so it was a tough trip for her, with a lot of seasickness. It was probably made doubly tough by my nonstop tales on the trip about the Alapa family in Kahuku and Lā'ie, as well as my Punahou pals, whom I bragged about endlessly.

We pulled into Honolulu Harbor. I didn't know where the Royal Hawaiian Band and the hula dancers, who usually welcomed tourists, were. Our greeting party was instead made up of my former football buddies in aloha shirts and shorts, unceremoniously climbing over the sides of the boat looking to hustle tourists and yelling, "'Ey, Schoenke!" and "Hoooo-eeee," which is how *Hūi*, a traditional Hawaiian greeting, is spoken.

We rented a car, and the rental agent said, "I went to Punahou, too!"

Nancy and I on our honeymoon in Hawai'i

As we made our way to the Ilikai Hotel, Nancy couldn't suppress her sarcasm. "Oh, you Punahou guys are *really* successful," she said sarcastically. "I'm impressed!" I had implied to her that graduates of Punahou were the leaders of the business and political world in Hawai'i.

That night, at the hotel, a former teammate, Vernie Hoke, showed up on a police motorcycle below my balcony and yelled out, "Hey, Ray! Welcome home!" This only reinforced again Nancy's questioning of the high-level career paths of Punahou grads that I had depicted to her.

No matter. It was a homecoming for me, really fun. I couldn't take Nancy around the island as much as I wanted because she had morning sickness. But I did take her to Kahuku to meet some of the family. The first time I met them, I felt an instant sense of belonging, but nothing could have been further from Nancy's experiences at her family home in Greenwood, Louisiana. Even being surrounded by her entire family hadn't prepared her for the exuberance and size of my Polynesian family as they came out to greet her with leis. At least a dozen people surrounded her, hugging her, and kissing her. Everybody was talking at once. I told them she was pregnant, and they all patted her tummy, which wasn't even a bump yet. It must have seemed very invasive. To them, she was family. To her, they were strangers.

After that initial visit, we returned often to Hawai'i for vacations, staying at the Ilikai, which overlooked the Ala Wai Boat Harbor. After we started bringing our children, we stayed at the Hilton Hawaiian Village, with its lagoon, swimming pools, and beach access, because the children had more things to do. Beach boys, young local Polynesian men, took them catamaran sailing and taught them how to surf.

Going to Hawai'i was always emotional for me. Once I realized as a teenager that I was Hawaiian and that I had this incredible history, I led with it from then on in every situation if people asked me what nationality I was. And I couldn't wait to get back. It pulled at me. When there were several years in between trips, I got off the plane, fell on my knees, and started crying. There was a deep connection there that I missed and needed. Nancy sat and held me, somewhat bemused by how much Hawai'i meant to me.

My kids, except for Page, don't understand why I am so enraptured with Hawai'i. Eric, our oldest child, was conceived before our first trip in 1965, but he's very hā'ole-looking. As a child, he had blond hair, and his eyes are green. He is a strong swimmer—he swam competitively all the way through college. He loved the ocean swimming in Hawai'i, but he was a little shy when he was young and became sensitive to attitudes toward ha'oles, so he didn't feel at home in Hawai'i because he doesn't look like a native Hawaiian. Page and Holly are great swimmers like Eric, and as swimmers, they were drawn to ocean sports such as paddling and surfing.

Eric shares Nancy's theatrical bent. He sang and danced on the stage in high school even though he couldn't sing. He attended the College of Wooster, a small liberal arts college in Ohio. He appreciated the good academic environment and the good swim team, for which he was the captain his senior year. He never took to football. I couldn't believe it because he was a big kid, smart, athletic, and could have been a good-to-great football player, but Nancy was determined that he wasn't going to be a football player, and she worked on him by supporting his swimming career. Swimming was his sport, and he excelled at it from the age of seven. Nancy became very involved in the swimming program at the club where he swam. He also saw me all banged up after games, and I also suspect that he had no interest in competing with me. He vehemently chose not to go out for football in high school, describing the coach pitching the program as an "idiot." He did spend a lot of time on the road with me during my gubernatorial campaign, so he at least appeared to engage with that side of me.

Page, who was born in 1967, fit right in when we were in Hawai'i. She's darker than Eric and has brown-black hair. Her coloring makes people see her Hawaiian heritage, but she is the spitting image of Nancy. Of the three kids, she has been the one to explore her "Hawaiianness." She and Nancy shared a love of fine arts, and Page showed the sensibility of an artist from an early age. She now has lived in Waimānalo, on Oʻahu, for the better part of three decades, where she has built a varied art career. She started studying art at SMU, and while she loved the rigor of the coursework there, she had a disdain for many in the SMU student body, who she felt were not just entitled but also racist. So, it appears that some of my experiences at SMU were echoed in hers. Eric said if she would swim, he could get her into the College of Wooster. She did indeed join the swim team at the College of Wooster and graduated as an art major. She loved Hawaiian paddling, too, and eventually became a paddler and steersman and raced in the Molokaʻi race in Hawaiʻi, the same one I had raced in, which she did several times.

She met her husband in Honolulu. They married, started a family, and sent their kids to Kamehameha, a prestigious private school for native Hawaiians, during which time they moved to Waimānalo. Because Kamehameha was viewed as an institution that would improve the lives of native Hawaiian children, this school was permitted legally to restrict enrollment to students who were of Hawaiian descent unless there was space available for others.

Not only did Page feel "in her skin" in the islands, but as she became a visual artist, she became interested in Polynesian themes. Page has said that she grew up with an identity conflict—living in the suburbs of Washington, DC and longing for a stronger, authentic connection to Hawai'i. She has indicated that she feels a particular affinity for her grandmother since she was also an artist. She has immersed herself in the Native Hawaiian cultural practice of *kapa* making, which involves growing plants for dyes and making her own sheets of traditional Hawaiian bark cloth, which is a stamped fabric made from the bark of the *wauke*, or mulberry tree, which she uses to make large tapestries, jewelry, and modern Hawaiian fashions. In ancient times, the cloth was used for clothing, blankets, and sails.

The passion that both Page and her husband feel for their heritage has been passed to their daughters, one of whom is enrolled at the University of Hawai'i, which allows her to continue her commitment to hula, which she studies in a traditional *hālau* (school).

Like Eric and Page, Holly was an outstanding swimmer—a natural, but not as outstanding as a student in high school as she was a swimmer. Born in 1972, Holly is a brunette, five foot, 10 inches, with blue-green eyes. She's really a blend of Nancy and me but resembles me more. Nancy suggested she consider culinary school since she had attended and enjoyed summer programs at local restaurants. With Nancy's wholehearted support, Holly enrolled in Johnson and Wales Culinary School in Providence, Rhode Island. After finishing culinary school, she went to work in a restaurant in Charleston, South Carolina. We saw a young person beginning to blossom.

To our surprise, several months later, she called enquiring whether the rule still applied that we would pay all college tuition and living expenses if she were in school. I said, "The rule still applies." She enrolled at the College of Charleston and surprised us all by turning into an accomplished political science student, which was a huge contrast to her earlier academic performance in high school. She was an All-Conference swimmer and captain of her swim team, which competed against all the top teams in the Southeast. Her senior thesis was entered to compete with top papers from students across the state for the best philosophy paper, at universities like Clemson, Furman, Citadel, and 30 others. Holly's paper won top honors and was presented at the annual meeting of the South Carolina Society for Philosophy, the state-wide collegiate association of philosophers. I think her enormous transformation had everything to do with Nancy telling her, "It's OK for you to go to culinary school." We both encouraged her to enroll in college when she expressed an interest in doing so. I think that it ultimately was Nancy's encouragement to go to culinary school that led to her transformation because she developed the discipline to succeed academically.

After graduating in 1996, in 1998, Holly became Assistant Deputy Campaign Manager when I ran for Maryland Governor. The other consultants were impressed with her skills, and she eventually became the Executive Director of the American Association of Political Consultants in Washington, DC.

HĀʻOLE GIRL IN HAWAIʻI

Over time, Nancy became ambivalent about our trips to Hawaiʻi. She somewhat reluctantly went out to the rural areas of Hawaiʻi with me where my family lived, and she tried to blend in with everybody in my family, or at least accept her role as an in-law. But she, of course, was always an outsider. On one of the early trips, we were visiting with my cousins underneath a carport, drinking beer.

They kept saying, "Those fuckin' hāʻoles, they shit on us."

She's sitting and watching and listening, and finally, she says in her most polite Southern way, "Excuse me, gentlemen. I'm a hāʻole. So would you quit referring to them as fucking hāʻoles?"

They sat up in surprise. "Oh, but you don't count!" She tried to be cool about everything, but it wasn't always easy. She also felt that I was so consumed with Hawaiʻi that I had begun to love it more than I loved her.

When the kids got older and didn't always come with us, Nancy and I started staying on what is called the Gold Coast, all the way at the east end of Waikīkī, by Diamond Head. We stayed at the Colony Surf, or at the Kaimana Beach Hotel. Both were next to the Outrigger Canoe Club. We ate breakfast on the Hau Tree Lanai, right next to the beach, and I worked out across the street in Kapiʻolani Park.

Nancy often took what is a lovely walk along that end of Kalākaua Avenue, along the park, all the way to the foot of Diamond Head, where there is a little beach community with bungalows from the 1920s and 1930s. The homes are charming, the vegetation thick. She came back one day and told me about a remodeled home that was for sale. She said, "You're gonna love this place." I went down there, and it looked very cool. But they wanted close to a million for it.

I decided to pay a call on my old high school baseball buddy Larry Johnson, who had been a year ahead of me at Punahou because I thought, as the president of the Bank of Hawaiʻi, Larry might be of some help with the purchase of the house. Larry was good-looking, blonde, blue-eyed, nice, and obviously *not* Hawaiian. In high school, he was a substitute pitcher, and I became the backup right fielder and occasional pinch hitter. (I could hit a baseball from the backstop in Lower Field all the way over Dillingham Hall, almost to Middle Field 500 yards away.) But the starting right fielder, Hiram de Fries, was lighting up the scoreboard with his hits. Coach Doole kept saying to me, "We're gonna get you in," but he never seemed to be able to.

Finally, we're playing for the baseball championship against 'Iolani. It's a tight game, and the coach calls me up to pinch hit to see if I could hit one out of the park. I get up near home plate, feeling great, and Larry walks up, taps me on the shoulder, and gives me the thumb, like, "You're outta here."

I look over, and Doole is putting his head in his hands. I walk over and say, "What's going on?"

He says, "Ray, I had a premonition, a dream, that Larry's gonna win the game for us." Larry struck out, and I was so mad I couldn't see straight. We still won the championship. If you look at the team picture, after the game, Larry has on a shit-eating grin, and I look like the last wilting rose of summer.

After Larry Johnson pinch hit for me and struck out (we still won the championship)

So I went to see him about financing the house; we started telling war stories, hemming and hawing, talking about what a lousy batter he was. The secretary closed his office door because we were laughing so hard.

Instead of talking about financing a million-dollar vacation home, we talked about my insurance brokerage firm on the mainland. I explained that I did a lot of work with financial institutions.

Larry said, "That house isn't worth what they're asking for it. Japanese investors are screwing up the market here." Then he added, "I'll finance it for you, but I'm more interested in your business. We could use here what you do on the mainland. If you bring your business to Honolulu, I'll be one of your first clients."

I went to Larry to buy a house, and he talked me out of it. But he talked me into bringing my business to Hawai'i.

I had to go back home and figure out how I could set up a satellite operation. It seemed far-fetched. I talked to my staff and realized I would have to get a resident licensed agent. I returned to Honolulu and looked up Bob Corboy, another Punahou grad and an agent. He agreed to help. We were at the Plaza Club in Honolulu next to the Bank of Hawai'i, and Harrison Cooke walked in. Incredibly, he was the person who had underwritten half my school tuition and was a Punahou trustee on the board of the Bank of Hawai'i. I saw him and said to Bob, "Let's go and talk to him."

Bob said, "Oh, you can't do that." He felt that he was crossing a boundary. His perception of his position in Honolulu's business community didn't allow him to interrupt someone as important as Harrison Cooke in a social setting. Hawai'i's history had created a pecking order. The original missionaries who came there to Christianize the Hawaiians became powerful land owners and eventually dominated the business community. Harrison Cooke's family was one of these original families.

I said, "C'mon, we're Punahou grads. Let's say hello."

There was a pecking order at Punahou as well, and there is indeed a pecking order in the business community in Honolulu. It is still a small town, a place of "The Big Five" Hawai'i companies run by the descendants of missionaries—a kind of oligarchy. You don't go walking into someone's office who's above you. But I had gotten everywhere I'd gotten to by being aggressive, by being a salesman, by going after big fish, and by building relationships. I was like, "Where I come from, those aren't the rules."

I went up to Harrison Cooke to say hello, and he remembered me once I introduced myself. He said he was delighted to see me and wished me well in doing business in Hawai'i.

I started going to Honolulu every other month for a week for many years. I brought my associates with me—the tax, finance, and numbers guys who talked to the clients. I soon realized that my competitive instinct wasn't enough. In addition to the right licensed agent, I needed some

way of penetrating what was still a small, old-school, insular community.

Catching some R&R on one of the frequent trips to Hawai'i

My desire to spend more time in Hawai'i started to cause friction in our marriage. Nancy felt Hawai'i was my mistress and came to resent it. Nancy preferred the Southwest. She discovered it when I had an insurance conference in Santa Fe. She loved the feel of that part of the country the way I love Hawai'i. Santa Fe became her refuge from any turmoil in our relationship. She went so far as to ask me if she could buy and furnish a townhouse in Santa Fe. It was beautiful, up on Palace Avenue on a hill overlooking the city. Any time we had a serious conflict, she would pack up and leave me with the kids. One summer, she got a job in a high-end dress shop on the square and hung out with all the artsy women for the entire summer. She left me to take care of the two girls. Page was in college by this time. I often took them to Hawaiʻi with me, but sometimes I left Page in charge. I would often come back and find beer bottles discarded in the bushes by Page's guests. I realized that I had to be more vigilant.

Eventually, the friction between Nancy and me over Hawaiʻi became a really big problem; she said that I preferred Hawaiʻi over her. We became increasingly more distant. I spent more time away from her, and she spent more time away from me. I was building my company, trying to slay the world, and taking off for stretches to Hawaiʻi.

In a way, Page played a role in stitching Nancy and me together when our marriage was frayed over Hawaiʻi. Page enjoyed doing sketches featuring Hawaiians, even having me pose for her. She became pumped about going to Hawaiʻi with me on vacations, and on one trip, she told us she wanted to live there. Nancy started to feel a little more open to coming to Hawaiʻi again because Page was there.

FINDING MY WAY TO THE OCEAN

Page played a role in deepening my ties to Hawaiʻi, too. Her work was in an art show at the Bishop Museum, Hawaiʻi's premier historical and cultural institution. I attended the opening with my sister, Marilyn. We were wearing nametags, and the museum director came up to me. "I'm Donald Duckworth," he said, reaching out his hand to shake mine. "I used to work at the Smithsonian in Washington, DC, and I followed you in football."

We chatted, and I told him I was trying to figure out how I could establish myself in the business community in Hawaiʻi. He started to tell me about something he was working on—trying to get two drawings to Hawaiʻi from England. They were original ink-and-watercolor drawings by John Webber, an eighteenth-century Englishman who was the official artist on Captain James Cook's third and final voyage to the Pacific.

Seeing an opportunity for the museum, Duckworth invited me to lunch. We met at the beachside restaurant at the Colony Surf. "Let me help you," he said. "If you can help me get these paintings here, I'll get a story in the paper, which will present you to the community as a Hawaiian coming back and establishing a business."

I became entranced with the exquisite drawings. One was a red-and-black charcoal sketch of two men in a canoe, sail unfurled, with one of the men bailing out water. The other was a rare, small drawing of a young man sitting, knees up, on a two-man raft, *Huinapapalani*. There was a large bunch of bananas and a cluster of coconuts in the middle of the raft.[110]

I told Nancy about Duckworth's overture. She was lukewarm. She was doing her thing in Santa Fe, and I was doing my thing in Hawaiʻi. I decided to buy both drawings and donate them to the museum.

So, in May 1990, I returned to the museum for a presentation of the gift. I had donated them in my mother's name, and she was there with me, along with members of the Oliwa-Alapa clan, as well as Bishop Museum trustees, the activist Moanikeala Akaka, some prominent Honolulu matrons, and John Dominis Holt IV (a grandson of an officer of King Kalākaua who was also on the military staff of Queen Liliʻuokalani). Ronn Ronck, the art writer from the *Honolulu Advertiser* was there, as was the acclaimed muralist John Charlot and the Native Hawaiian artist Rocky KaʻiouliokahihikoloʻEhu Jensen.

A reporter from the *Honolulu Star-Bulletin* was there, too. The paper ran a two-page spread in the sports section with the headline "Schoenke Does Honor to His Heritage." I thought, "Here I am, I

---

[110] *Ka Wai Ola*. "In Acknowledgment of Patrons." June 1990, vol. 07, no. 06, https://kawaiola.news/issue/199006/, p. 17.

established my business on the mainland, and now I'm bringing it here. I can be part of this." Another person who showed up that day ended up being pivotal to my efforts to reconnect.

Tommy Holmes was a Punahou grad, a hāʻole boy, skinny. He knew everybody. He came from money, but he didn't have any money, being sort of the black sheep, a misfit. He had run the Honolulu Marathon barefoot. As a bodysurfer, he could catch 25-foot waves, and all the Hawaiians said, "Are you frickin' crazy?" To prove he was as tough as they were, he went out when nobody was out and went straight down the wave, the wave crashing down on him. They figured he was dead, and then he popped up and went back out again. He was renowned as a "lolo" (crazy) hāʻole boy who was tough as nails.

Tommy Holmes came to the presentation and introduced himself to me. He was still skinny, but now he wore a toupee. He presented himself as an authority on Hawaiian history and lore. He was one of the founders of the Polynesian Voyaging Society, a nonprofit research and educational corporation founded in 1973 to perpetuate traditional Polynesian voyaging methods. The thought crossed my mind that he might be able to help me. And the same thought may have crossed his mind. He probably saw me as a good mark, and I saw him as someone who knew a little bit about everything and might give me a starting point. I started hanging out with him, and he told me what to do and who to reach out to.

I was trying to make a splash, trying to figure out how to establish my business in Hawaiʻi. Buying the paintings helped. Another idea I had was to get involved in paddling again. Tommy became my advisor on everything Hawaiʻi. He and I went to dinner every night—on my dime.

Tommy came up with a scheme. He took me to the Outrigger Canoe Club, where he was a member, at the Diamond Head end of Waikīkī. He said, "You wanna join this club. But you don't want to paddle for them because they're rich and White and stuck up. We want to join

Anuenue, a club made up of local paddlers, mostly Hawaiian and Asian, and paddle for Nappy Napoleon. We want to do the Moloka'i race."

I'd always wanted to do the Moloka'i race. So I went with Tommy and met Nappy Napoleon, the coach at Anuenue Canoe Club, which was based in the backwater of Waikīkī, on the Ala Wai Canal. I asked if I could do the race. Nappy was a man of few words. He said, "You gotta come here and practice. You can't just show up for the race."

At 50, I was still a fairly formidable athlete. I had a physical presence, and I was fit. I still had a little of that cachet from having played in the NFL. The only guy who didn't give a shit about all that was Nappy Napoleon. All he wanted to know was *could I paddle?*

One of my first outings with Nappy involved paddling in Honolulu Harbor. Some of our guys were waiting on the pier, and he wanted me to get out of the boat and for one of them to get in. He said, "Schoenke! Get outta da boat!" What he wanted was for us to pull up to the pier, so I could climb out. I didn't know what he wanted. So, I jumped out of the boat. I was swimming around, looking for a way to get out of the water, and he was looking at me and shaking his head. "Boy," he said in his gruff Pidgin, shaking his head, "Dat is one *dumb* Hawaiian."

Like many watermen, Nappy believed in action. When it came to knowing how to maintain a competitive edge or how to be a great paddler, he had a stock answer. "You know what the secret is? Get in the canoe and paddle."

There are six paddlers in each boat, sitting evenly spaced. The steersman at the back controls the canoe's course with his paddle. The lead sets the pace. At predetermined intervals, the person sitting in the second seat calls for paddlers to switch sides. That's a little tricky, but nothing compared to "changes," which is when fresh paddlers, who are traveling nearby in an escort boat, swim up to the boat and get hauled in to relieve other paddlers. The boat does not slow down during changes.

Training for the Moloka'i race

The first time I practiced changes, I pulled myself up, and my hand slipped, so I grabbed the hull again and threw myself back into the canoe, dislocating my shoulder. I went to Straub Clinic and was told the shoulder was stuck, that they couldn't pull it out. They said they'd have to give me a shot to relax it. Finally, that's what they did—deadened the muscle, popped it back in, and put my arm in a sling to keep everything in place until they could operate on it.

The next day, back at the Ala Wai Canal, I'm walking along the sidewalk next to the canal in my sling, following the canoes. Nappy caught up with me and looked at me with his narrow eyes.

He says, "'Ey, Schoenke, ey, why you not in da canoe?"

"I can't do the changes," I answer.

"I no care what you *can't* do. Can you paddle? If you no can paddle, get outta here!" If you grow up on the mainland and come to Hawai'i late in life saying you are Hawaiian, you may not be accepted until you prove your authenticity by your ability to surf, to paddle, to dive, play and sing Hawaiian music, and communicate with your fellow Hawaiian brothers in Pidgin. My strong physical presence was not enough. You get tested. I looked at him, took the sling off, and got in the boat. I realized if I kept my hands close to my chest, I could keep my shoulder from popping out. So I got into the canoe and started paddling. In my head, I could hear the ghost of Lombardi—SCHOENKE, THAT'S NOTHING BUT A GODDAMN PUSSY INJURY! PADDLE! After the practice, I went to a medical supply store and got a brace that would prevent my arm from extending so far out as to make it pop back out.

I liked Nappy, and he liked me. I have incredibly warm, wonderful feelings toward him. He had been paddling the Molokaʻi since 1958, when he was 17. At this time, he was in his fifties, already a legend. He knew everything about going in between the islands. In 2022, he paddled his 60th consecutive race. His beloved wife, Anona, was home during the race after having experienced a stroke, and he hurried home to her after the race.

I made the senior crew. I thought Nappy was going to steer my boat, but at the last minute, his five sons decided to paddle the race, and he decided to steer their boat. However, my good friend, Tommy Holmes, a veteran of many crossings, and I paddled together.[111]

Wearing cotton floral-printed swim trunks and an Anuenue Canoe Club tank top, I crossed the beach off the west side of Molokaʻi barefoot carrying my five-foot-long koa paddle. I had traded a football uniform for the uniform worn by a crew of six paddlers. We hopped into a trim, 40-foot-long outrigger canoe. A 10-foot-long float, connected to the canoe by two wooden struts, balanced the canoe and helped the canoe move easily and quickly through the waves and also improved its buoyancy.

Over 40 canoes were lined up and about to cross the Kaiwi Channel from Molokaʻi to Oʻahu. I was excited and confident in the same way

---

[111] Kohn2. "Legendary Paddler Joseph 'Nappy' Napoleon Steers His 60th Consecutive Molokai Hoe." *KHON2*, 9 Oct 2017. https://www.hawaiibusiness.com/kalama-evp-weinberg-foundation/.

Native Stories (podcast). "Nappy Napoleon of Anuenue Canoe Club." *Nappy Napoleon of Anuenue Canoe Club – Native Stories, Native Stories*, 15 Dec 2019, nativestories.org/nappy-napoleon-of-anuenue-canoe-club/.

I was just before going onto the football field. I had prepared myself, but I was still nervous that I might not be able to perform because I had a shoulder injury and had never done this before. Still, I was out of my mind with excitement and ecstatic because I was about to fulfill a lifelong dream and connect with my heritage in a brand-new way. As a team, we were going to paddle a channel that has strong winds, waves, and even the possibility of storms, and I, as a novice, was racing against highly experienced teammates. It was overcast, and the swells were high. One and only one thought raced through my mind—*Paddle, and paddle hard!* Within an hour after the race began, you couldn't see any of the other canoes because each steersman chose a different route across the channel. I relied completely on my teammates when it came to handling the weather and wave conditions. As I paddled, Tommy constantly yelled at me and pointed out dolphins, flying fish rising out of the water, sharks, whales, and birds—an amazing array of wildlife.

We had 40 miles and five hours before we'd get to Waikīkī. I think we placed 12th. Outrigger Canoe Club beat us. After we pulled our canoe onto Duke Kahanamoku Beach, we put on red tank tops for the closing ceremonies. Nancy came for the race, but she was sickened that I was doing all this with a torn shoulder. All the rest of my family was there, with lei for me—maile leaves and ʻilima and puakenikeni and tuberose flowers and even a haku lei garland for my head.[112] My teammates saw me on the beach, decked out with all those lei. "'Eh, brah," they said, "First time, yeah?" Most of them had already paddled the race many times, so they were ribbing me.

That put me in my place. There was a little fanfare about my desire to reconnect to Hawaiʻi—a segment on a TV station showed me paddling with the crew. For me, though, it was a thrill just to do the whole thing—to finish, even though I was injured—and to be accepted by Nappy.

---

112 "39th Annual Molokai Hoe 10-7-1990." *OCC Sports*, Outrigger Canoe Club. photos.outriggercanoeclubsports.com/Outrigger-Canoe-Club-1990/1990-Molokai-Hoe/.

Celebrating finishing the Moloka'i 32-mile canoe race

Of course, being committed to my Hawaiian heritage would involve a lot more than paddling in a canoe race. I didn't want to just be a rich guy who helicoptered in. I wanted to be a part of the Hawaiian community. Being from Kahuku and Lāʻie, being an Alapa, gave me legitimacy. At the time, the Hawaiian Cultural Renaissance was blooming; Hawaiian Studies at U.H. was booming, and there was political agitation over rights that were owed Hawaiians. I wanted to figure out how to be helpful.

I met two important people through First Hawaiian Bank. The first was Walter Dods, who was president of the bank. Walter is a self-made man, who came from humble roots and rose to being a hugely successful financial business executive. We were simpatico. And he was a trustee at Punahou even though he wasn't a graduate. Walter had a saying: "Strive to achieve your goals and aspirations, but never forget about your community."[113] The second was Corbett Kalama, who helped finance my early banking needs. Corbett grew up in one of the oldest Hawaiian families in Kailua, but he was one of 11 children in a 900-square-foot home with a family that relied on welfare, food stamps, and the kindness of others.[114] At First Hawaiian Bank, since I had met him, he had climbed from supervisor of the organization's personal banking and small business banking segment to leading the Wealth Management Group, directing 250 employees, and managing approximately $10 billion in assets. He was on many charitable boards and community organizations. He was a paddler, too.[115]

Walter was a savvy businessman. Corbett was astute, kind, and involved with various civic organizations. Larry Johnson encouraged me to bring my business to Hawai'i. If my football coaches taught me how to be a businessman, these three men taught me how to be a *Hawaiian* businessman.

ECHOES

Football was never far behind me. While I was establishing my business in Hawai'i, I continued to maintain my relationship with the Redskins. At that time, the new general manager was Bobby Beathard, who was a friend of my daughter's father-in-law. Bobby had worked

---

113 Gelber, Gina, et al. "Talk Story: Corbett Kalama, Executive VP and COO, Harry and Jeanette Weinberg Foundation – Hawai'i Office." *Hawai'i Business Magazine*, 6 Aug. 2019, www.hawaiibusiness.com/kalama-evp-weinberg-foundation/.

114 Ibid.

115 Wilcox, Leslie. "Corbett Kalama The Long Short Story with Leslie Wilcox." *PBS Hawaii*, Feb 2010. https://www.pbshawaii.org/long-story-short-with-leslie-wilcox-corbett-kalama/.

with June Jones, a well-known college coach who was one of the originators of the "run and shoot" offense. I wanted to learn more about it. At one of the many Redskins events I attended, where Bobby was also often present, during a conversation with Bobby's wife, Christine, I mentioned June Jones, and she said she knew him. She called Bobby over, and he said he would be glad to call June and set up a meeting. I thought at the time that June Jones was coaching at the University of Hawaiʻi. However, to my surprise, Bobby told me that he had just accepted the head coaching job at SMU.

I contacted June and set up a time to meet with him in Dallas. I flew down and planned to spend a weekend with him. He invited me to attend all of the practices and team meetings. I found it enlightening and fun to watch a coach who didn't scream, yell, or threaten the players. He was softspoken, and when he gave a directive, he expected the players to respond immediately. In one situation where the offense and defense were running live scrimmage, the play called in the huddle was a deep pass. The offensive players executed the play, and the defense covered the receiver closely, but the quarterback was able to execute the pass perfectly. The receiver sprinted down the field to the end zone.

Coach Jones blew his whistle, brought the players all together, and said, "Gentlemen, did you understand what I said? I said this is *live*. Do you understand what that *means*? OK. Let's run it again." Within seconds as the play began, a war broke out. There was total physical engagement and mayhem on the playing field. After the play was over, June said, "Thank you, gentlemen. Let's continue."

June's approach was simple and direct. I was impressed with the simplicity of his directives and how his team responded to his words. I extended my stay and spent the week with the team and then traveled to a game they won. My interest in the "run and shoot" technique was what had driven my desire to meet June Jones. However, it was our connection to Hawaiʻi and to each other and mutual respect that ultimately propelled our relationship, which endures to this day.

After donating the eighteenth-century drawings to the Bishop Museum, I was asked by Donald Duckworth to chair the Hawaiian Arts and Culture Board. He specifically gave me the task of working with certain Native Hawaiians who were recipients of funds channeled through the museum. They were artists and craftspeople doing research and bringing back traditional arts. One of my main jobs was to help monitor funds for the *Hōkūle'a*, the sailing canoe that had traveled throughout Polynesia without the aid of Western instruments.

Senator Daniel Inouye allocated $20 million in federal funds to the museum, and the museum directed it to the committee, which in turn managed the finances for the *Hōkūle'a*. Duckworth wanted me to work with Pinky Thompson, who was a real patriarch in the voyaging community. He was a physically small guy with incredible influence, which made him larger than life in spite of his stature. I observed that when he walked into a room, everyone stood up. When he talked, everybody shut up. He was regarded with enormous respect. His full name was Myron Bennett Thompson, but everyone knew him as "Pinky." The nickname came from his mother, who was so convinced during her pregnancy that she would have a girl that she bought pink baby clothes and decorated the baby's room completely in pink.[116]

Pinky graduated from Punahou with a bachelor's degree in sociology from Colby College and a master's degree from the University of Hawai'i at Mānoa. He was president of the Polynesian Voyaging Society. The premise of this organization was to prove that ancient Polynesians traveled throughout Polynesia and traveled thousands of miles without instruments back and forth, particularly between Hawai'i and Tahiti. The society's first project was to build a replica of a double-hulled voyaging canoe, the *Hōkūle'a*, which was used to prove that this was in fact possible.

Pinky had multiple interests and dimensions. In addition to being a social worker, he was involved in state land use issues. He was also

---

116 *Vimeo*. "Visions in the Dark: the Life of Pinky Thompson." n.d. https://vimeo.com/461983925.

a state administrator and a trustee of the Bishop Estate (now known as Kamehameha Schools). He helped create the Hawaiian Health Care System, as well as a group called ALU LIKE. This group's focus is on on-job training, health, housing, education, and the rights of native Hawaiians.[117]

Pinky grew up in an extremely large household full of "at-risk" foster children. "I grew up living with kids who were less fortunate," Pinky once said. "We became close. I felt their pain. I wanted to find a way to help and that began my process of entering into social work."[118] Pinky was very proud of being Hawaiian, and he channeled his anger about the treatment of Hawaiians into developing methods to help them and to encourage them to share his sense of pride in his cultural heritage.[119] Pinky was a visionary and a leader, but he didn't tend to step into the limelight—that is, unless he was coming to ask me for money. In the early 1990s, my job was to manage Pinky's requests for the *Hōkūle'a* and make sure there was enough money left over for other projects. I needed to make sure that the money didn't go just to the *Hōkūle'a*. And once he got his share, I had to make sure Pinky didn't spend it all right away.

Pinky passed his social values on to his son, Nainoa, a 1972 Punahou grad who was becoming renowned as a navigator in his own right. His first solo voyage from Hawai'i to Tahiti in 1980 put him on the map as the first modern Hawaiian to master the art of Micronesian navigation:

Navigators like Thompson and his mentor, Mau Piailug, rely on information such as the color, temperature, and salinity of seawater, floating plant debris, sightings of land-based seabirds flying

---

117 Childs, Shelley. "RE: HENRY NAINOA THOMPSON." *Genealogy.com*, 29 Apr 2010. https://www.genealogy.com/forum/regional/states/topics/hi/3251/.

118 Low, Sam. "Myron Bennett 'Pinky' Thompson (1924-2001), A Life of Service." *Hawaiian Voyaging Traditions*, 1 Jan 2002. https://archive.hokulea.com/index/founder_and_teachers/myron_pinky_thompson.html.

119 Shapiro, Treena and Omandam, Pat. "Ex-Trustee 'Pinky' Thompson Dies at 77." *Honolulu Star-Bulletin Hawai'i News*, Honolulu Star-Bulletin, 26 Dec 2001. archives.starbulletin.com/2001/12/26/news/story2.html.

out to fish, cloud type, color, and movement, wind direction, speed, and temperature, the direction and nature of ocean swells and waves, the position of stars in the sky. Incredibly enough, the "compass" they use is not magnetic, but rather a mental model of where islands are located and the star points which one could use to navigate between them—an extremely complex and difficult task that takes years to learn and memorize.[120]

Nainoa became the lead navigator on many voyages of the *Hōkūleʻa*. When Pinky died in 2001, Nainoa took over his role as the president of the Polynesian Voyaging Society. Hawaiian society was based on the ocean, so the ocean was never viewed as an enemy or as a threat because my ancestors had to migrate thousands of miles throughout the Pacific on its surface to locate land and food sources. This became a cultural skill set. What I came to realize was that my history was the history of the Polynesian people. I had the great honor of being part of all of this because I helped these navigators get their money through the Bishop Museum. Through this process, I also gained something as I became more connected to my own heritage and to my own relationship with the people, the land, and the ocean.

Pinky adored his son. Nainoa represented everything good about Hawaiʻi's past *and* its future. He was a star, big time. He was giving credibility to Polynesian history. I feel privileged to have become his friend.

He invited me to various sailing trips or sometimes just to come down and clean the boat. He came to Washington, DC, and we spent time together. One night, we were sitting outside having dinner in Georgetown. It was a clear September night, and he looked up at the sky and started telling me about the stars, how they looked different in different places in the world because to navigate at the level he did without instruments, he had to rely heavily on the stars.

---

120 Munatones, Steven, "Master Navigator Nainoa Thompson Recognized." *WOWSA*, 25 May 2015. https://www.openwaterswimming.com/master-navigator-nainoa-thompson/.

Once, I was able to ask Nainoa to do *me* a favor while I continued to help him. The Alapas were having a family reunion, and Page was one of the cousins organizing it. Nainoa was looking to train his crew by going on training trips, and I was overseeing his expenses in my role on the museum committee. I asked whether there might be a chance that he and his guys could train on the other side of the island. He said, "Yes." In exchange, I asked him if he could take some of my family members out on the boat while he was at it.

He said, "Sure, I'll do that."

He met me at Kualoa Bay on the windward side of Oʻahu. Off in the distance, you can see majestic mountains that reach 2 to 3,000 feet in the air covered with deep green foliage. In the valley below is Kualoa Ranch, with its beautiful green pastures dotted with horses that provide tourists with treks through the valley. Our cousin worked as a ranch hand there.

When we got there, the *Hōkūleʻa* was waiting out in the bay. There were 16 of us all together—my brother Walter and his son, my sister Marilyn and her kids, Page and her husband, and various cousins, including Harvey Alapa and Eric Keawe, the son of singer Genoa Keawe. We crossed the grassy expanse of the park and then swam or rowed out to the boat—the bay is shallow, a mixture of reef and sand pockets.

We sailed past Kahana Bay, passed some of our family on another beach, and waved to our cousins. Then, we sailed back to Kahana, where my grandfather had brought my mother a century earlier, after they returned from Iosepa, Utah, and before they left for a homestead on the Big Island. On that sailing canoe, my entire family had an opportunity to merge with their own history. As I steered, I entered into a euphoric state where I felt connected with my brothers navigating the islands of Polynesia without modern instruments. In that moment, I incarnated my own heritage fully for the first time on this historic vessel, steering it with the wind coursing past me over the same waves my ancestors had moved over centuries before. I connected emotionally with my warrior

Nainoa Thompson and I after I sailed on and steered the Hōkūle'a

bloodline, the Alapas. Time stood still, and for that brief moment, I embodied my ancestors as I moved gradually toward the lagoon to the sound of my cousin Aunty Dawn standing on the beach—dressed up in a beautiful *mu'umu'u*, with a shell lei, chanting a Hawaiian welcome to the visitors to her home, which now, for the first time, felt truly like my home as well. One of the *Hōkūle'a* crew members waiting on the beach for us with my aunt was Māori, and he greeted each of us in the old way—by touching noses and breathing in, sharing breath.

For the family, it was a memorable event and incredibly exciting—and fun. For me, it was deeply meaningful at almost a primal level.

I said to Nainoa a grateful, "Mahalo nui." Thank you.

And, boom, he was off training.

THE COST OF KEEPING MY GOOD NAME

As far as my business was concerned, I was in an unusual and very fortunate position. I could sit in the garage and drink Primo with my Hawaiian brethren, and I could sit in a corporate boardroom. I also could paddle in the Ala Wai Canal with my Hawaiian teammates and invite Governor John Waiheʻe to my Redskins suite in Washington, DC. By the year 2000, Schoenke & Associates had picked up just about every major corporation in Honolulu as clients: Bank of Hawaiʻi, First Hawaiian, Bank of the Pacific, Maui Land & Pineapple, Hawaiian Electric, you name 'em. It was frickin' fantastic.

Through professional contacts like Larry Johnson, Walter Dods, and Corbett Kalama, I started meeting people at the Office of Hawaiian Affairs. This self-governing corporation was founded to right wrongs suffered by Native Hawaiians. Grassroots leaders proposed that income from land taken from the illegal overthrow of the Hawaiian Kingdom in 1893 be used to benefit Hawaiians. My great-grandfather Oliva Alapa was a beneficiary of an OHA program intended to help manage lands that had been set aside as homelands for native Hawaiians. My half brother Stanley's daughter, Luana, is an OHA delegate.

One unforgettable leader in OHA was Haunani Apoliona, who in her late 60s still holds a leadership position with the Bank of Hawaiʻi.[121] She was elected to the OHA Board of Trustees and became its chairperson. She has held federal offices and was appointed to the US President's Advisory Commission on Asian American and Pacific Islanders and the US Census Bureau Race Ethnic Advisory Council. Apoliona is also a composer and a slack-key guitarist. She performed for years with the popular group Olomana. Her intelligence and tireless efforts to improve the lives of Hawaiians impressed me. We spent time talking about Hawaiian issues and how native Hawaiians could improve their economic and political status. When I returned to the islands, she often met me after one of her performances at one of the local hotels, and we caught up.

I had political contacts in the Washington offices of both of Hawaiʻi's senators—Daniel Inouye and Daniel Akaka. One big issue at the time was a bill arguing for nation status for native Hawaiians. It was

---

121 Bank of Hawaiʻi, Board of Directors. "S. Haunani Apoliona." n.d.; https://ir.boh.com/board-member/s-haunani-apoliona.

labeled the Native Hawaiian Government Reorganization Act, but it was eventually called the Akaka Bill after Daniel Akaka, who was the first Native Hawaiian elected to the US Senate and was spearheading the bill. Akaka was friendly, warm, and very likeable, but he wasn't the type of guy who got "out there" and promoted his bill. The Akaka Bill proposed establishing a process for the US government to recognize Native Hawaiians similar to that applied to American Indian tribes in the continental 49 states—although it prohibited Indigenous Native Hawaiians from gaming, it did offer them some benefits.

I realized that I might be able to use my political contacts in Washington to help get the Akaka Bill through. For starters, I got OHA to hire my law firm, Patton Boggs. After retaining Patton Boggs, a whole new world had opened up to me. I paid them big bucks, but Tommy was protecting my business. He knew everybody.

Basically, in Washington lobbying circles, Tommy had access to the Democrats, and Haley Barbour, Tommy's good friend, a Republican lobbyist, had access to the Republicans. In spite of the fact that we were very close friends, and we were both Democrats, Tommy and I didn't run in the same political circles. My involvement with Eastern Liberals like the Kennedys began because I was politically involved as a professional football player. I added value to them because I was able to support and express liberal views I was committed to that were at the forefront at the time, and I was involved with the Special Olympics. I became part of the inner circle—Eastern liberals who attended the parties I was invited to at Ethel Kennedy's home, who I rubbed shoulders with—politicians, business people, celebrities, athletes, some very wealthy, some not. Tommy ran in the hardcore, nuts-and-bolts circle where legislation was passed the political world on the Hill. His views, although Democratic, were moderate and conservative. He and his supporters were typically not invitees at the Kennedy home, but they knew each other and respected each other. His father, Hale Boggs, was a powerful legislator, which gave Tommy total access to the Democratic machine and indirectly, to the Republican machinery. Because of Tommy's relationship with Haley Barbour, he was able to reach over the aisle and gain Republican support on major legislation.

I managed to talk OHA into retaining both Boggs's and Barbour's firms. But then, when the Hawaiians came to town to lobby Congress, they all showed up at Tommy's office at once because they had nowhere else to go. OHA would bring *all* the delegates—people who had major leadership roles in the Hawaiian community like Clayton Hee, and also women who were strong leaders in the Hawaiian community like musician Haunani Apoliona and political activists like the Trask sisters. I got desperate phone calls from the law firms.

"They're expecting us to entertain them," the secretary said. "What do we do?"

I was really helpful. "Give them a cup of coffee."

"I've already given them coffee." Most clients don't send the whole entourage. I eventually had to cancel my appointments and run down there and take them out to lunch.

It was quite a scene, but in the end, some of it worked. Senator Akaka was instrumental in the passage of the 1993 Apology Resolution, which acknowledged the 100th anniversary of the US overthrow of the Kingdom of Hawai'i. But although he proposed various forms of the Native Hawaiian Government Reorganization Act starting in 2000, the bill never passed.[122]

My efforts to get the Akaka Bill passed didn't work out. The most laughable failure, among several I experienced, may have been something I did with a Samoan who was a 1962 graduate of Kahuku High School. His name was Eni Fa'aua'a Hunkin Faleomavaega Jr. (Eni Hunkin).

He called me and said, "We've got a lot of Hawaiian athletes coming into the NFL, and there's nobody there to advise them. I'm working with a group of people—one of them was Jack Thompson,

---

[122] The Federalist Society. "The Akaka Bill." 21 Apr 2009. https://fedsoc.org/commentary/publications/the-akaka-bill.

The Throwin' Samoan—who would like to be the first out of the gate to help them. Would you talk to them?"

I sat down and talked to them and eventually put up some money to help this group get started. Each time I checked in with them, they told me they had met with different athletes from different schools, but they hadn't signed anybody. Then, they came back to me and said that they had come up with this idea to do a basketball game they were calling "Who's Got Game?" It was a version of the schoolyard game known as HORSE, where competitors take turns attempting shots from anywhere on the court, often with tricks mixed in, with the objective being to force an opponent into an effort they can't convert. If someone makes a shot, then everyone else must replicate the feat. If they can't, they gain a letter. Once someone gets all five letters of the word "HORSE," they're eliminated from the competition. It's also played as PIG for those with short attention spans—or not much time on their hands. Of course, when it's not being played on a schoolyard, there are all kinds of different names for it, like TAXES, or STUPID, or something more pejorative.

The game is best when players can hit long-range bombs or get crazy with between-the-legs and behind-the-back attempts. You want versatile shooters. Eni Hunkin's group from Seattle said they wanted to get the NBA involved, and I said, "If you get the Seattle SuperSonics involved, then maybe we've got something."

They did get the SuperSonics involved. They started envisioning the event as a national Christmas TV show, with all these great former NBA players flying to Hawai'i. I gave them seed money. They started lining up NBA players, and I got word back: "It'll be a huge success, and we'll return all your money through the sponsors they will secure!" I called my Punahou friend John de Fries, cousin of my baseball teammate Hiram. John represented the Ritz-Carlton Hotel on Maui, and he was able to secure the hotel for the event.

I called one of the organizers and asked, "How are we doing?"

They say, "It's great, NBC has agreed to televise it; it's going to be a Christmas special; they're going to build a basketball court; they have all these former NBA players coming in. Everything's cool."

I called a friend in Bethesda who worked in sports at NBC to confirm everything, and he explained how much it would cost to air it on NBC. We're talking megabucks.

Then, when the time comes, I fly to Hawai'i, and I can see a strain on the faces of the organizers. I see John de Fries, and I say, "John, how're we doing?"

He sits me down and says, "Ray, I think we might have a few problems."

I talk to the guys. "Well, we don't have any sponsors," they say.

I say, incredulous, "What? Who's paying for this?"

The whole thing caved in. My friend, John Miller at NBC, said, "Ray, get your ass out of there. Close your books, walk away; fuck them; they screwed you."

"I can't. My name is on it!"

I went back to Honolulu to Harlan Cadinha's firm, where I had some of my investments. I paid everybody, and they televised it. I got some of my money back but still lost a bundle. It cost me over a half million dollars. That was the price for me keeping my good name. I didn't want anyone to ever be able to say my word wasn't good.

I was in Hawai'i first because I was an athlete, second because I was a paddler, and third because I was part of the Bishop Museum committee. At one point, I held the purse strings for the Polynesian Voyaging Society, but it went beyond that. I felt a genuine connection with them. There was a new sailing canoe, the *Hawai'iloa*. After it was built in 1994, it was launched from Honolulu, to end up at Wai'anae for a christening ceremony. Eni Hunkin was there. I spent the night out there, camping in the hills, and in the morning, the crew took us out on a ride along the leeward coast in the *Hawai'iloa*. Nainoa asked me if I'd like to steer, and of course, I wanted to. I got to be part of that whole world, which was wonderful.

CHAPTER NINE

From One Blood Sport to Another (1992-2006)

PRESIDENT CLINTON AND THE FUTURE

While thrilled to be involved with the *Hōkūle'a* and the paddling community, at the same time, I was getting more involved in Hawaiian civic and cultural and political affairs, and I was itching to play a larger role in campaign politics. Ever since the McGovern campaign, I'd stayed active in Democratic politics. I really thought that politics, not business, was my calling and that success in business might enable me to build a network and run as a candidate myself one day. By 1991, I was hearing buzz about Bill Clinton, the former governor of Arkansas, and it sounded like he would have a lot more skill than Carter at winning hearts and minds. But when I attended parties with primarily guests who were Democrats, and I expressed support for Clinton, the people at the party disagreed with me, expressing skepticism about the "new" Democrat.

Leading up to the 1992 Democratic Convention in Chicago, I still had doubts. I remembered that a good friend of mine at SMU, Rudy Moore, had worked in Clinton's campaign for Governor. I called him. Rudy wasn't going to the convention, but he said, "I'm gonna have someone meet you there. A judge."

When I got to Chicago, I had breakfast with the judge. Whether it was the judge, Rudy, or someone else, somebody must have said something positive about me. I signed with the Clinton campaign feeling like a political veteran amidst the sharp young minds supporting his election.[123]

I picked up the gauntlet since it was clear that in the political world, money is what makes the world go around. I started raising millions in campaign contributions for Clinton. The first time I raised half a million dollars at a dinner, I knew I had become what I call "a big dog."

After the campaign, I get a call from President Clinton. We talk, and he is incredibly cordial. He says, "Come on down to the White House." I do. I get there, and I am really nervous. Erskine Bowles, his Chief of Staff, invites me to sit in his office, and I have the feeling that I am in a holding pen, as if I don't have the clout to meet with the president.

Clinton comes out and sees me there and says, "Erskine, what's Ray doing in your office? Come on over here and get in my office." So we sit down, and first thing you know, we're laughing it up and having a big time. He's just that kind of person. Incredibly friendly.

Clinton was very charitable. He reached out and invited Nancy and me to a lot of events—the Presidential Gala, the National Finance Breakfast (twice), the Clinton-Gore Dinner Dance. He even invited me to one of his infamous 'coffee klatches.' Clinton was criticized and accused of selling access to the White House to the attendees of these coffee klatches in exchange for political donations.[124] However, I felt that when I attended one of these events, I was closer to Clinton than anyone else there. These get-togethers at the White House were in fact a lucrative part of Democratic fundraising. One of the hastily scheduled coffees might bring in bring a few hundred thousand dollars, and it has been reported that altogether, the coffee klatches brought in millions.[125]

---

123 Joyce. "The Game Beyond the Game."

124 *Las Vegas Sun*, "LV men part of coffee klatches." 05 Feb 1997. https://lasvegassun.com/news/1997/feb/05/lv-men-part-of-coffee-klatches/.

125 Jackson, Brooks. "Lincoln Bedroom Guests Gave $5.4 Million." *all politics*. 24 Feb 1997. https://www.cnn.com/ALLPOLITICS/1997/02/26/clinton.lincoln/.

Weisskopf, Michael and Babcock, Charles R., *The Washington Post*, "DONORS PAY AND STAY AT WHITE HOUSE", Dec 1996. https://www.washingtonpost.com/archive/politics/1996/12/15/donors-pay-and-stay-at-white-house/5e0cad1f-5e9c-42c5-8fae-a549508f8388/.

Hanging out with the President in his office

Up to the point of attending the coffee klatch, I had been pretty good friends with reporter Bob Woodward. We had hit it off when he was working for a local Montgomery County weekly paper, a client of mine in my insurance business. We remained pretty good friends socially.

After I attended the coffee event, he called me and asked me about my attendance and asked if I was promised anything. I was taken aback and told him so. I gained nothing from the event except my camaraderie with Clinton himself. I was probably the only person at the event who actually had a social relationship with Clinton. I sat next to him, and we hammed it up. In my innocence, I had no idea that by attending one of these events, I would be considered someone who was seeking influence. However, I think that attending the event clearly made me suspect in Bob's eyes. I didn't personally hear Clinton promise anything to anyone. It was strictly social.

Nancy was involved with Emily's List, a political action committee focused on helping elect Democratic female candidates in favor of abortion rights to public office. Once we attended an event with

Clinton as a keynoter. I didn't approach him—it would have been almost impossible to do so.

I'm talking to Ellen Malcolm, who runs Emily's List, and a man in a dark suit with an earpiece comes up, taps me, hands me a phone, and says, "The president wants to talk to you."

"The president of what?" I ask.

"*The* president."

Ellen looks at me, puzzled. I realize the guy is Secret Service.

I say hello into the phone, and Clinton says, "Hey, Ray, I saw you in the crowd. How ya doing?"

Clinton called me occasionally in my office. On those occasions, my office assistant came in and said, "The president is on the line—*The* president."

When I took the call, he said, "Hi, Ray. How 'ya doin'?"

I always wanted to answer, "Hey, Bill. How are you doing?" But I didn't. I always addressed him as "Mr. President."

Of course, incidents like this were incredibly flattering, but Clinton engaged in this behavior with a lot of people. That's why he was so popular.

We played golf. He didn't want to play at Robert Trent Jones, an exclusive golf club in Gainesville, Virginia, which I had joined for my business. He wanted to play somewhere a little more plebian. So we went to a private course where the public could also play. The president was playing with handcrafted, uniquely designed clubs from Russia made out of special metals. It was a fun outing, interrupted by a storm. Right before we took cover in the clubhouse, I said, "Go ahead and hit the drive with one of those Russian clubs, and see how far you can hit it. The wind is beginning to howl, and I bet you can hit it at least 400 yards." He took my challenge and sent that ball flying.

"Mr. President, you can hit the ball a country mile," I wrote to him shortly after the incident, in August 1999. "The one you hit right before the storm easily went over 300 yards. The Russian war club was fantastic and saved me when I used it on one hole."

Golfing with the President

This is an example of dozens of notes we exchanged. I wrote him letters, consistently, on topics ranging from thoughts in a 1995 meeting with Newt Gingrich, to a discussion of an article by James Fallows in *The Atlantic*, to invitations to go duck hunting. After another golf outing in which I'd praised his game, he wrote back, "Thanks to your gracious mulligan! It was all great fun!" I even had the audacity to reflect on Vince Lombardi's style and to share a few thoughts on leadership. The president's notes were always short and gracious —sometimes typed by his secretary, sometimes handwritten. I don't know whether Clinton liked that I had the nerve to write him and tell him what I thought or whether he just suffered fools gladly. I followed his moves closely, and I wasn't averse to getting into the national or international crisis of the day. When Serbia and Bosnia were at war, I said, "Bomb the shit outta them." He was already doing it and getting criticized for it. He didn't have to write back, but sometimes he did. That gave me confidence in the relationship.

I'm sure I was not the only person who had this relationship, but I did think to myself, "*I cannot believe that I, the son of the Olivia Haleaka Alapa Schoenke, am corresponding with the president of the United States.*"

Clinton's was the most important campaign I was involved in, personally and politically. You name it; I would do it for him. He was a cool dude. He went out of his way for me. I found him to be charming, intellectual, and a good politician. He knew how to work a crowd.

During his administration, I met with Vernon Jordan, the lawyer who was Clinton's friend, advisor, golfing companion, and go-between. Jordan, in spite of being intimidatingly large, conveyed warmth and friendliness. He thanked me for my effort in the campaign and said the president wanted to offer me the ambassadorship to New Zealand. I stupidly declined. At the time, I didn't appreciate what that would have meant: not just a great opportunity to see New Zealand, but a rare chance to expand my understanding of myself as a Pacific Islander by becoming acquainted with the Māori people and their culture. By the time I changed my mind, it was too late. The position had been offered to someone else. I then was offered the position immediately under the Undersecretary of the Interior—or under the under—which I turned down as well.

I had other ideas for myself.

In 1998, after 30 years, I sold my company, Schoenke & Associates, to Clark Consulting Inc. for $17 million, with the promise of deferred income of several million dollars. I was pushing 58 years old.

THE RUN FOR GOVERNOR

That's the year I decided to run for Governor of Maryland. Politics had always excited me, and I'd nurtured a dream of running for public office since my days at SMU. I even dreamed of representing Hawaiʻi in some way and actually considered running for office in Hawaiʻi.

I had invested time and energy in building a reputation, and I had raised enough money through business to be independent. I had considered running for the US House from my district, but I had known for a long time that I didn't want to be one of 400. I wanted to be one of one. Did I want to spend five to 10 years earning my spurs in the state house, run for office in Hawaiʻi, or take a long shot, run for governor, and risk a lot of money?

I had built a network of people, and I had previously hired lobbyists for my insurance business, so when it came time for me to jump in and seek the highest office in Maryland, it was hard for them to say no. But rallying behind me would mean stepping on the toes of other Democrats.

Tommy Boggs, who was then the #1 lobbyist in Washington and a dear friend, said, "Ray, that's crazy. You don't wanna do that. It's so hard; it's high-risk, and you're gonna piss everybody off in the Democratic Party, particularly in the state of Maryland." But Governor Parris Glendening was getting bad press. He seemed weak, so I persisted. Eventually, Tommy promised, "I'll do anything for you if you decide to run, but it's a long shot. You're climbing up a steep hill. All our friends are calling me and begging me to convince you not to run because they don't want to help you. I told them, 'If he runs, we're helping him. I don't give a shit what you say.'"

Bill Clinton also told me not to do it. In spite of him and other naysayers, I decided to take the risk.

I remember walking along the C&O Canal with Nancy and Hazel and George Solomon when we told the Solomons I was going to run for governor. They said they couldn't believe that I was going to do it, but if I did, they said they would support me.

That day on the canal, the four of us were talking about what it meant to run for governor, how difficult it might be, and why I was doing it. I sounded George out about what kind of reception my candidacy might get from *The Washington Post*. I also knew Ben Bradlee, Executive Editor at the *Post*, from parties. I think he was the one who said, "Hey, Ray, this is life. If you're gonna get out there, you could get your ass handed to you."

Donald Graham, the paper's high-powered publisher, was an occasional tennis partner after we happened to vacation with our families at the same resort one year. I also won a Mercedes at the *Washington Post* golf tournament, which I still drive. I had taken Graham into confidence about my desire to run for office, and he had encouraged me to run for office in Maryland, where I lived, not Hawai'i, because I had spent most of my adult life in Maryland. He certainly didn't let our on-court parrying or our friendship influence his treatment of my candidacy. He managed the editorial board and encouraged me to have a sit-down with them. They chopped my butt up. Michael Barnes, the governor's campaign chairman and a good friend of mine, stated that he regretted "having to fend off these kind of potshots." He was referring to my criticism of the governor, and Amy Argetsinger with *The Washington Post* also described me as "not being plugged in enough to the state political hierarchy to gain much support in the long run."[126]

By this time, I had hired two national political consultants, Bill Hamilton and Ray Struthers, who held focus groups to see whether or not a Democrat like me, coming out of left field, could run against an incumbent Democrat governor and win. The results revealed it was a long shot, but not impossible. Political consultant Matt Reese indicated to me that voters were reacting favorably to the idea of a candidate who was a tough-minded Democratic businessman even

---

126 Argetsinger, Amy. *The Washington Post*. "Against Long Odds, Ex-Redskin Is Ready to Challenge Glendening." 19 Jan 1998, B01. https://www.washingtonpost.com/wp-srv/local/longterm/library/mdstateleg/govrace/schoenke1.htm.

though I did not have any electoral experience.[127] It would cost a lot of money, but I decided to run.

My daughter Holly started doing preliminary research for me. I suggested she be my assistant campaign manager, working directly with my campaign manager, Cheryl A. Benton, an African American woman out of Baltimore. Holly was living at home with us and could tell me what was going on with the staff. There was time when it became a little intense for both of us. I loved it, but I'll never forget the morning when I was sitting in the bathroom while she was brushing her teeth and combing her hair, putting on her makeup, trying to get ready. She finally walked up to Nancy and said, "I gotta get outta here. Dad is driving me nuts." She got her own apartment.

Holly stayed through part of the effort, though, and soon she was joined by her brother Eric, who was back from Guatemala, where he had been in the Peace Corps.

Eric was comfortable scouting the scene, getting a sense of the crowd and a feel for the program and telling me what he saw and heard. When there was a big meeting, maybe 300 or 400 people in a room, he walked around, got a feel for the crowd, then came back. "Hey, Dad," he'd lean in and whisper in my ear. "Just be aware…" He was very good.

We primarily targeted Baltimore, which was my kind of city—down-to-earth, a working man's town. We did some advertising in Montgomery County, where we live. Laytonsville is far from downtown DC and the wealthy suburbs, but the entire county is considered by many in the rest of Maryland to be its own universe. However, my main advertising focus was around Baltimore. If you can get communities and counties around Baltimore behind you, as well as the city of Baltimore, you have a good chance of winning the primary. I threw $2 million at it. I curried strong favor in ethnic communities, particularly among Blacks and Italians. Overall, though, I got a

---

127 Ibid.

lukewarm reception. I was making some headway in the polls, but I wasn't getting up to the numbers that I needed. I was paying a pretty penny to my staff and consultants and had an interest in continuing, but they were honest. They tried to show me what the odds were and urged me to throw more money at it.

I went at it differently, seeking and garnering publicity. Unfortunately, not all of the attention was positive. I had been dealing with reporters all my life, and because of my relationship with George Solomon, I trusted them. I guess I shouldn't have. *The Washington Post* branded me in such a way as to destroy any blue-collar appeal I might have had by focusing on my relationship with Clinton and my bank account.

Nevertheless, I still felt I had a shot against Glendening. He had made some bad decisions in his first term and was not especially popular in 1998. The daughter of Bobby and Ethel Kennedy, Kathleen Kennedy Townsend, was his Lieutenant Governor. This did not work in my favor. Ten years earlier, I supported Jimmy Carter's reelection campaign when Teddy Kennedy was considering running, and Ethel Kennedy hadn't forgotten it.

She felt it was a betrayal; she actually confronted me during my campaign and chewed me out. She said, "How dare you run against my daughter."

"I'm not running against your daughter," I responded.

Others were more supportive: "Ray understands the underdog role," Billy Kilmer told *Baltimore* magazine at the time and showed me that he had more understanding of my character than I had realized. "He was always the guy who had to scratch and claw to show that he could get to the top."[128]

In the same article, the journalist Wil S. Hylton seemed sympathetic, too, describing my smile as "a strikingly sincere grin somehow combining the innocence of childhood and the reassurance of a parent."[129]

---

128 *Baltimore Magazine*, June 1998, 48.

129 Ibid, 50.

Looking the part and trying to be the part

Once I covered Baltimore with paid media, we moved to Montgomery County and the greater DC markets. We set up offices around the state. It was a full-fledged campaign. My strengths in my insurance business were leadership, motivation, and running things. I had built a successful company in a discipline that I was not an expert at. I could sit and make sure everybody got their answers, and I could close a complex deal. I knew how to walk in, introduce myself, discuss the problems at hand, and offer a solution. That's what I pitched that I would do as governor.

The finer points of my campaign concerned education, families and children, and the economy. I was dissatisfied with the status quo. The state needed real leadership, especially when it came to economic matters. I argued for a reduction in state income taxes and, controversially, proposed that the state finance public school initiatives through slot machines at horse racetracks.[130] I campaigned with the average taxpayer in mind. Curiously, Art Modell, the guy who owned the Cleveland Browns when I was there, who'd tracked me down to the Redskins locker room to apologize about cutting me, now owned the Baltimore team. He wanted the state to take over building the stadium, but I was against using taxpayer dollars to essentially underwrite a profitable sports franchise. I didn't want to be seen as an ex-player; I wanted to be something more than that. I was saying, "This isn't the way to spend our money. Let the owner build that." Of course, Modell was pissed at me, but we later made up.

I tried to highlight my issues, but I wasn't getting the traction that I needed. I got pigeonholed as an out-of-touch millionaire. I wanted to say to everyone who called me that, "Screw you, man. I came from nothing!" I was constantly fighting that type of criticism, and it hurt my campaign. I was never a winner in the polls. I got close a couple of times, but for the most part, Glendening continued to lead. The polls indicated I would finish second. Ellen Sauerbrey, a former minority leader of the Maryland House of Delegates, was running on the Republican side, but she had lost to Glendening in 1994. I proposed we run together, but she was reluctant to do so. I was told that if I dropped out, I could get a major state position from Glendening. The position I wanted was economic development. But that wasn't offered; in a meeting before I dropped out, the Baltimore stadium authority post was offered. That was ironic, if not downright

---

130 Bubeck, Chris. "His Drive, His Dime Fuel Schoenke Campaign." *Capital News Service*, 3 May 1998, 11. https://cnsmaryland.org/1998/04/29/schoenke-runs-campaign-for-governor-on-his-drive-and-his-dime/

disrespectful. I said to Glendening, "Did you see my ads?" I left the governor's office incredulous and very angry.

My run for governor was over. It was July 6.

I felt, in many ways, positive about the whole thing. I was willing to take the risk, and I was willing to risk big money. But I was also disappointed. I kept reliving it, wondering what I could have done differently. Could I have started at a lower level, run for congressman, and bided my time for 10 years in Congress before moving out? I felt that wasn't for me. I saw the life that they lived, constantly running for reelection and fighting over issues that I found unimportant. That was their life, not mine.

That being said, I learned that you have to get in the trenches and build yourself up over time. Having economic independence was not necessarily a good thing. If you come out of left field, as I did, everything has to line up perfectly. I decided to stay in the game by pursuing other projects—just not by running for political office.

CONNECTING WITH MY PRIMAL SELF

My infatuation with American Indian culture that began when I was 10 in Weatherford, Texas, in part had to do with my being dark-skinned and wanting to find my "tribe." But I was genuinely fascinated by the hunter-gatherer culture. I was absolutely immersed in the whole idea of hunting: the patience required for tracking, the skill of marksmanship, the thrill of the bounty. This fascination carried me for the next 40 years. It was *nothing* for me to sit in a blind for four or six hours, or even longer. I just sat there and waited patiently, trying to outfox the animal I was hunting. As I waited, I watched a stream of interesting wildlife passing by and ignoring me as I sat in silence, waiting with my dog, Boone, often in bitter cold covered with snow, for a bird to land on a body of water next to my blind or a deer to wander past my blind to get a drink of water.

Boone was my partner and my companion. He was a roan-colored poodle pointer, bred for every aspect of hunting—one dog that could do everything—track, point, and retrieve. He spotted game for me. He kept me warm when I arrived at my hunting site before daybreak. I slept in the unheated car, and he served as my blanket and my heater. He was constantly with me. I couldn't rely on friends to hunt with me because I had to fit hunting in when I had free time, which didn't always fit with their schedules. Depending on the time of year, in warm weather, reptiles or lizards might slither by near enough for me to touch (or avoid, if, like water moccasins or rattlesnakes, they were poisonous). Like the American Indians, everything I killed, I ate. I didn't hunt for trophies, fur, or skins. Being a hunter was part of my identity. I retired Boone to civilian life when he started having hip problems, and he roamed my property with Duke, our bichon frisé, who became his buddy. They both died around the same time, and Boone is buried here on my property with Duke's ashes. I pass by their grave every day when I walk past my tennis court.

When I was with the Redskins, I learned about hunting on the eastern shore of Maryland. The Chesapeake Bay was a big center for waterfowl—Canadian geese, snow geese, Atlantic brant, and more ducks than you can imagine. There are dabbling ducks and diving ducks, sea ducks, and wood ducks. There are mallards, canvasbacks, redheads, goldeneyes, buffleheads, surf scoters, red-breasted mergansers, and hooded mergansers.[131]

It is amazing. I let it be known that I liked to hunt, and I started to be invited to places to hunt. One day in the early 1980s after I'd hired Tommy Boggs to do my lobbying, I called up and asked for him. His secretary said, "He's out on his hunting farm on the Eastern Shore."

"He has a hunting farm?" I asked, incredulous. "He's nothing but a Gucci-wearing, hotshot lobbyist! *I'm* a hunter."

"Listen, buddy, get over there and check it out," she said.

---

[131] "Chesapeake Bay Waterfowl." *Chesapeake Bay News.* https://www.chesapeake-bay.org/index.php/chesapeake-bay-information/waterfowl/.

Looking the part

I got Tommy to invite me, and as I was going down a gravel road to his cabin, off in the distance, I noticed cultivated ponds surrounded by embankments. Hundreds and hundreds of ducks jumped into flight as I drove through.

When I finally arrived at the cabin, there was Tommy holding a drink. He said, "What do you think of this, baby?"

"I want one of these!"

Tommy entertained lobbying clients at his farm, and he invited me to some of the outings. His guests arrived on Friday evening for a night of drinking, eating, laughing, and telling stories. Then they were up at 5:30 in the morning. He sent anywhere from 10 to 20 people out with guides to go hunt ducks. They came back and enjoyed a big feast of wild game; then they departed. He was able to get a law passed in Maryland allowing you to raise ducks that were banded and identified, and there were no limits on them. By law, they could not be used to attract wild birds, but because there were so many of those ducks, the wild ducks came in anyway. It was, of course, very difficult to determine which birds were wild and which were released. When game wardens came by, it could be very dicey trying to determine if we were breaking laws. They were not understanding, and they would throw the book at you if they found any irregularities.

Politicians loved hunting there because they didn't have to work that hard. They could go out and play like they were hunters. It was a huge production. Tommy was there lobbying, taking care of his clients, and entertaining senators and congressmen. I became enamored with Maryland's Eastern Shore. Within 90 days, I bought a 300-acre farm down the road. I built a magnificent hunting lodge near Tommy's property. The area was gorgeous, and I invited colleagues who liked to hunt to stay at the lodge and enjoy the amenities. Family, colleagues, friends, and clients drove to Maryland's Eastern shore, walked in, and immediately entered the great room—three stories of wall-to-wall barnwood paneling with exposed beams and a massive stone fireplace that ran from floor to ceiling. It had a very rugged, masculine ambiance. It slept 14 people.

I hosted opulent dinners that could be likened to Viking parties in terms of food, drink, raucous conversation, and off-color joking among the men in attendance. Guys came in on Friday night around five. We had drinks around the fireplace involving excited conversation that ranged from politics in DC to sports and the anticipated hunt the following day. We had a huge meal and then got up before daybreak the next morning to hunt. Some of the guests said, "I don't wanna get up that early." So I took their sons out or friends who came with them. Then, everybody came back in, and we had a huge hunter's breakfast. Some stayed for the afternoon when we released pheasants out in the woods. They hunted some more; then, they went home. I helped clean up the place with the staff and headed home to Laytonsville to be with Nancy on Saturday night.

During hunting season, Tommy didn't always have room to accommodate everyone who wanted to hunt at his place, so occasionally, he called me and asked me if I could accommodate some of his guests. Tommy typically had between 10 and 20 guests. I typically only had half a dozen. Tommy asked me once if I could accommodate some military guys. I agreed, and among these guests were Joe Reeder, a prominent lawyer who became Under Secretary of the Army under Clinton and later worked for Patton and Boggs. He brought with him Congressman Chet Edwards, Steve Joseph, former Assistant Secretary of Defense for Health Affairs, John Dalton, Secretary of the Navy under Clinton, and 4-star Admiral Bill (Bud) Flanagan, who became Senior Managing Director of Cantor Fitzgerald, which was housed on the two top floors of the World Trade Center. I got to know them over time, and we became friends. Bud invited me up to meet Howard Lutnick, the CEO of Cantor Fitzgerald, and I invited Lutnick to the farm to hunt. He came to the farm by helicopter. I started courting Cantor Fitzgerald and made an effort to do business with them.

Once when I was visiting Bud and had a meeting with Lutnick, out of curiosity because he was so high in the building, I asked him what would happen if there was a fire below him. He said that he had a helicopter on the roof that he could use and that he could get everyone out of the building. They had fire escapes on both sides of the building and a variety of mechanisms to protect the building in the event of a fire, and he could also get helicopters to come pick people up.

On September 11, 2001, I was in my office trying to reach Senator Akaka regarding the bill I was assisting him with. Nancy was nearby and called me into the family room where the TV was showing the second plane go into the World Trade Center. I immediately thought of the people I knew who were working there. I tried to call, and naturally, I didn't reach anyone. Later, I found out that Bud was running late and that Howard had dropped his son off for his first day of kindergarten, so he was delayed getting to work that day. Bud later told me that as he walked to work, he first saw ashes like burned paper floating in the air, and as he got closer, there was more debris. When he saw the tower, he noted that everyone at Cantor was above the fire. He witnessed the second plane hit the tower. Of the 960 employees, 658 who reported to work that morning at the World Trade Center died. The escape routes that Howard had told me about unfortunately were not an option.

NOT NANCY'S CUP OF TEA

Hunting and hanging out with the guys wasn't Nancy's thing, but I started getting her to come out to the farm, even when the place was teeming with corporate bigwigs. These guys are used to being powerful, controlling every situation, and, in settings like this, being waited on hand and foot by the women hired to do so. This led to some incidents. There were women on staff who made breakfast, and once, one of my guests, Father George from Georgetown Prep, saw Nancy as she came in from her study to get some coffee for herself, gestured to get her attention, and said, "Hey, Miss, would you get me a cup of coffee?" not realizing she was my wife.

Nancy looked at him straight in the face and flashed the mischievous look Ethel Kennedy knew so well. "I don't do coffee," she said. "See that big guy over there?" She pointed to me. "He does coffee," she said as she walked away.

Father George was mortified, and Tommy Boggs, who was his good friend, laughed hysterically over the incident.

My little piece of paradise

There were five bedrooms, some with bunks. Eventually, we brought the kids out, too. They loved the place. We spent time as a family there, and over time, we also spent time with and celebrated Christmas and other holidays with our close friends at the farm.

We owned the farm for about 20 years, and I rented it out for corporate retreats. I could never convince Nancy to live there. It was gorgeous, but was too isolated for her. It was out in the middle of nowhere surrounded by water. Nancy preferred our home in Laytonsville, which she had transformed into a paradise. Nancy helped keep both us and our home understated. When we bought it, it was a modest ranch house off a small highway, situated on a hill surrounded by five acres. To enter the property, you crossed over a creek and climbed up a hill, reaching the residence toward the back, at the top of a rise. When we bought it, the lot was scraped clean of all vegetation other than a few trees; there was a four-bedroom ranch house, a gravel driveway, and a bridge.

Nancy set to work and redesigned the entire property. She was a master gardener, but rather than create opulent formal gardens, she designed naturalized perennial beds filled with seasonal flowers and blooming shrubs—azalea, rhododendron, and hydrangeas. I tended to want to showcase the visible evidence of my achievements, but she wanted to keep everything understated. She planted trees to ensure our privacy, which also helped understate the house and guest house. The property is surrounded by the original trees, which now tower over the entire landscape. The pool and tennis court are shielded from public view by magnificent mature 40-foot bamboo screens and fences covered with purple wisteria.

At Nancy's house, everything was set. Everything had to be just so; you had to conduct yourself just so. I had to deal with that. We had dinner at 6 o'clock, and you'd better be there. I tried to always be there. She didn't like to hold up things because she had the kids to feed. She ran a tight household, and I had to adhere to it. For the most part, I didn't fight her. I was the king of the house. She was the queen of the house. She ran everything, and I went along with it.

But there came a point when I felt Nancy had put me in a straitjacket. And I didn't like being in a straitjacket. I said, "Enough's enough." We argued, and I got really steamed. There were times I got up, packed up, and walked out. She had good intentions, and the things she asked for were reasonable, but it was just so rigid. No flexibility, no room for error. My life was not that way. My life was full of error. I didn't always make it the first time around.

Nancy's and my differences eventually over time became so overwhelming that I left. She came home one day, and all my clothes were gone. We formally separated, and I rented a townhouse in Gaithersburg. It was 20 minutes away, close to my office, and the kids could come and visit. But the kids started out stunned and never got used to the arrangement.

In hindsight, I realize that my obsessive drive to succeed in my business took a terrible toll on our children and my marriage. I realize how much my children suffered because of the effects the discord and turbulence in our marriage had on Nancy. The separation was especially tough on Page and Holly. After Page graduated from college, she had to step in and assume a lot of family responsibilities because Nancy was not functioning well as a mother and moved to her townhouse in Santa Fe in the summer of 1990, leaving her to supervise Holly, who was 15 at the time.

I was around, but I was totally focused on paddling because I was preparing to paddle in the Molokaʻi Race. I set up a dummy canoe in my pool in Laytonsville and tied it to the diving board so that it wouldn't go anywhere. I practiced paddling every spare minute I had. I even turned on the pool lights and practiced in the evening. Even when I *was* at the house, I was somewhat distant in terms of my role as a parent. The girls weren't in school. They invited people over to go swimming, and the kids who came brought alcohol onto the property. I tried, but this was very difficult to control when so many kids were coming and going. Nancy and I were both failing to be engaged in our roles as parents. In August, I took off for Hawaiʻi to train in earnest. Page and Holly came with me at first and then returned to Laytonsville because Holly had to return to school. Nancy joined them. I stayed in Honolulu and focused solely on the race because the race was in October. I have been guilt-ridden for years since that time due to my failure to fully assume my role as a parent during this difficult period in my marriage.

Despite the difficulties between Nancy and me, I continued to feel an enormous attraction and love for her—and an obligation to my family. I came back. Nancy took me back, and we worked hard to resolve our differences. We consistently went to marriage counseling. I don't know what the turning point was, but finally, in the mid-nineties, it was all resolved. She accepted me, and I accepted her. After building a business, I sold it, ran for political office, and lost. We started to spend some especially meaningful and wonderful time together.

BATTLING THE NRA—AND LOSING

During this period, I had accepted a position on Glendening's advisory commission on gun violence, and I managed to rankle Chairman Vincent DeMarco by voting against a recommendation to license gun owners. I wanted to ban assault weapons, but I didn't like the wording. The measure failed in the legislature.

Meanwhile, Nancy had gotten involved with the Brady Campaign, which was started by Sarah Brady, wife of James Brady, who was wounded in an assassination attempt on Ronald Reagan. The Brady Campaign advocated for gun control and against senseless gun violence. Once Nancy got on board, I supported her and went to several functions. But they were seeking supporters who weren't gun owners, and I disagreed with this approach.

"You need to talk to people who own guns," I told the board. "Most people who own guns are hunters and shooters. They're law-abiding, not vicious." I felt that gun control needed hunters' support to be successful, and I told them I'd be pleased to help them in that arena. I addressed the great divide that occurs in families where partners disagree about the role of guns. I had to reconcile this issue in my own family. Nancy didn't like guns, but she shared my love of the environment.[132]

Curious, I hired some lobbyists and pollsters to see if there was any truth to my suspicions. Turns out I was right. Most gun owners want to make sure that people who own guns won't hurt themselves or others. Reasonable gun owners don't believe in assault weapons. Sportsmen and a good number of Republicans wanted an organization they could turn to that was interested in protecting their gun rights while making sure that their communities were safe.

Satisfied with these results, I believed that the most efficient way to take on the National Rifle Association was not with liberal organizations, but with people who own guns, who understand that you

---

132 Schoenke, Ray. "A Typical American Family on Guns: Figuring Out How to Work Together for Change." *The Huffington Post*, 11 Sep 2008. https://www.huffpost.com/entry/a-typical-american-family_b_125665.

don't need an assault rifle to hunt. In 2005, I founded an organization called the American Hunters and Shooters Association. I hoped it would bridge the gap between urban liberals and rural gun owners. We called ourselves a "progressive gun rights organization" and tapped into the concerns of rural hunters and shooters over the NRA's failure to address environmental issues that affect hunters. We also appealed to conservationists, linking their interests with those of hunters.

It was a gun organization that we believed in. We wanted to show some of the positive things about hunters, about people who own guns—that they care deeply about the land and about conserving special places, but at the same time, we wanted to advocate for preventing someone who could harm himself or others from owning a gun—and made the argument that background checks are important. And we argued that you don't need an AK-47 to shoot a deer. Responsible gun owners believe that.

We had an early success in 2006 when we threw our support behind Claire McCaskill in the hotly contested 2006 Missouri US Senate race.[133] She won.

I envisioned AHSA as a rival to the National Rifle Association but failed to realize how much power the NRA truly had. I had gotten used to battling bullies, but the NRA wasn't just a bully; it was a truly evil opponent. They started with disinformation, labeling AHSA as "anti-gun." Then NRA lackeys went after Bob Ricker, AHSA's cofounder and Executive Director and one of the nation's top gun policy experts. He was a former assistant NRA general counsel and top lobbyist for the gun industry who stepped forward and went public about the NRA/gun industry conspiracy of silence and its refusal to address the problem of corrupt gun dealers who sell guns to criminals.

NRA leaders didn't stop there. They fought efforts to restrict armor-piercing handgun ammunition dangerous to cops; they opposed

---

133 Schoenke, Ray. "Oh, What a Mighty Web the NRA's Leaders Weave, When They Practice to Deceive." *The Huffington Post*, 03 March 2008. https://www.huffpost.com/entry/oh-what-a-mighty-web-the_b_89646.

background checks on all sales at gun shows; they opposed voluntary industry efforts to provide free child safety locks with all new guns sold; they opposed efforts to keep guns out of the hands of terrorists; they wanted to repeal restrictions on keeping guns out of bars and restaurants when liquor is served; they wanted to force employers to allow guns in the workplace; they opposed the efforts of big-city mayors to stop illegal gun trafficking; and, incredibly, they wanted to criminalize efforts by law enforcement to share traced information about guns used in crimes, calling them "jackbooted thugs."[134] AHSA filed a brief in the landmark US Supreme Court case *District of Columbia v. Heller*, which was cosigned by 11 senior military leaders and was written by the national powerhouse law firm Greenberg Traurig. Joe Reeder, who had hunted at my farm and with whom I had developed a friendship, assisted with this project.

I figured there would be gun owners who would support our efforts, but I knew I would have to raise money to keep the program going.

In an attempt to make an impact on a national scale, I created a promotional video for AHSA and flew around the country.[135] I went to an NRA meeting in St. Louis and set up an area in the ballroom right across from them, trying to become a thorn in the NRA's side. I had a table and all my literature and signs. I had one interesting conversation with a woman at the airport in an NRA jacket. She picked up two rifles, and I asked if she was on her way to the convention. She said she was a long-distance hunter and was leery of AHSA as a "gun control organization." She respected my opinion, but she was still adamantly pro-NRA. The NRA paid little attention to AHSA. It was nothing to them.

It didn't take long for me to realize I would need tremendous financial support to take on the NRA on a national scale. I reached

---

134 Schoenke, Ray. "Oh, What a Mighty Web the NRA's Leaders Weave, When They Practice to Deceive." *HUFFPOST*, 03 March 2008.

135 *YouTube*, "Introducing the American Hunters & Shooters Association." 2009. https://www.youtube.com/watch?v=TURyJiOdD8Y.

out to Eli Broad, the billionaire entrepreneur and philanthropist. He gave $100,000 through his foundation and helped arrange another $200,000 through Geller & Company. I reached out to Michael Bloomberg, who contributed about $200,000 with the understanding that I would travel around the country for him to major cities where he was trying to prevent gun violence.

Bloomberg was encouraging. He appreciated my voice. But he was focused on gun violence in the cities while I was trying to take on the NRA. I assisted him with the understanding that he would also take on the NRA, but I was disappointed. He used me for his cause, but he wasn't willing to contribute the kind of money that seriously opposing the NRA would take. Anyway, for me, he was too far to the left. I wanted my organization to be closer to the center.

People liked the idea of working against gun violence, but when it came time to take on the political arm of the NRA, everybody cowered. The Obama Administration voiced support. They asked me to run a national ad about gun ownership and gun control[136] indicating that Obama did not plan to take their guns away. Later, after the ad ran nationally, I asked them for help with AHSA. They did nothing, and nobody responded to my phone calls. I realized I would need not just money, but huge and *sustained* political alliances. The NRA wasn't Goliath; it wasn't a gorilla; it wasn't King Kong—it was an unimaginably big and impenetrable monster, and it was mean, mean, mean.

American Hunters and Shooters Association ceased to exist by 2010. I was spending a lot of my own time and money, but I alone just couldn't take on the NRA. I was known to take risks like this. I'd come out of left field, start a project, and go for it. If it was a worthy cause, I wasn't afraid to face failure. But I also wasn't going to ignore failure.

---

136 Graham, Chris. "Ad Watch: Obama and the Second Amendment." *Augusta Free Press*. 17 Sept 2018. https://augustafreepress.com/news/ad-watch-obama-and-the-second-amendment/.

THE PRICE PRO ATHLETES PAY

I've thought a lot about success and failure in my life. I sometimes think I was lucky to have faced difficulty early and to have acquired the grit to keep going. Although my football career ended in 1975, football and sports have continued to provide me with metaphors that have meaning in other areas of my life. Football has had an impact on everything I have done. If I hadn't played, would I be where I am today? It got me to where I am. It was an essential, integral part of my journey.

But football has had repercussions. I've had seven operations on my knees. I've had both knees replaced. I lost track of the number of dislocated fingers, which point in directions other than straight forward. My shoulder was dislocated several times. It might be the cause of nerve damage in one shoulder that makes my left hand frequently fall asleep, which wakes me up at night and causes me to toss and turn. The other shoulder has little or no cartilage, which causes the bones to rub on each other, is extremely painful, and also disrupts my sleep. I refuse to get another operation, so I live with it. My back gives me trouble. I go to an orthopedic doctor. I've got a shoulder doctor, a hand doctor, a knee doctor, and an ankle doctor, and they move me around depending on what area hurts the most. I go to therapists for experimental treatments to relieve pain. Did I pay a price? You're goddamn right I did. If you ask me would I do it again, knowing what I know, and knowing what it takes to get where I am, you'd better believe I would.

Hard hits and physical injuries go along with the territory, and we all knew we signed up for that. But something else—damage to our brains—didn't come to light until after I'd left the game. In 1994, the NFL created a Mild Traumatic Brain Injury Committee. In 2002, forensic pathologist Bennet Omalu identified chronic traumatic encephalopathy (CTE) in a former NFL player. It took many more years for the significance of findings about degenerative brain disease to take hold. *The Washington Post*'s Leonard Shapiro wrote in 2018 that the NFL has conceded it expects almost a third of its retired players to develop cognitive problems at "notably younger ages" than the rest of the population and that Boston University researchers have found CTE in 99 percent of the brains from deceased NFL players that they have studied.[137] "One sign of CTE is judgment and impulse-control issues," Shapiro writes. "Memory loss is another, though it's impossible to confirm that CTE is the cause since it can only be confirmed through an autopsy." Redskins, he adds, "have paid a staggering price for their still-flickering fame."[138]

I have former teammates who tell me their memory is shot, and one who has to rely almost entirely on his wife as his memory bank. Interestingly, my granddaughter Lucy, who is attending Virginia Tech and studying sports journalism, is involved with the school's nationally recognized Virginia Tech Helmet Lab, which provides unbiased helmet ratings based on rigorous testing that allow consumers to make informed decisions when purchasing helmets for all types of impact sports and activities that require helmets.[139] It appears that some of my grandchildren are vicariously taking after me. Her sister, Milena, is planning to help manage her high school football team.

CTE is a repercussion of playing football we need to be paying attention to. There are some horror stories, all sad commentaries on the reality of the game. Nancy and I were good friends with a family who lost a son. Aaron Hernandez killed a man. Junior Seau killed himself. Seau is a particularly interesting case. He was a handsome, jovial person, beloved in the NFL. But after 20 years as a linebacker, he became increasingly detached, violent, and self-destructive. He drank compulsively and gambled away millions. I think he got overextended.

---

137 Shapiro, Leonard. "They were the first Redskins to play in the Super Bowl. Decades later, they're paying the price." *The Washington Post*, 2 Feb 2018. https://www.washingtonpost.com/outlook/they-were-the-first-redskins-to-play-in-the-super-bowl-decades-later-theyre-paying-the-price/2018/02/02/05d967c0-ff88-11e7-9d31-d72cf78d-beee_story.html.

138 Ibid.

139 *VIRGINIA TECH HELMET RATINGS.* https://helmet.beam.vt.edu.

I don't know if he was embarrassed about it, or depressed, but in 2012, he put a bullet through his heart. His last act says a lot about the man. He knew he was suffering from CTE. And he wanted to preserve his brain for an autopsy.

For years, I used my head as a battering ram. So, I've taken the time to research the early symptoms of CTE. Based on current evidence, I am convinced that I'm one of the lucky ones. By my age, if I had CTE, I would be experiencing some of the more serious problems, like those experienced by Junior Seau. Fortunately, I am not.

You pay a price to play this game. There are the injuries. And the idea that you are set for life, when you're not. The idea that the fans will always be there for you, and they're not. But the biggest, deepest price you pay may be the cognitive issues that some of us may suffer over time. A teammate will schedule a golf game on such and such a day at such and such time, and when I call to confirm, he doesn't remember anything about it. If I misplace my phone, which happens to literally *everyone*, it scares me. I never know which of my injuries is going to flare up if I engage in vigorous exercise. Trying to stay fit is difficult because of this. Players sustain tremendous injuries to knees, tendons, and damage to joints in general. But the brain injuries are the most alarming. The idea that you could be developing any of these issues hovers over you like a drone poised to drop a bomb. I am grateful every day for the fact that I still have a short-term memory. Some of my friends are not so lucky.

CHAPTER TEN

To Have and to Hold (1986-2020)

In 1986, Schoenke & Associates was doing business with the insurance company First Virginia, which hosted a trip every few years for their top producers. They called us and said, "Hey, you guys won a trip." It was a two-week safari in Kenya. My partner at the time said he couldn't go. I called home. "Nancy, you don't wanna go to Africa, do you?"

Her answer was immediate. "Yeah, I want to go to Africa!"

Neither one of us had traveled to the continent, but she was so focused on the children that I didn't think she'd leave them. But she said she could sort it out. My niece Ohelo, the daughter of my half brother Stanley in Hawai'i, had come to live with us for a while, so Nancy and I took off.

Nancy and her family had been very insulated. They didn't go anywhere, other than to visit family in Greenwood, Louisiana. She had long been the perfect daughter, and I'm sure part of her attraction to me was my worldliness. I'd been a military brat and had traveled all over the country and Europe. My life with Nancy was filled with drama, and at times, the drama was more tumultuous than joyous. (Four years later, we formally separated.) But, by this time in our marriage, she was ready to seize the opportunity to see the world. I had traveled quite a bit for business, and sometimes she'd joined me at conventions, but I hadn't realized that she had this thirst for adventure. And I hadn't realized that she would be the perfect traveling companion for me—she was so excited about everything, so gung-ho. She just wanted to taste everything.

With a young Masai warrior in Kenya

FREEDOM AND AFFECTION

Kenya was breathtaking. There were about 100 people, agents with their wives, broken into three groups. Each group went to a separate part of the country, changing every four to five days. We went through three different places, each at a different elevation, each with different animals in the wild. We saw mountains and jungles and rivers and deserts, crocodiles, giraffes and elephants, zebras, baboons, and monkeys. It was mind-boggling. We skirted the edge of danger.

I was sitting next to the pilot as we flew over Mt. Kilimanjaro. His hands were squeezing the controls as we climbed. We had to get up 15,000-20,000 feet, and we just barely got over the mountain, and then we dropped down. One of the groups we arrived with was not as fortunate. Their plane had slammed into the mountain on the return trip. All 30 on board perished. Needless to say, the news was overwhelming. I had some experience piloting a small plane, and I had decided not to pursue my pilot's license because I realized that the sky is not always clear, and the wind currents are not always forgiving. My group sat up all night talking about how we came on this trip to have fun, and we could have all easily died. We were nervous about the next day, when we would ride in an even smaller plane. We talked long into the night about how we could have orphaned our children and about how these exciting journeys can have some serious downsides we didn't anticipate. We knew there could be complications on such trips, but dying or actually being seriously injured was not really on our radar. We might have anticipated the possibility of being eaten by a lion, but we had guides armed with rifles to protect us from encounters with wildlife, so an animal attack didn't seem likely. We've all seen the YouTube videos of people who don't listen to their guides and get attacked while trying to take photos, but we were not that foolish. We certainly had not considered plummeting to our deaths while flying over the highest mountain in Africa. It was a sobering thought.

Being out in the field could also be scary—but it was thrilling. Every time we went out, we had a gun bearer—there might be a leopard up in a tree that had just made a kill. Or we were in these hollowed-out log canoes, with crocodiles everywhere. It evoked a combination of fear and exhilaration. At one of our locations, we found dead hippos in a river, and lions and crocodiles came out of nowhere, jumped in the water, and began eating the carcasses while fighting with each other over them.

All my childhood infatuations with hunting came back to me. We went out at night, and a leopard ran alongside the open Jeep as we moved through the tundra toward a herd of antelopes feeding in the grass. The leopard was using our open Jeep as a shield, hiding behind us so he could attack. You could reach out and almost touch the leopard. I loved it. We went out one night to see an albino deer. The guide went to sleep, but I stayed up all night in the blind, hoping to see this animal. I didn't. I talked endlessly to the guides about hunting—how dangerous it could be, but how exhilarating. Also about how they tracked animals, about how most safari junkies just wanted to bag the big five. It was obvious these hunters didn't have a feeling for the animals or the African way of hunting.

The last day, Nancy said, "We gotta bring our kids here." Once we had the chance, we did, taking Eric, Page, and Holly for a month and traveling to Botswana, Zambia, and Zimbabwe.

After our separation a few years later, some of our friends were devastated. Roger and E.J. Mudd were concerned about me, and they were reluctant to invite Nancy, as a single woman, to their parties. But then, when we got back together, they immediately had us over, and we started up again. Such experiences do bond you to friends. Nancy and E.J. Mudd traveled to the Caribbean together, and we continued to socialize with them. They often invited Jim Dickenson, a reporter for the *Star* and the *Post*, and his wife Mollie to dinners and parties at their house as well as other interesting guests. Roger and Jim were very close, and we ran together a lot. In fact, after he retired from the *Post*, Jim worked for a political consulting firm that I hired during my campaign for governor.

Once I sold the business, folded my political campaign, and Nancy and I rekindled our relationship, we had few, if any, responsibilities. We had enough money that we could live comfortably for the rest of our lives. Our kids had launched their own lives and families. Traveling became our deal. I like to think that we brought each other something much more than heartache.

Our first trip to China had been in 1996, when we went to visit Eric, who was teaching at a school in Beijing. The tour company had set up a trip to go down the Chang Jiang River on a steamboat. It was being billed as the last trip because the government was going to shut off the Chang Jiang and build a dam to give electricity to a major part of China. They stopped at different points, and you could see farms on

Traveling together in China

the sides of the cliffs. There were men who carried you on their backs in chairs up and down to small villages. I declined that privilege, but there were large, overweight men who didn't want to walk up the hill who rode in the chairs on the backs of these small Chinese men. We also visited the Great Wall where Eric was acting in *Macbeth*.

Nancy and I developed a new routine. We decided that we wanted to go somewhere—Australia, New Zealand, Italy—and off we went. Places in the States, too. You name it, we went. Nancy signed up for cooking schools sometimes she took me; sometimes she took the girls. Often on trips, Nancy took the lead. She wanted to do things that were meaningful, see things that were difficult to get to, and take risks. We hung a big map and marked all the places we'd been.

In Australia, we started in Melbourne and wanted to go to Sydney, and one was on the south and one on the west. I said, "Let's go! It can't be that far." Well, it was. You had to drive through the mountains, and all we saw were sheep and kangaroos. Then, I said, "Let's go to New Zealand! It can't be that far away." Well, it was.

Nancy loved the Cotswolds, in the southern part of England—lovely, romantic coastal towns. After our separation, Nancy told me she sat and daydreamed of being there with me. So when we got back together, immediately, I said, "C'mon, we're going to the Cotswolds." We spent a couple of weeks in beautiful inns.

Nancy had come to accept my need to succeed. She realized that I wanted to prove that I could amount to something in the business world—that I was more than just a jock. I wanted to show her that we could do anything we wanted to do, that I was so successful I could take her anywhere. Part of that was my ego, but I also knew that she wanted to see the world, and I wanted to give her that.

The early 2000s marked one of the most pleasant periods in our life together. We had money, freedom, and our kids were doing well. The politics went by the wayside as we traveled and enjoyed our freedom. Nancy and I became incredibly close. Our marriage finally became stronger and better.

Even as we got older, and she started to have physical difficulties, we traveled. Nancy said, "Let's go to the top of the Andes. Let's climb Machu Picchu!" We arrived in Peru and moved each day closer to the Forbidden City, getting adjusted to the higher elevations. Two days before the last leg, she collapsed, and there was no water. I went down and got water from a stream for her.

When we got back to the cabin, I said, "We have to rest." She cried the whole night—she didn't think she could make it. The last day, when she was climbing up the final set of steps to get into the Forbidden City, she was afraid she wouldn't be able to make it. I got behind her and followed her all the way up. Then, when she got there, I hugged her, and we shouted out across the top of those mountains in the Andes, "We made it!" I have pictures of us hugging, drinks in the air.

Then, we went to Pantanal in Brazil to see the jaguars.

We went anywhere we wanted to go. It was so much fun. We had freedom. We had affection. She loved me, and I loved her.

THE HARSH REALITIES OF FACING AN INCURABLE DISEASE

One day in 2008, Nancy came back home, and she'd knocked off the mirror on the car. Shortly thereafter, I was driving with her, and I noticed that she was driving over the traffic cones that had been placed on the road in front of our house by road crews. She was clearly unable to maintain her position in the lane. I pointed it out to her, and she dismissed it as minor. Nancy's mother had died from Parkinson's, and we were alert to the signs. Shortly thereafter, our worst fears were realized when she was diagnosed with Parkinson's.

Later, Holly came in after riding in the car with Nancy at the wheel, and she told me she was alarmed.

"Nancy, you can't keep driving," I said.

"I can still do it," she answered. I even gave her a test, which she failed.

Then, Page came in and said, "Dad, Mom is scaring me." We all knew that she had to stop and that she was stubborn.

Nancy reluctantly gave up driving, and that depressed her. Parkinson's is characterized by depression and anxiety, and the disease can be very isolating. Because of Nancy's mother, I had an idea of what we were in for. It would be a long, slow decline. Nancy would eventually become bedridden, and I knew she might stay that way for an interminable length of time. I knew it was going to be a struggle.

"Don't worry, baby. I'm going to take care of you," I told her. And I did. This is a wheel you get on, 365 days a year, morning and night, and it lasts for YEARS. In Nancy's case, it was ten. There is no vacation or respite from a partner with Parkinson's. It is a constant challenge that comes at you from many directions. I embraced this monster like I did the most challenging opponent I had met on the football field. I faced Parkinson's like I faced Buck Buchanan and Lyle

Alzado. I committed the same way I had committed to football and my business. It was total engagement—total commitment. I was all in. I reminded myself of the true meaning of the vows I had made to her when I married her: *'til death do us part.* Just as I had become an expert on pass blocking, I became an expert on Parkinson's. I was determined to save her, and I was playing the game to win. I wanted to prove I could defeat Parkinson's.

This was the Super Bowl, and the final score depended on whether or not I could take down this disease. I was determined to keep her alive. "I don't care how tough it gets," I told Nancy. "I'll never leave you."

I'm sure I presented myself as kind of a superman to anyone offering help because I felt guilty for any ways I had failed Nancy or our marriage, and I felt that I needed to take care of her myself. I felt it was my responsibility. I kind of martyred myself. Because our marriage had been troubled at times, and it affected her and the family, I felt I owed her—a sense of indebtedness, obligation. I faced the guilt I carried with me about things that I had contributed to the problems in our marriage, and I also embraced and honored the years we had spent together making up for it after we got back together after our separation when we both recommitted to our relationship. Caring for her was atonement, but it was also an act of love, and I loved her with kindness, gentleness, and constancy. I was determined to be the best nurse she could ever have. But, eventually, I realized that I had bitten off more than I could handle. My effort to do penance had prevented me from asking my children for the help I really needed.

I remodeled the house so that it would be easier for Nancy, taking out the different levels on the main floor, putting in an elevator, and making the bathrooms more accessible. Unfortunately, at the end of the remodeling, the house burned down, and we had to do the whole thing over again.

Ironically, that was the occasion for our last international trip together, to China in December 2013. It didn't appear that the insurance would cover the million dollars that it would take for us to rebuild the house after the fire, so we decided to sell some paintings we had purchased in New York in 1984. The gallery we bought them from said that to get the best price, we needed to go to Beijing. They would help us sell them at the Poly International Auction and pay our expenses while in China. We called Page to see if she wanted to come with us, partly because she is an artist, and we wanted her to be part of the experience, and partly because Nancy needed more help than I could provide by myself.

Nancy was still lucid, and she could still walk, though she needed a little help. But I had to give her medicines on time and do things like catheterize her when we were in situations where taking her to a bathroom was difficult or highly inconvenient. Her doctor and her nurse taught me how to do it. It was very difficult, and at times it hurt her. I was increasingly becoming a professional nurse. On the trip to China, Page was great—she was constantly thinking of Nancy and her needs. And she was aware that if I perhaps pushed Nancy to do things, Nancy matched my drive with a competitive spirit of her own.

We stayed at the Four Seasons in Beijing, where the auction was being held in a massive ballroom with a giant screen behind the podium. It's one of the largest auctions in the world, and there was art from all over—calligraphy and Chinese paintings, but also canvases from across Asia and Europe. The focus is on modern and contemporary art. Page is a person who can just devour art, whether in an art history class, a museum, or in this case, the magnificent auction catalog. She says she spent hours in "room after room" of art. She was also fascinated by this window into the international art market, especially at this moment when China had opened up to capitalism, and the halls were flooded with young Chinese buyers.

The day of the auction was very intense. I'm telling Page, "We gotta get her downstairs," down into the auction room. She helped Nancy and me get positioned in the right spot. Finally, our painting came up on the giant screen. Beside each painting was a list of the bids—in

RMB, US dollars, Hong Kong dollars, and Euros. With each bid, all the numbers changed—it was like some kind of crazy Las Vegas slot machine. Our two paintings, both by the exiled artist Cheng Danquing, came up on the screen. We paid $7000 for *Shepherd with a Flute*. It sold for $554,649, or a profit of $547,649. *Going to Market* we paid $10,000 for; it sold for $783,034. A total profit of $1,320,683.

We also went to one of the best-preserved and best-known sections of the Great Wall of China, outside of Beijing, which had breathtaking scenery. We had been told that a "trolley" would get us to the top, but when we got there, we found that the "trolley" was actually a rickety old chair lift.

"Watch what I do," Page said, and went to the top ahead of us. I strapped Nancy in next to me at the bottom with the help of the attendants.

As we made our way up, over the static of the ancient PA system making announcements in Chinese, I was yelling up to Page, "You gotta be there when we get there. Make sure you're there." When we arrived—the chair didn't stop moving—Page ran up, and we struggled to unstrap Nancy. Nancy threw her arms around one of the attendants. Somehow, we got her out of the chair. That was scary. Then we realized we were on top of the world. We walked along the top of the wall, and there were people dressed up as Chinese guards. You got an immediate sense of the history. Then we realized we had to get *down*. After some negotiation, we managed to get permission to go down in what they called a toboggan, a sled that goes down a chute, twisting and turning almost like a roller coaster. Nancy enjoyed the ride. I was panic-stricken.

We stayed in Hawai'i on the way back from China. Page was painting, and Nancy put on her overalls and went to the studio with her and tagged along with Page when she worked on commissioned projects.

Over the next seven years, I watched the slow deterioration of Nancy's movements and her mind. She also had Lewy body dementia, a degenerative condition similar to Alzheimer's disease. Initially, this showed up in little ways. She would "lose" things in the house that she swore she had placed somewhere, and I would have to hunt around and find them. Table settings were missing critical items. She was trying so hard to maintain the status quo, and it was a struggle. Eventually, we laughed about it when we sat down at the table and noticed that important implements like forks were missing. She maintained her sense of humor through all of it. We always tried to lighten the mood.

She started having difficulty dressing herself. She developed a tremor in one hand, which at first she tried to hide by holding the shaking hand down with the other hand. But eventually, it shook so much she couldn't conceal it. I was told by her doctors to keep her moving so she wouldn't become bedridden, so I encouraged her to walk. I tried to keep her mind active. She slept a lot, but when she was awake, I read to her, watched TV with her, and discussed current events with her. I sang to her. I encouraged our children, relatives, and friends to come see her.

I went from helping Nancy to the bathroom, to having to help her use a bedpan, to changing diapers. She was humiliated and embarrassed about all of it, and for a while during each stage of loss of autonomy, she was angry and hostile. It was a struggle to help her accept her situation. I had to go into public restrooms with her, which was an issue. At night, I had to help her use a bedpan, clean up after her, or catheterize her so she didn't have to get up. I had to be up and down during the night if she wanted to use the restroom or became restless and uncomfortable and made loud sounds or called out my name indicating that she needed something.

I made her comfortable and cleaned up after her if she didn't make it to the bathroom or had to use a bedpan. I felt that my job was to keep her comfortable and let her know that I was there for her any time she needed me. I tried to make her life as rich and as full as I could. It was incredibly difficult. I developed a special method to take Nancy to the bathroom—facing her, lifting her up by her armpits, walking backward in front of her, holding her up with my head in order to pull her pants down. We laughed a lot because it was all so crazy. This went on every day for four or five years, multiple times a day, and I had to make adjustments and try not to embarrass her or frustrate her. It was hard on both of us. After a few years, it got to a point where Nancy couldn't make it to the bathroom at all.

I bought a golf cart so I could take her around the property to see her gardens. It was almost impossible for me to get a night's sleep and virtually impossible to find competent help who were gentle and proficient at even the most basic requirements to keep her comfortable. I started trying to find a caretaker to help relieve me, especially at night. The first caretakers I hired to help me at night fell asleep and failed to care for her at all or even to be kind. When she began to hallucinate, instead of gently indulging her or treating her with kindness, one caretaker (who didn't last long) told her she was crazy. The nights became almost unbearable. I couldn't sleep. My sleep pattern became severely disrupted because I was constantly aware of her movements in our bed, and I was afraid to sleep in a different room once I had a caretaker because when I tried to sleep downstairs, I could hear movement upstairs, and when I checked, the caretaker was often asleep, and Nancy was struggling to get up or move on her own.

Even several years after her death, I still sometimes have trouble sleeping through the night, and I have to deal with the physical problems caused by such a long period of poor sleep as I am gradually returning to normal. I was looking for every possible way to slow this menace down, to overcome it. This was a battle to which I was going to bring every bit of fierceness I had developed withstanding the pressure put on me by Vince Lombardi. I looked for new medicines; I invested in companies that were coming up with new therapies. I took Nancy to lectures on new medications and alternative treatments for Parkinson's. I flew to Hawai'i to meet a guy out of Hong Kong because I had heard that he had discovered a cure. We took her to a place where they put her in a hyperbaric chamber several times a week. She hated it. I tried everything. But this wasn't football. I couldn't take down this monster.

I had resisted hiring professionals, wanting to take care of Nancy by myself, and probably choosing to stay in denial of the seriousness of her illness. However, I realized that I simply couldn't go without sleep forever, so I was constantly looking for a suitable caregiver once she demanded round-the-clock care. For years, we had a Salvadorean housekeeper, Ana. She and Nancy were devoted to each other, speaking to each other in Spanish. After I had gone through several caretakers and had failed to find anyone even remotely good at the job, Ana said she had a niece, Cordelia, who might be able to help. Cordelia asked me for the job description. I said, "Your job is to love Nancy."

That's exactly what she did, beautifully, for the last six years of Nancy's life. She was incredible—just so intuitive about Nancy's needs and naturally kind and thoughtful. I trusted her completely. At first, Cordelia also had to help *me* because, during all of this, I had surgery on my knee.

On Nancy's last trip to Hawai'i, Cordelia came with us. It took both of us to get Nancy to the restroom on the plane. Cordelia had to stand up on the toilet behind her as I pulled her up. All three of us were laughing hysterically because the bathroom was so small that what we were trying to do was virtually impossible, the three of us crammed into this tiny restroom on an airplane. We stayed in Page's house in Waimānalo. Cordelia slept in my granddaughter's room, and I slept with Nancy, but when I had to get up in the night to take Nancy to the bathroom, Cordelia ran in and jumped up on the toilet behind her. Or we'd both jump in the shower and wash her off.

The doctors were telling us not to stop. Don't let her fall back, they'd say. Mostly for her mind, but she also fought hard physically. I tried to get her to walk, and she wanted to. She went around the house. She used a walker, then a wheelchair.

Until death do us part

We had always entertained a lot, and Nancy knew the people in the community. She was so thoughtful and friendly. She had a lot of friends, and they were aware of her disease, and happily, they wanted to stay a part of her life. Before she was bedridden, we'd often have friends over—we'd even have dinner parties, and Nancy watched to make sure I did things right—using the cloth napkins, the right plates, serving our guests, doing things the "Mrs. Schoenke way."

Cordelia frequently reminds me how kind Nancy was, how she didn't care about how much money you had or where you came from. The bond between them was incredible. Nancy relied on Cordelia, but Cordelia also talked to her and asked her for advice—for herself and her entire family. She was far more than a caretaker. Nancy told her that she was another daughter. Cordelia speaks excellent English, but she indulged Nancy and talked to her in Spanish, which Nancy preferred. Cordelia paid me the highest honor one day when she told a friend, "When I watched Mr. Ray take care of Nancy, I believed in true love."

While Nancy could still communicate, we did everything we could to make her feel that she was still part of things. We didn't limit her. She was never left alone.

Finally, toward the end of 2019, the hospice people came. They played music and tried to make her last days comfortable.

"How's she doing?" I asked frequently.

"I think she has several weeks, maybe months," the hospice nurse said. Then, just like that, it changed.

I went to Hawai'i, and when I left, she was good. She was having difficulty, but she was communicating. Her face was beginning to get drawn, but she still had some zip. I had to rush back from Hawai'i because Cordelia couldn't wake her up one morning, and she had been taken to the hospital. Shortly after she returned home, the doctor said she was on her deathbed. I was shocked at how quickly it all happened. I was stunned.

Nancy died on February 11, 2020. I don't remember the specifics of the last conversations I had with her. After her last hospital visit, she had quit talking altogether. I just wanted to love her, to make her comfortable. Eric and his wife were living in our guest house; Page had come from Hawai'i, and Holly was here, too. Very early in the morning, just after midnight, Page came and found me downstairs. She said, "She's going."

I ran upstairs into the master bedroom. Nancy's face was drawn, and she was very still, barely breathing. Shortly after I got upstairs, Page said, "She's gone." A long guttural moan left my body involuntarily, and I cried out in grief with what sounded like a primal howl. The snow weighed down the branches of the sycamore trees outside the window, trees she had planted four decades earlier. My ten-year Super Bowl, me versus Parkinson's, was over, and I had lost.

We had an online service with family due to the pandemic, and we went around the property and sprinkled some of her ashes on different gardens that she had designed and planted. The rest of her ashes are here in the guesthouse she designed in a beautiful Southwestern earthenware Hopi jug she loved.

I couldn't have had the life I had without Nancy. She was a strong woman—principled, fair, and forgiving. I played football—a tough business. She didn't love it, but she was in there. She knew everything about it. She kept all the letters I wrote to her from football camp. She got to know the wives, and they loved her. She wasn't afraid to criticize a coach when I wasn't being played. And while she was doing everything else, she was expanding her mind. She was a renaissance woman. I loved that she was so accomplished. She had so much spirit. After her death, I began to assess my entire life and future. Confronting death will do that to a person.

When Nancy left me at the age of 20 that awful day in Dallas in that garage apartment and drove away, I felt that everything that made me who I was had walked out with her. I came to realize as the days went by, however, that I had the strength and confidence to stand on my own. Even though at that time, I felt more perfect when Nancy and I were together, I learned that I could be alone and face and address my own imperfections. I found that all the things I thought had walked out with her actually had not, and I unknowingly already had the foundation of the successful man I would become. After Nancy's death, I was faced with this realization again. I could go on without her, and I have.

CHAPTER ELEVEN

Still Stomping in the Puddles

I have tried to figure out how the sensitive kid who was made fun of and called "Fat Girl" evolved into the fierce lineman that I became, the schmoozer at Ethel Kennedy's, the lone 'gun' willing to take on the NRA, someone who wasn't afraid to reveal my political stance in the context of the NFL and eventually run for political office. I know that I inherited my mother's outsized ambition and her belief in me, and I'd like to think I inherited my father's calm temperament, but I'm sure there are those who would disagree with that.

After Nancy's death, I started considering where I got the confidence to do all of this. Although I was aware of standing on the broad shoulders of men like Charlie Ane, I often felt like a lone warrior in my early years. Something got me through and even allowed me to take risks, whether on the playground, the football field, in the boardroom, or in the political arena. Having convictions, going for what I wanted, tussling with bullies, and going out on limbs have been the story of my life. I always chose to do things that required risk.

I also realize now that Fat Girl was the underlying internal force that helped me overcome the challenges I consistently faced during my life and career that required taking these risks. Fat Girl was the part of me that taught me how to stand up to bullies and also taught me that I alone was the only one who could meet my unique life challenges, as I did at the age of 12. Many events in my life helped me believe in myself, and both early failures and successes prepared me for the struggles I would face in my marriage and as I built a prosperous business. I grew more confident as I survived life's knocks just as I did as a chubby little boy.

I also eventually evolved my own philosophy with the help of Fat Girl. You take what you are given—in my case, athleticism, drive, ambition, intellect, and raw courage—and use it to achieve what you perceive to be meaningful accomplishments. Being bullied taught me that even if you are afraid, you take bullies on, or they will not stop. Football taught me that you don't quit after early failures. During my football career, part of my philosophy was also that you had to figure out how to be perfect when you *can't* be perfect, which is an odd, uncomfortable paradox. There's absolutely no sympathy when you make mistakes, as is often the case in life. So if I made a mistake, I had to make sure, personally, that I didn't let that render me helpless. It was a mindset. In life, as in football, it has been impossible for me to be perfect. Yet I have had to figure out how to walk off the field victorious in my internal struggle against my own imperfection.

SNAPSHOTS: IT AIN'T OVER 'TIL FAT GIRL SINGS (1949-2023)

At the age of seven, I have learned something *very* important: Don't start fires.

At 12, I know it's OK to be nice, loving, thoughtful, caring, and kind. I have to hold onto that. That's who I am. I thought the world was good, but there are a lot of people out there who are *not nice*, who can be mean, and my niceness seems to be viewed as a weakness. And I don't have any idea *why*. I just don't *understand*. I can't fathom why I have been singled out to be laughed at, taunted, bullied, humiliated, punched, hurt. I know I don't deserve it, which is really hard, but I have to learn to deal with it, and I can't let them destroy me. I'm not comfortable telling my parents or my teachers. I have to take care of *myself*. I'm on my own. I'm so confused. Why are they *doing* this? I didn't do anything to *them*. I don't even *know* most of them. They don't even know *me*.

At 14, I can't trust anyone. I have to stay on guard at all times. I can't run. I have to hold my ground. No matter how scary it is, I may have to fight, and I can get hurt. But I'll be stronger for it. It will be empowering, and it will carry me. I *have* to do this because I keep being faced with these challenges. People look at me and think I don't deserve to be a winner. I have to believe in myself and overcome the fact that as I go through life, there will always be another bully waiting around the corner. They are everywhere. I have to be willing to take risks because it is scary as all get out when these people come at me. And they just keep comin'. I can't be afraid. I am stronger than I think I am. If I *have* to hit someone, I'll take 'em out of play.

At 18, I feel strong, confident, and successful. But now, I'm facing a whole new challenge with varsity players who don't like me, who want to embarrass me and put me down. It's still going on. I'm still having to defend myself…and this is more complicated. I can't punch frat guys who pick on me in the student union in front of everyone. I just have to endure public humiliation. Does the bullying ever *end*?

At 21, I now know I don't know how to pass block, and nobody will help me. Please, *somebody* help me? Oh, I forgot, I have to help *myself*.

At 24, in a team meeting, Lombardi yells, "WHO'S THAT?" and the coaches quickly respond "62! Schoenke!" I know I had a bad block, so I'm just going to put my fingers in my ears and hold my breath, hope he doesn't have them turn on the lights, and wait until he quits yelling.

At 35, thank god, I can finally flush those pills down the toilet. I finally get to be like everybody else…or NOT. Maybe I don't *want* to be like everyone else.

At 45, I have mistakenly gotten the idea I am through with bullies. Guess what? They wear designer suits instead of football pads, but they are just the same. I hope they like walking. They don't know who they are messing with.

At 57, I have retired and don't know who I am. I think I may have lost myself somewhere along the way. I'm so angry. It's OK to be nice, loving, thoughtful, caring, and kind. I have to hold onto that. That's who I *am*.

At 81, today, I think the world is basically good and that people are fundamentally nice. I have to believe this in spite of how messed up the world is now. There are good people out there who will take risks, deal with all of this chaos and cruelty and not let it destroy them. I cry a lot these days when I think about the wild dog that has chased me my whole life. I have lived almost an entire lifetime running scared and not trusting anything to be stable—believing that everything good will get ripped away from me. Still, I have been fearless in the face of all of it. I have taken down my worst enemies. I have been standing up to bullies and competitors since I was knocked off of my bike when I was 12 years old, punched in the face and taunted and embarrassed by kids who didn't even know me. That's 69 years of anxiety. It has taken a huge amount of energy for me to always be prepared for war, and I'm tired. But to be Hawaiian is to be a warrior. There is a certain amount of strength and natural fortitude that arises from my cultural mindset. I have channeled all of that strength and energy into the battle I have waged on the field of life. But now that I have stepped off the battlefield, I have found the gentle, loving, optimistic person I am, that I have *always* been…and finally, I don't have to run anymore looking over my shoulder. The only thing behind me now is the wind at my back.

Image Credits

My little league baseball team (it's not hard to find me)
The Weatherford Democrat, 1953

My Punahou football team—I'm #76
Punahou staff photographer

With my high school girlfriend, Janet, and friends in Weatherford, Texas
Adrian C. Cowan, promotional photo for Texas Christian University, Weatherford, Texas

Me with some of my Weatherford High School teammates
Weatherford yearbook student photographer

I was accused of murder in a mock trial at SMU, and I won an ugly man contest in this outfit
SMU campus newspaper student photographer

When I used my head as a battering ram (my face took a beating)
Laughead Photographers, Dallas, Texas

All American and All-Southwest Conference lineman for SMU, 1962
Laughead Photographers, September 1962

Nancy and I on our way to a college dance
Laughead Photographers, 1962

Everyone was crying, hopefully not because Nancy was marrying me
Laughead Photographers, 1964

Made the team, but YIKES! I don't know how to pass block
Laughead Photographers

Blocking against the Kansas City Chiefs
Dick Darcey Sports Photos, *The Washington Post,* via Getty Images

Program for the Polynesian Football Hall of Fame induction ceremony
The Polynesian Football Hall of Fame

Coach Lombardi telling special needs children about football
Nate Fine, 1969

Plaques sold in Rodman's Drug Store to benefit the DC Special Olympics
Nate Fine Productions, 1974

If he can't find you, he can't yell at you
Arnie Sachs / CNP

Campaigning for McGovern
Photographer unknown, Montgomery County McGovern campaign

Celebrating with Coach Allen after a big win
Nate Fine Productions

Leading the charge for Larry Brown
Photographer unknown, *Newsweek*

Going from the locker room to the boardroom
Chase Studios, Bethesda, Maryland, 1988

Chatting with President Carter at a White House lawn event
White House photographer

After Larry Johnson pinch hit for me and struck out (we still won the championship)
Punahou staff photographer

Training for the Moloka'i race
Promotional photo for Ānuenue Canoe Club, Honolulu, Hawai'i

Hanging out with the President in his office
Bob McNeely, White House photographer, 1998

Golfing with the President
White House staff photographer

Looking the part and trying to be the part
The Washington Post, 1998, via Getty Images

Looking the part
Barry Smith, farm manager

About the Author

Ray Schoenke was among the earliest Polynesian NFL players and was inducted into the Polynesian Football Hall of Fame in 2015. He had a 12-year career as an offensive lineman with the Dallas Cowboys and The Washington Redskins. In 2002, he was selected as one of the top 100 players in the history of the Redskins. He is the retired CEO of Schoenke & Associates, a firm specializing in design, funding, and administration of executive compensation and benefit programs for large, private- and publicly traded companies in the Mid-Atlantic Region and Hawai'i. During his business career, he was very active in public and civic affairs, including playing a significant role in the founding of the Special Olympics and serving as the Executive Director of the Mid-Atlantic Region. He actively campaigned for three US presidents. He was appointed as Chair of the Hawaiian Arts and Culture Board for the Bishop Museum in Honolulu, HI, and also ran for public office. He currently resides in Maryland in the home he shared with his late wife.

Made in the USA
Las Vegas, NV
08 June 2024